"This book is a must-have for anyone seeking to learn innovative, creative, and effective ways to work with death and dying. The authors share personal and professional experiences of using experiential and other methods of change combining an Eastern and Western wisdom and knowledge. Readers will walk away with immediately useful new interventions while having their own souls renewed."

—*Kate Hudgins, PhD, TEP, clinical psychologist and director of training at Therapeutic Spiral International*

"The authors have developed a powerful, user-friendly 'how to' manual for those who are doing grief work. The section on critical incident stress management (CISM) is so strong and reflects the authors' extensive experience and wisdom. This book will be a valuable resource for all practitioners involved in grief work."

—*Brian Cahill, LCSW, former clinical director of Catholic Charities in San Francisco, CA; author of* Cops, Cons, and Grace

"I'm not sure if this resonates more for me as a career child welfare social worker who has seen a lot of trauma firsthand, a supervisor and manager responsible for taking care of first responder staff in a large government agency, or 'civilian' me, who has experienced loss and trauma in my personal life. The connection of mind, body, and well-being is an essential component to the roadmap to healing. The detailed techniques, action steps, and example vignettes make this an easy and informative read for clinicians and lay readers alike."

—*Jonathan Weinberg, child welfare social worker; former adjunct professor, San Jose State University School of Social Work*

"An important contribution to the literature base—to my knowledge, this is the only book dedicated to psychodramatic work with grief and loss! The experiential techniques outlined by the authors, including sociometry and psychodrama, foster connection after loss while helping clients get unstuck and renegotiate their grief. A blend of practical recommendations, theoretical considerations, and personal experience, this is a must-have publication for professionals working with grief and loss."

—*Dr. Scott Giacomucci, DSW, LCSW, CTTS, CET III, PAT, director and founder, Phoenix Center for Experiential Trauma Therapy; co-editor,* Autobiography of a Genius *by Jacob L. Moreno*

"Comprehensive and wise throughout, Darrow and Childs' book provides a creative and compassionate guide to using active and expressive techniques in working with grief and loss. This wonderful and original book takes a direct and healing approach, and the clinical examples are moving and useful. The authors convey a deep understanding of the nature of loss, the power of group-work in healing, and the benefits of using active and expressive techniques with both individuals and groups."

—*Nancy D. Whiteside, LCSW, former manager at Worcester Youth Guidance Center*

"Experiential Action Methods and Tools for Healing Grief and Loss-Related Trauma **provides sensitive and real methods for navigating the grief journey. Kindness and an open heart are fully present in clearly described psychodramatic and sociometric tools for helping people access their internal, interpersonal, and transpersonal strengths. This book is absolutely essential for those who want to support others on the complex path of healing from grief and trauma."**

—*John Olesen, MA, TEP, psychodrama trainer and former hospice therapist*

"This book combines insights from grief and loss literature with a practical, four-tier structure developed by the Centre for Living with Dying that provides sequential components to guide practitioners in helping clients manage grief and loss and the stressors that accompany them. The addition of psychodrama as the methodology for exploring these components (acknowledge, express, act, and reconnect) offers an innovative approach to this work that is cognizant of current neurological research demonstrating the efficacy of action methods for promoting post-traumatic growth."

—*Mario Cossa, RDT/MT, TEP, co-director of Therapeutic Spiral International with an international reputation as a psychodrama trainer and practitioner*

"This fine book states clearly that grief is a natural life experience we all go through in healing the reality of loss and change. The authors teach us that each grief journey is unique and how reaching out to others for support and being kind to one's self can enable us to survive the pain."

—*Charles Garfield, PhD, author,* Life's Last Gift: Giving and Receiving Peace When A Loved One Is Dying *and founder, Shanti Project*

EXPERIENTIAL ACTION METHODS AND TOOLS FOR HEALING GRIEF AND LOSS-RELATED TRAUMA

Experiential Action Methods and Tools for Healing Grief and Loss-Related Trauma introduces innovative psychodramatic and creative expression methods for helping those affected by bereavement and trauma.

Each section focuses on a particular acute or secondary grief issue, providing supportive and explanatory material that can be given to clients, and experiential action methods for providers. Real-world vignettes and psychodrama tools delineate a unique approach to unlocking and shifting entrenched perspectives related to persistent grief and loss-related trauma, with chapters organized for practical use and application by counselors and therapists. The book also includes critical incident stress training material specifically for first responders, a frequently overlooked population.

The practical guidance offered in this book will be of great interest to all who work with grief and trauma, including practicing and trainee psychologists and therapists, counseling centers, hospice organizations, bereavement support programs, and ministers.

Lusijah S. Darrow, LMFT, CP, is a licensed marriage and family therapist. She is nationally certified in psychodrama and group psychotherapy and is a continuing education provider. Previously, she managed a biomedical research lab at Stanford University and served as the state chairperson of her spiritual community. She maintains a private practice in Soquel, California.

Rev. Janet Childs, DD, is the director of the Bay Area Critical Incident Stress Management Team at the Centre for Living with Dying program, Bill Wilson Center, San Francisco, USA. For over forty years, Janet has dedicated her life to providing support, education, and crisis intervention to people facing loss, grief, and serious illness, as well as to responders and caregivers on the front lines.

EXPERIENTIAL ACTION METHODS AND TOOLS FOR HEALING GRIEF AND LOSS-RELATED TRAUMA

Life, Death, and Transformation

Lusijah S. Darrow and Janet Childs

NEW YORK AND LONDON

First published 2020
by Routledge
52 Vanderbilt Avenue, New York, NY 10017

and by Routledge
2 Park Square, Milton Park, Abingdon, Oxon, OX14 4RN

Routledge is an imprint of the Taylor & Francis Group, an informa business

© 2020 Lusijah S. Darrow and Janet Childs

The right of Lusijah S. Darrow and Janet Childs to be identified as authors of
this work has been asserted by them in accordance with sections 77 and 78
of the Copyright, Designs and Patents Act 1988.

All rights reserved. The purchase of this copyright material confers the right on the
purchasing institution to photocopy pages which bear the photocopy icon and
copyright line at the bottom of the page. No other part of this publication may be reproduced,
stored in a retrieval system, or transmitted in any form or by any means, electronic,
mechanical, photocopying, recording, or otherwise, without prior permission in
writing from the publisher.

Trademark notice: Product or corporate names may be trademarks or registered trademarks,
and are used only for identification and explanation without intent to infringe.

Library of Congress Cataloging-in-Publication Data
A catalog record for this title has been requested

ISBN: 978-0-367-27503-7 (hbk)
ISBN: 978-0-367-27502-0 (pbk)
ISBN: 978-0-429-29749-6 (ebk)

Typeset in Stone Serif
by Newgen Publishing UK

In our lives, we dance the balancing wheel of life and death, sorrow and joy, peace and turmoil. We dance between being in control of our lives, to experiencing total loss of control, when we are confronted with life-changing events. We then, many times, can go through the 'secondary trauma' of guilt and anger, blaming our own inadequacy or the outer events or people connected with the change for our misery.

If we can allow our dance to be an adventure, rather than a recrimination of choices made in the past, we might be able to make meaning from painful experiences. Just about every spiritual and psychological tradition focuses on the ultimate healing we can work towards when we open our heart and being to the process of journeying through our emotions and circumstances with hope, love, and honesty.

I dedicate this book to Husain Chung, a wise and loving soul, healer, and master psychodramatist who has been my teacher both in his life and death. The lived experience and many gifts I received and keep from my relationship with Husain are the basis of my contribution to this book.

Lusijah Sutherland Darrow

I dedicate this book to the people who have inspired me as I have walked beside them in their courageous journey of transforming profound loss into healing and hope. This gift sustains my life.

Janet Childs

CONTENTS

List of Figures		xiii
Preface from Janet		xv
Acknowledgments from Lusijah		xvii
Acknowledgments from Janet		xviii
List of Abbreviations		xix

Introduction		1
CHAPTER 1	Approaching the Grief Journey: Four Components to Healing: Acknowledge, Express, Act, Reconnect	3
CHAPTER 2	Centre for Living with Dying Grief Program	8
CHAPTER 3	Psychodrama and Sociometry with Grief Work	12
CHAPTER 4	The Beginning: Sharing the Story	18
CHAPTER 5	Tools for Coping	23
CHAPTER 6	Loneliness	36
CHAPTER 7	Fear	45
CHAPTER 8	Sadness	49
CHAPTER 9	Anger	55
CHAPTER 10	Unfinished Business	62
CHAPTER 11	Frozen Moments	70
CHAPTER 12	Guilt	77
CHAPTER 13	Mementos: The Power of Action Steps in the Aftermath of Loss	82
CHAPTER 14	Unique Issues after Violent Death and Suicide	84
CHAPTER 15	Grief Work beyond the Acute Stage	94
CHAPTER 16	Faith and the Grieving Process	103

xii Contents

CHAPTER 17   Creative Expression Activities for Larger Groups and Day-Long Retreats   110

CHAPTER 18   Grief Work with Fragile Populations   122

CHAPTER 19   Family Dynamics in Loss and Change   132

CHAPTER 20   Stress, Trauma, and Critical Incident Stress Management   141

CHAPTER 21   Grief Training for Clinicians and Caregivers   167

Conclusion: Final Thoughts   177

Appendices
  I Research Overview of Psychodrama   179
 II Relationship of Experiential Action Methods and Theory with Other Models of Psychotherapy   182
III Special Aspects of Grief   185
Index   189

FIGURES

1.1	Cascade effect of trauma/support	4
2.1	Centre for Living with Dying program and contemporary grief theories	9
3.1	Spectrograms and locograms	15
6.1	Social atom	38
9.1	Guilty–angry	55
10.1	Unfinished business backpack	66
14.1	Feel wheel	89
15.1	Life-meaning atom	99
17.1	Essence/expression	114
17.2	Heart hotel	116
18.1	Role atom	126
20.1a	Typical reactions in the aftermath of a tragedy	143
20.1b	Personalized reactions in the aftermath of a tragedy	144
20.2	Past trauma backpack	148

PREFACE FROM JANET

My experience with sudden and traumatic loss inspired me to work in death and grief counseling. While my parents were open and loving in so many ways, when my Aunt Betty was murdered when I was eleven years old, I was not allowed to attend her funeral in Los Angeles. They truly felt that it would be difficult for me, as she was my favorite aunt. She was a jazz singer, and was well loved and admired in the musical world. Her boyfriend strangled her in a fit of rage, and never was found or brought to justice. My father was never the same after that loss of his beloved sister. His family life had been rough, and my Aunt Betty was the one anchor of love and support he could count on.

Literally a year and a half later, my father died of a massive heart attack. I believe he died of a broken heart. He was in the law enforcement profession, and never being able to bring completion to my aunt's tragic death devastated him. He was experiencing a classic grief reaction, but I sense he felt he was going crazy. He became withdrawn and depressed. And after his death, I was given one day off from school for his funeral, a long all-day affair. I felt ill and depressed afterward. When I returned to school, no one knew what to say to me. It was an isolating and difficult time. My mom went back to work, and I took care of home duties, along with my grandmother who now lived with us.

When I graduated from college, I worked with the Suicide and Crisis Hotline in San Jose and became even more fascinated with the way we deal with death and grief in America. Training to become a healthcare professional, I was struck by the fact that grief and the process of dying were totally ignored. There existed a conspiracy of silence. I began to feel that the isolation and alienation of grieving people were caused by the way we treated them in the aftermath. And while we couldn't control what happened in terms of grief, trauma, or loss, I realized we could control how we responded to the crisis. Then, I was to meet an incredible woman, MaryAnne Kelly, who after several deaths in her own life, including the suicide of her first husband, and the heart attack death of her second husband, dreamed of beginning a service to support those going through the grief process, either after or during a process of dying, serious illness, or trauma.

In my tenure at the Centre for Living with Dying, I have subsequently lived through the deaths of my brother, my mother, my uncle, and my stepson. What each of these deaths has given me is a new awareness of the preciousness of life and how important it is to have a safe place to grieve, to begin the healing process.

For over forty years, I have had the privilege to walk with people facing grief and trauma, spiritually as a Reverend and emotionally, as a founder of the Centre for Living with Dying. The Centre is the most comprehensive bereavement counseling organization in the country. Founded in 1976 by MaryAnne Kelly, the Centre provides support, intervention, and education for all age groups and professions on the life issues of loss, serious illness, death, grief, and trauma.

As I have observed clients, volunteers, communities, and nations face the reality of building the 'new normal', I have noticed the comfort that a structure brings to the daunting task of moving forward in making meaning from the loss. I have defined four essential components for managing the difficult dynamics of unexpected change, loss, or trauma. These four components—acknowledge, express, act, reconnect—can create a framework for healing, and a sense of empowerment and satisfaction, even in the midst of overwhelming chaos. All dimensions of human experience touched by loss—physical, emotional, mental, social, and spiritual—can be supported in the journey towards healing by this structured framework, which also allows for the unique individual experience.

I wish that the thousands who have touched my life, as I have witnessed their courage to explore the spectrum of issues in their life-changing loss, will know the fruits of their labors in this declaration of discovering hope.

My wish is that I might devote my energy and focus on synthesizing the many gifts that have been bestowed on my heart and mind, by a world beyond the shadows of grim appearances, that does hold a candle. May we witness its light.

Reverend Janet Childs, DD
Director of Education, Training and Bay Area Critical Incident Stress Management Team
Centre for Living with Dying program of Bill Wilson Center

ACKNOWLEDGMENTS FROM LUSIJAH

I want to express deep gratitude to the people who offered their incredible skills in my training as a psychodramatist. The sensitive and caring artistry in their practice of psychodrama gave me the first-hand experience to know the power of psychodrama to work with grief. Heartfelt thanks to Sylvia Israel, Mario Cossa, and John Olesen from the Bay Area Moreno Institute in San Rafael, California, Rebecca Walters and Judy Swallow from the Hudson Valley Psychodrama Institute, and Kate Hudgins, Clinical Psychologist, Director of Training at Therapeutic Spiral International. I also want to acknowledge Lisa Herman who taught me the power of creative expression with traumatic experiences. I am grateful to my sensitive group co-facilitator, Joan Russell, who completely jumped on board with using experiential action methods.

I want to acknowledge my co-author Janet Childs. The first time we met, I knew there would be important learning from her—which turned out to be very true and in ways I didn't anticipate. Deep thanks to Janet for her loving presence and support at the death of my beloved partner. I am grateful to have had the privilege to participate in the wonderful grief program she co-created.

I feel gratitude to my husband, Marc Darrow, who has encouraged me every step of the way with this book. This includes his positive feedback on the material as a fellow therapist, his suggestions as a skilled and published writer, and most importantly, that our love has shown me that the human heart is ever expanding in capacity to love again. Many thanks to my daughter, Alena Rott, who made the figures to illustrate our work.

ACKNOWLEDGMENTS FROM JANET

My lifetime has been filled with teachers, mentors, family members, friends, and colleagues. There are so many beings, two-legged and four-legged, who have touched my heart and informed my river of experience to be this—a woman who has the deep honor to work with those walking the grief road. If you have known me or worked with me, you are a part of this manuscript. There are thousands of first responders and caregivers who tenderly and courageously allowed me into the catacombs of their broken hearts. Their stamina to do this work in a world that so often ignores or vilifies their duty is inspirational.

I would not be at this moment in my growth, if not for MaryAnne Kelly and her vision and direction in founding the Centre for Living with Dying. Reverends Tom and Mary Garry, beloved spiritual teachers, who embraced me into their spiritual community over thirty years ago, encouraged and nurtured my soul self and grounded that soul into the world.

Special gratitude to the healers, to the organizers, to my fellow co-workers, and to the responders who have stood by me over the years to bring meaning and quality of life, as well as encouragement to pursue this path. Deep appreciation to Marc Darrow for his editing magic, and gratitude to my co-author, Lusijah, in birthing this concept of profound healing.

And to my family—heart and blood—and my love, my spouse Corry Gott, whose courage, wisdom, and strength have become my roots and wings, propelling me forward into joy and full life, even as we have survived heartbreaks and loss, I say thank you.

We both make the following acknowledgments with enormous gratitude:

Thank you to our editor, Anna Moore, who believed in our book and provided kind and skillful feedback and suggestions to make our book stronger. Many thanks to Ellie Duncan and Dawn Preston for their guidance and support in helping us through the publishing process. Thank you to Liz Williams for providing meticulous care towards catching important ommissions and needed corrections.

ABBREVIATIONS

CBT	cognitive behavioral therapy
CISM	critical incident stress management
CISR	critical incident stress response
CLWD	Centre for Living with Dying
EMDR	eye movement desensitization and reprocessing
EMS	Emergency Medical Services
ICISF	International Critical Incident Stress Foundation
IOP	Intensive Outpatient Program
OIS	officer-involved shooting
PHP	Partial Hospital Program
USAR	Urban Search and Rescue

INTRODUCTION

The death of a loved one is part of the human experience. Despite the universality of experiencing loss, the felt grieving process is unique to each individual. It is impacted by the nature of the relationship, whether in romantic partnership, as a parent or child, and the circumstances of death of the loved one. For example, loss after illness, sudden death, or suicide creates unique aspects to grief responses. Complex or ambivalent feelings that were present in the relationship carry over to the grieving process. Issues that were unresolved in life have run out of time and can no longer be resolved. In addition to more expected reactions of sadness, loneliness, and isolation, there are grief reactions that form the basis of what is called 'complicated' grief that include anger, guilt, frozen memories, and unresolved issues. Talking about the issue does not necessarily create integration of new insights. The action methods presented here effectively work to change narratives around the most difficult grief issues.

Intellectually, we all know loss is part of life, and yet the strength of the grief experience is unexpected in intensity. People who begin attending the grief groups are initially overwhelmed, experiencing intense acute-stage grief. Compassionate normalizing of the intensity of feelings and issues is an important start towards working on grief issues.

People in grief experience difficulty in bridging the gap of their own intense feelings with friends and/ or family who have not had the experience of loss. It becomes clear to those grieving that our society copes poorly with death as something to be feared and pushed away. Everyone who has experienced loss has heard well-meaning statements of friends and family that are just not helpful. "He's in a better place," "at least she didn't have to suffer longer," or "isn't it time to move on?" may be well-meaning but are completely disconnected from the experience of the bereaved. The societal discomfort with death means that friends and family often don't know how to support someone who is grieving, creating isolation for those who have experienced loss.

Often the loved one who has died was interwoven into the life meaning of the survivor or had a role as a life ballast. There is a sudden vacuum, the person providing companionship and support is gone, and there is loss of purpose related to how the survivor had previously organized his or her life. On top of dealing with acute grief issues, life-meaning issues have often collapsed. Recovery from grief includes envisioning and taking steps toward creating a different life that has meaning to the client. We provide suggested action methods to support clients as they move beyond acute grief into a new normal.

Faith, lack of faith, and loss of faith influence the grieving process. People who have experienced loss and who have an active religious or spiritual practice seem to have an easier time. Beliefs about life after death, specifically the continued existence of the soul, are comforting. In our experience, people who do not have religious or spiritual practices often experience a profound sense of absence or emptiness and face existential questions related to their own human mortality and the meaning of life. A common theme is fear about the life and contributions of their loved one being forgotten. These are huge questions.

The death of a loved one can shake the foundation of faith, creating a sense of being lost at sea, as beliefs and expectations are shattered. Chapter 16 on faith and the grieving process presents ways to support and comfort those with and without a defined religious or spiritual belief, and those who are experiencing a crisis or loss in faith.

This essence of the loved one is part of the survivor on a cellular level through stored memories and feelings. When clients are sharing happy memories, they smile. When activating these memories, it is as if they are re-experiencing them in the present moment. The biological mechanisms that store the knowing of the loved one, feelings of connection and love continue to exist. The survivor can and does experience memories of how the loved one spoke, their sense of humor, how they dressed, what they liked to eat, and how it was to be cared for, touched, loved, and kissed. They can connect with a felt sense of love, care, and wisdom of the one who has died. As will be seen later, this is a powerful resource in coping with grief issues. Survivors can call forth the wise and supportive voice of their loved one in the here and now. In the grief groups using action methods, clients were not asked to theorize what the loved one might say; they were asked to step into the role of the loved one and speak from their voice.

The methods presented in this book support bereaved individuals to stay connected to the sweetness of shared experience and to honor what was good in their relationships. There is a bitter/sweet integration in grief—sadness in conjunction with remembering and honoring memories, personal growth and life experience that only occurred because of the place of the deceased in their life, and gifts of the relationship that are carried forward. Clients want to remember the stories and experiences they had with their loved one, and to honor what the deceased brought to their own lives and the lives of others. The grief process is an integration of tolerating the pain of loss with what was good.

Family and friend networks generally cannot deeply hold and provide support for the extended grieving process of another. It is useful to seek counseling, and group work offers benefits that individual therapy cannot. Sharing stories that are heard and supported by others with similar experiences reduces isolation. Issues of grief are fully unpacked and individual stories are held by others with empathy and tenderness. Group members see hope in other group members' steps towards recovery.

We present in this book a process toward working with grief that encourages individuals to acknowledge, express, find action steps, and reconnect with others. Each chapter contains material that can be used as handouts for specific acute grief topics and associated experiential action methods that have been used in grief groups and individual therapy. Many of the exercises, methods, and information material are placed in specific chapters, yet have broader applications for other grief/trauma topics. We encourage readers to use these tools where they will be helpful.

CHAPTER 1

APPROACHING THE GRIEF JOURNEY

Four Components to Healing: Acknowledge, Express, Act, Reconnect

What Is Grief? What Is Stress? What Is Loss?

All of us, at some point in our lifetime, have experienced loss or change. It is the one thing that unites us as human beings. Grief and stress are the natural responses to any loss or change in our lives—even positive change. Even getting married can be a grief process. For example, when we cry at weddings, we experience joy and a sense of loss and change. Life will never be the same.

Grief is a spiral of feelings and reactions. It is not a line with a beginning and an end. It can be a rollercoaster of surprising triggers. We refer to them as landmines, because they are sudden and unexpected. There are three types of landmines:

1. Sensory triggers
2. Memory triggers
3. Time triggers.

Trauma and grief know no time. James Baldwin (2011) offers this particularly relevant wisdom for the process of recovery from grief: *Not everything that is faced can be changed, but nothing can be changed until it is faced*. It doesn't matter how long ago the grief happened; sometimes, when we hit a landmine, it may feel like it happened yesterday.

The Backpack Effect

Present grief can tap into grief that has occurred in the past. So, we are not only dealing with present loss, but that loss can touch the past as well. The truth of grief is that it is eternal. All our grief meets in the moment of our present loss or trauma. What may help is to identify what has been brought up from the past—realizing it may have as much emotional impact as the present. We call this activation of feelings from past loss and trauma the backpack effect.

The Cascade Effect

In the experience of grief and loss, one loss often creates a cascade of additional losses. For example, with a job loss, we can potentially lose our home, our relationships, our self-worth, our financial security, our sense of meaning, our sense of purpose and well-being, and that can lead to depression, anxiety, substance use/abuse, and suicide. We also have the capacity to build a positive cascade, by providing support,

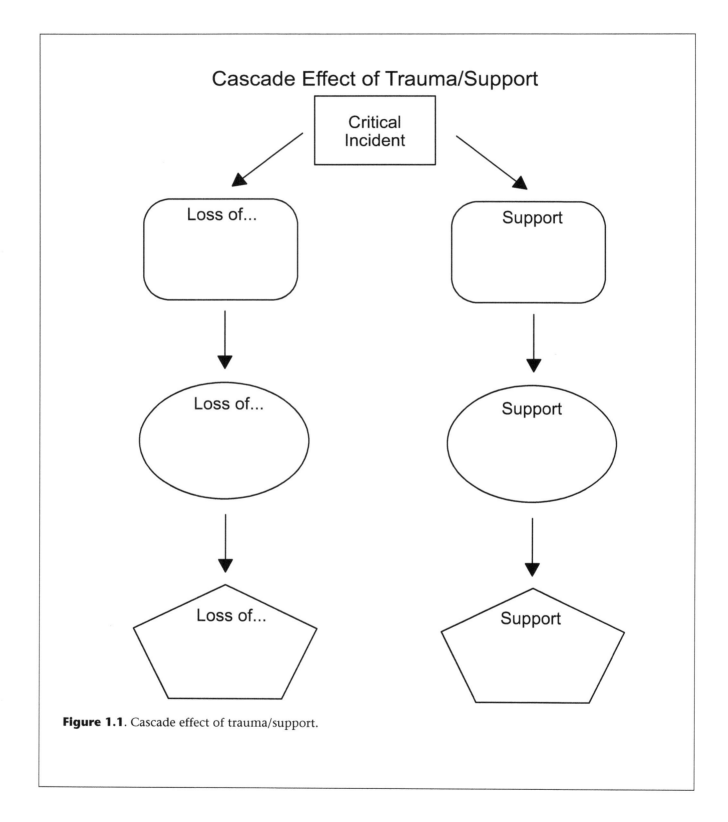

Figure 1.1. Cascade effect of trauma/support.

presence, resources, and community in the aftermath of loss. Figure 1.1 provides a worksheet for clients to identify their own positive and challenging dimensions of the loss cascade.

The Heart Hotel

One of our clients said it very well:

> My heart is like a hotel. Everyone I love has a room in my heart hotel. When they die or go away, no one can take their room in my heart hotel. I can fill up the empty room with the love and the memories that neither death nor separation can take away. However, I can add new rooms to my heart hotel as I meet new people to love and care for.

This is the work of grief—to let go of the pain, trauma, and grief and keep the love, memories, and good times. It is like a sifting process. It takes time and patience, and understanding that you are a normal person having a normal reaction to an abnormally stressful event.

In our modern society, great emphasis is placed on what we do as a gauge of our worth as human beings. When we experience change, loss, or transition in the work environment, it can have far-reaching effects on our personal lives and our self-esteem as well as our beliefs and values. Dealing proactively with change in the workplace and in our personal lives can be a key factor, both in individual and team performance, and job satisfaction.

Symptoms of Grief/Stress

What happens? A review of research studies on physiological issues associated with bereavement indicates systemic impact after loss (Knowles et al., 2019). Also, survivors of loss have increased incidence of cardiology problems, a phenomenon known as the broken heart syndrome (Mostofsky et al., 2012). Here are a few of the feelings, behaviors, thoughts, body reactions, and belief systems brought about by loss.

- Guilt
- Suicidal feelings/thoughts
- Substance abuse
- Strained relationships
- Inability to function at work or at home
- Depression
- Apathy—I just don't care
- Anger, hostility
- Craziness
- Memories/flashbacks
- Sleep disturbance
- Eating changes/disorders
- Loss of belief
- Feeling shaky
- Loss of friends and support systems
- Yearning and missing
- Loneliness
- Isolation
- Disbelief
- Despair, hopelessness, helplessness

6 Approaching the Grief Journey

- Physical pain in the gastrointestinal tract, headaches
- Disorientation
- Sadness
- Numbness
- Anxiety and panic—feeling out of control
- Relief
- Gratitude/appreciation for life.

These responses and reactions are normal.

We think stress is different from grief. Actually, it's the same—it's our natural response to loss and change. Grief and stress management is a way of taking care of ourselves and one another in the aftermath. We can't control the traumatic event that caused our stress, but we can provide a safe place to share the details of the pain with each other and explore tools for coping and survival. This perfectly reflects the Centre's goal since its inception in 1976.

Grief management is a tool all of us can use, whether we are individuals going through a grief situation, first responders, or a community in crisis. It is not therapy. It is a positive acknowledgment of the different feelings and reactions we go through. Its structured guidelines create a non-critical and confidential atmosphere that builds comfort and support, helping us all realize we are more alike than different. Even though trauma and grief feel crazy, we are normal.

One of our wonderful volunteers at the Centre said it very well:

I will never be the way I was before my daughter was killed. But I have learned to build a new normal by acknowledging and expressing my grief. In some ways, I am a better, more compassionate person, because I have survived and made meaning out of the loss.

The Centre for Living with Dying has identified four components (not to be confused with stages of grief) that help to manage grief and stress—acknowledge, express, act, and reconnect.

Acknowledge the Loss and the Impact of the Grief Process

Honor your grief. It is a reflection of the depth of your love and caring. Don't minimize or negate your grief. The first step is to accept that you are a normal person living through an abnormally painful time. You are entitled to your feelings. Much of the grief response is very physical. Your body can react in many different ways. Grief impacts us on a daily basis—emotionally, mentally, socially, and spiritually.

- Your journey through grief is individual, even though the feelings associated with grief are universal. Don't let anyone tell you how to grieve or how to survive. Grief is something one never truly gets over. You simply build a new normal, by taking one moment at a time.
  - List your fears—both real and imagined. Be specific and write them down.
  - Focus on what is most difficult to handle right now.
  - What do you need to do to help the situation right now?

Express Your Feelings and Issues

- Express your feelings through talking, writing, speaking into a tape recorder, or physical movement. Writing a letter to the person you are missing or have unfinished business with is an excellent way to release bottled-up emotions.

- Talk with others who are sympathetic and/or who have experienced similar losses. It helps to know you're not alone.
  - Talk with a co-worker or supportive person.
  - See a non-judgmental support person/counselor.
  - Physically express through your body, by exercising, or doing some activity that requires exertion.

Act

- Create as much meaning and ceremony as you can to bring closure to the event of loss. If you are breaking up, have a ceremony of separation. If you are facing an anniversary date, light a candle by a photograph of your loved one. Do something active that will acknowledge your pain and help you to transform it into the remembering of the love.
  - Do specific, concrete actions to facilitate the changes you are experiencing. Creating your own ceremonies can be very useful, often combining traditions that are meaningful with your own inspirations.
  - Complete and bring closure to any unfinished business or unclear interactions with family, friends, or important others.
  - Do something playful, fun, and relaxing that is totally disconnected from life responsibilities to balance the stress.
  - Normalize the rest of your life as much as possible. Do not change too much at one time. If there are other life changes you have no control over, acknowledge them. Realize that you only have to deal with the most pressing issue right now.

Reconnect

- Give yourself the opportunity to acknowledge your victories. Look back at what you have survived and accomplished.
- Do something fun and life affirming which rewards you for a job well done.

The components to approaching grief—acknowledge, express, act, reconnect—are repeated many times in the course of working with and supporting each person's grief journey.

MaryAnne Kelly, founder of the Centre for Living with Dying, often said: "The pain never goes away, but the memories are what I can keep. And the pain changes —from the gut-wrenching anguish to the bitter-sweet sorrow. The pain of grief is the price for having loved."

Bibliography

Baldwin, J. (2011). In R. Kenan (ed.), *The cross of redemption: uncollected writings*. New York: Vintage International.

Grollman, E. (1995). *Living when a loved one has died*. Boston, MA: Beacon Press.

Knowles, L., Ruis, J., & O'Connor, M.F. (2019). A systematic review of the association between bereavement and biomarkers of immune function. *Psychosomatic Medicine*, 81(5):415–433.

Mostofsky, E., Maclure, M., Sherwood, J., Tofler, G., Muller, J., & Mittleman, M. (2012). Risk of acute myocardial infarction after the death of a significant person in one's life. *Circulation*, 125:491–496.

Sandberg, S., & Grant, A. (2017). *Option B*. New York: Alfred Knopf.

Tatelbaum, J. (1980). *The courage to grieve*. New York: Harper & Row.

Zuba, T. (2014). *Permission to mourn: a new way to do grief*. Rockford, IL: Bish Press.

CHAPTER 2

CENTRE FOR LIVING WITH DYING GRIEF PROGRAM

The Centre for Living with Dying (CLWD) program offers an approach to grief work that is practical, with curriculum developed by people who have experienced loss and grappled with universal issues of grieving. CLWD provides support through grief groups to those affected by the death of a loved one, violence, and tragedies, and to first responders. The Centre has served over a million individuals since its beginning over forty years ago.

Kübler-Ross (2014) must be acknowledged with deep respect as the first to start the important discussion of the grieving process with her stages of grief model. Further work examining the grief process suggests that grieving is an individual process that does not have stages. Kübler-Ross herself acknowledged (in personal communication) that her stages of grief model was problematic because it served to put people in categories and in a conceptual linear process rather than supporting and acknowledging the individual grief experience of healing.

The CLWD program honors the unique process of each person—a process that has no linear timeline or sequential steps to the grieving process. The program works in a direct way with feelings that universally come up after loss and with issues that contribute to complicated grief. The CLWD recognizes the helpfulness of peer support, the address of universal themes or topics faced by people who are grieving, and the movement toward finding a new normal. The initial issues that we work with, in no particular order, are:

- Tools for coping
- Loneliness
- Fear
- Sadness
- Anger
- Unfinished business
- Frozen moments
- Guilt
- Mementos.

We continued working beyond the acute issues of grief, on what we called secondary grief. These issues pertained to envisioning a life with meaning and satisfaction, honoring the memories and gifts from the relationship, working with dreams, and creating new narratives, among others.

The CLWD program did not evolve from academic theory, and yet it is consistent with work of contemporary grief theories which we show in Figure 2.1 and discuss below.

Stroebe and Schut (1999) recognized two distinct processes in mourning: *loss orientation* and *restoration orientation.* In our work these two distinct processes would be found in the initial eight-week program addressing acute issues of grief, explained in Chapters 4 through 13, and grief work beyond acute issues or secondary grief, detailed in Chapter 15.

Contemporary Grief Theories

Kübler-Ross's Stages of Grief Model was the first exploration of healing from grief. Contemporaty grief theories have moved away from a model with defined and sequential stages of grief, instead highlighting important aspects of successful grief work. Below we list contemporary grief theories and the relationship of these theories to the Centre for Living with Dying program described in this book.

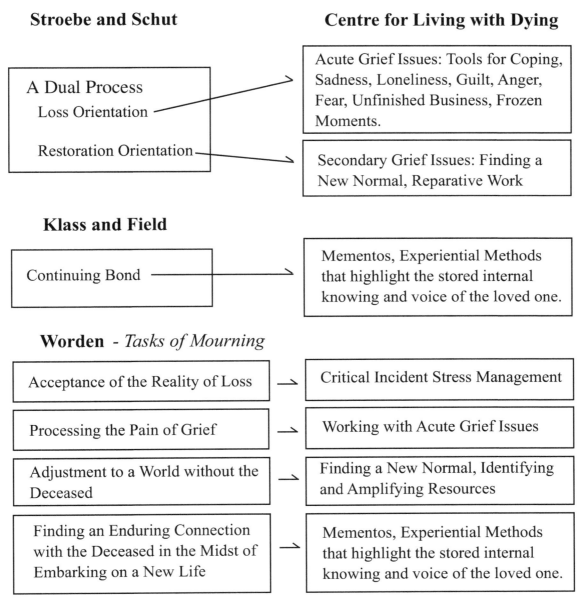

Figure 2.1. Centre for Living with Dying program and contemporary grief theories.

Life meaning vs. happiness has become prominent in popular media and within the field of positive psychology. This is also relevant to recovery from loss. *Meaning reconstruction* is described by Neimeyer and Sands (2011) as an important component of resolution of grief. The critical importance for identifying new life meaning after catastrophic loss and trauma is presented in *Man's Search for Meaning* by Viktor Frankl (1992), an account of his internment in a German concentration camp during World War II. As a psychiatrist, he was curious to understand what factors contributed to prisoners being able to thrive in these circumstances, while others did not. We frequently recommend this book for its message of the importance of finding new life meaning as a differentiating factor of whether people can thrive after horrifying loss.

More recently, Baumeister and Vohs (2002) explored meaningfulness in life as an important component to long-term well-being and satisfaction. Aaker et al. (2013) and Baumeister et al. (2013) looked at the importance of happiness vs. meaning, finding that the temporary feeling of happiness does not create the same long-term positive impact as compared to individuals who feel their lives have meaning. They found that life meaning gives individuals a valued sense of self and purpose in life and community.

Our work with clients supports finding a new normal and taking steps towards a life that has satisfaction and meaning, which is consistent with contemporary grief theory that recognizes the importance of life meaning in recovery from grief.

Our orientation is transpersonal. An important aspect of our work includes the concept of the *continuing bond*, first espoused by Klass et al. (1999). In agreement with Field and Worgrin (2011), we have found that it is healing for individuals to arrive at a different relationship with their loved one who has died, rather than pushing memories of the loved one away. Our concept of continuing bond includes honoring the gifts of the relationship that remain after loss and coming to know that the loved one is and will remain a part of the survivor.

The pain of loss creates landmines for the individual and their families. A conspiracy of silence can form, sometimes pictures are hidden, and mention of the one who has died stops for fear of setting off pain. Not only does this not work for the individual, but it robs other family members from having any relationship with the loved one through cherished memories. We met individuals in groups whose loss took place decades previously. They were referred by their individual therapists, addiction program, or primary care doctors to finally address unresolved grief. From a biological standpoint, the loved one is a cellular part of the survivor, encoded in memories. We frequently see that individuals seem to have a felt experience when talking of memories, as if the bereaved person is reliving amusement, respect, tenderness, love, and so on. Witnessing the manifestation of this cellular memory and consequent felt presence of the loved one is a key foundation of our work. We use this understanding with psychodrama and other action methods to bring the loving and compassionate voice and presence of the loved one into the here and now to resolve the more difficult grief issues and integrate the concept of continuing bond.

The tasks of mourning described by Worden (2009) are consistent with our work. Worden's tasks of mourning include:

1. Acceptance of the reality of loss
2. Processing the pain of grief
3. Adjustment to a world without the deceased
4. Finding an enduring connection with the deceased in the midst of embarking on a new life.

The CLWD approach addresses all of these tasks. The first task is addressed as critical incident support in Chapter 20. The remaining tasks are contained in the CLWD grief groups which are organized by type of loss. The groups have working topics. The first meeting is an invitation for group members to share their story. The following weeks cover a specific topic which we present as chapters. At the end of each session relevant handouts are given out that match the topic and which are included in each chapter. Group members appreciate the handouts for giving them further food for thought and helping to normalize their own experience.

The groups are a tender container for processing the life-shattering experience of loss of a loved one. The interpersonal connections between group members, knowing that they are not alone, is among the most helpful aspect of the group. And yet it is clear that the peer group format alone is sometimes insufficient to transform persistent and difficult grief issues. Repeating the story doesn't resolve or shift entrenched perspectives.

Individuals suffering from complicated grief are mired in the more difficult grief issues such as anger, guilt, frozen images, and unresolved issues. Psychodramatic techniques are powerful in shifting entrenched internally held narratives around issues of complicated grief. The next section describes the use of psychodrama tools and methods to work with the grief topics.

Bibliography

Aaker, J.L., Baumeister, R.F., Garbinsky, E.N., & Vohs, K.D. (2013). Some key differences between a happy life and a meaningful life. *Journal of Positive Psychology*, 8(6):505–516.

Baumeister, R.F., & Vohs, K. (2002). The pursuit of meaningfulness in life. In C.R. Snyder & S.J. Lopez (eds.), *Handbook of positive psychology* (pp. 608–618). New York: Oxford University Press.

Baumeister, R.F., Vohs, K.D., Aaker, J., & Garbinsky E.N. (2013). Some key differences between a happy life and a meaningful life. *Journal of Positive Psychology*, 8(6):505–516.

Field, N.P., & Wogrin, C. (2011). The changing bond in therapy for unresolved loss: an attachment theory perspective. In R.A Neimeyer, D.L Harris, H.R. Winokuer, & G.F. Thornton (eds.), *Grief and bereavement in contemporary society: bridging research and practice* (pp. 37–46). New York: Routledge.

Frankl, V. (1992). Man's search for meaning. New York: Buccaneer Books.

Klass, D., Silverman, S., & Nickman, S. (1996). (eds.) *Continuing bonds: new understandings of grief.* Washington: Taylor & Francis.

Kübler-Ross, E. (2014). *On death and dying.* New York: Scribner.

Murray, C.P. (2011). The historical landscape of loss: development of bereavement studies. In R.A. Neimeyer, D.L. Harris, H.R. Winokuer, & G.F. Thornton (eds.), *Grief and bereavement in contemporary society: bridging research and practice* (pp. 1–5). New York: Routledge.

Neimeyer, R.A., & Sands, D.C. (2011). Meaning reconstruction in bereavement: from principles to practice. In R.A. Neimeyer, D.L. Harris, H.R. Winokuer, & G.F. Thornton (eds.), *Grief and bereavement in contemporary society: bridging research and practice* (pp. 9–22). New York: Routledge.

Stroebe, M.S., & Schut, H. (1999). The dual process model of coping with bereavement: rationale and description. *Death Studies*, 23:197–224.

Worden, J.W. (2009). *Grief counseling and grief therapy* (4th ed.). New York: Springer.

CHAPTER 3

PSYCHODRAMA AND SOCIOMETRY WITH GRIEF WORK

Psychodrama and sociometry are powerful and effective experiential action methods. They were invented and developed by J.L. Moreno, a Viennese psychiatrist in the early part of the twentieth century. Moreno's core theoretical foundations of group psychotherapy and psychodrama are ubiquitous in today's field of mental health, existing in cognitive behavioral therapy, gestalt, family systems therapy, and drama therapy, among others. Blatner (2004) in *Foundations of Psychodrama* provides a thorough overview of the history, theory, and practice of psychodrama. Tian Dayton (2005) in *The Living Stage* presents a practical guide on therapeutic use of psychodrama with group psychotherapy, which demonstrates the applicability of psychodrama to a broad cross-section of mental health issues.

Psychodrama methods evoke compassion for self and others, which helps create new insights and narratives about relationships and events. This is especially important for healing issues that contribute to complicated grief. Sociometry methods highlight and enhance connections between people. The sociometry tools we describe below work well for promoting interpersonal connections and safety in the groups.

Psychodrama methods are catalysts for tapping into the survivor's internalized knowing and 'voice' of one who has died. The remembered and felt sense of the loved one—how they loved, their wisdom, caring, and compassion—become available to resolve difficult grief issues.

We describe here an overview of psychodrama and sociometry tools and techniques for those who are not familiar with this modality. Later chapters include specific ways in which psychodrama and sociometry can be used to work with specific topics of grief. Many of the psychodrama methods have broad applications for a variety of grief and trauma issues. We encourage readers to utilize methods as they will be helpful.

Role Reversal

The most commonly used psychodrama tool is 'role reversal'. Role reversal has a client speaking (or writing) to another (usually to the one who has died, but can include others, such as family members, or doctors), and then doing a role reversal, in which the client speaks from the role of the other. Role reversals continue for as long as there is productive exchange and closes with the client invited to speak in their own role to say the last words, for now, to the other.

When the role reversal is with the deceased, the client is tapping into their inner knowing of the loved one and speaking as if they are the other person. In role reversal, the words reflect how the person remembers or experiences the essence of the loved one. The client can also speak in role reversal with someone who is not as familiar. If the client steps into the role of someone with whom there are unresolved feelings, the client is placed in a here-and-now situation in which they can explore different possible and plausible points of view the other person might be feeling. This frequently creates a shift in how the bereaved holds a memory of a painful or disturbing event. In complicated grief, unresolved guilt and anger co-exist with the sadness of loss. Even in relationships that had complex feelings of anger, guilt, and unresolved issues, there remains a memory of the loving and caring aspect of the deceased. This compassionate aspect is available to the client, in spite of ambivalence or issues of complicated grief. When the client, in role reversal, becomes the compassionate, loving, and wise aspect of the one who has died, there is a transformation in the painful narrative and feelings.

Doubling

Another powerful psychodramatic tool is called 'doubling'. Doubling statements are offered as possible unexpressed inner thoughts. The statements are in service to the person doing the work, that is, statements that are consistent with the group member's story or perspective. However, effective doubling taps the empathy of the commonly shared human experience. The person who is doubling stands slightly to the side or behind the client and speaks as if they are the client, speaking in first person. The double statements mirror or amplify what the client is feeling or can make on open-ended statement inviting further internal exploration. Such a doubling statement might be "What I really need to tell you is…" Or the double can make an offering such as "Actually, I am furious at you because you left me." The person who is working on their story can correct or reject the doubling statement. One of the most important aspects of healing in grief groups is the connection clients feel with others in the group, to be fully seen by others, to know that they are not alone, and to have their own story held with tenderness by others. The tool of the double supports a greater connection.

Surplus Reality

'Surplus reality' is another psychodramatic concept that is particularly useful for supporting resolution of complex grief issues. Surplus reality means what might have been. The client can imagine and enact a plausibly different version of events or interactions. For example, the client might imagine that the one who has died has experienced redemption or rehabilitation, has a larger view of him- or herself, and is now able to see how hurtful his or her behavior was. In role reversal, the rehabilitated deceased person would plausibly feel and express sincere remorse at their actions. The bereaved who were hurt by issues such as addiction, mental health problems, or medical problems usually have multilayered memories that are both positive and negative. Surplus reality gives the bereaved person the experience of saying, in role reversal, and then hearing the deceased speak from their best self—no longer affected by the elements that had been such a painful burden in life.

Identifying and Amplifying Client Resources

Our work uses a strength-based orientation to work with grief and loss-related trauma. Revisiting the pain of loss without integration of new insights can be re-traumatizing. Psychologist Hudgins (2001) and Hudgins and Toscani (2013) developed an adaption to classical psychodrama, called the Therapeutic Spiral Model, which has been used effectively throughout the world in work with trauma survivors. One important aim of their work is to help clients stay in an emotional window of tolerance while working with trauma. They discovered the importance of identifying internal strengths and resources in preparation for work that touches trauma. This helps avoid flooding and allows for integration of new insights. This is relevant in grief work. When bereaved people are overwhelmed with grief and loss-related trauma, they lose touch with personal strengths and resilience, and lose the ability to integrate new insights. We invite clients early

14 Psychodrama and Sociometry

in our work to identify their interpersonal, intrapsychic, and transpersonal 'resources' or strengths, and further amplify them with role reversal into these strengths (described more fully later). As people move beyond an acute stage, we continue to underline client strengths. These, in turn, move clients towards finding a new normal that embodies satisfaction and life meaning.

Sylvia Israel (2019) and Scott Giacomucci (2019) provide an excellent overview of important safety and containment structures that are part of the Therapeutic Spiral Model. In addition to identifying and amplifying resources, the containing double and the body double, variations on the classical psychodrama double, are especially important for helping people reground themselves in the midst of intense feelings that come up with grief work.

Our grief work with clients has been influenced by personal experience with loss, and the transformative experiential aspect of psychodrama. Experiential action methods are used to amplify positive memories, create new and more compassionate narratives, and celebrate the influences of the loved one and the gifts of the relationship that are carried forward—with a sense of gratitude. Our approach doesn't try to find ways to distract or to only define coping strategies to avoid pain. Action methods support holding the sweetness of memories alongside the inevitable bitterness of loss. Our work supports acceptance of ambivalence, the possibility that tears may always be present on anniversary days, and that there may well be joy and satisfaction in the future as clients seek to redefine a new normal with life meaning. We are able to hold joy and sorrow simultaneously. We are complex beings.

Interwoven into each chapter are examples of the use of action methods/psychodrama with specific grief issues. All of the vignettes in the book describe what actually happened with clients who volunteered to work in action on the grief topics. We find that adequate warm-up with sociometry tools (see below) paves the way for group members to comfortably volunteer. We also find that group members who do not choose to actively participate often benefit greatly by observing the work of others. All vignettes use false names.

Sociometry Tools for Group Building, Assessment, and Warm-Up

Warm-up is a key component to doing deep emotional work. Group members enjoy sociometric warm-ups, which in turn facilitate readiness for work. The warm-ups promote group members to learn more about each other, revealing points of common experience, and possibly identifying what Moreno called 'tele', a feeling of resonance or being drawn to another person.

The sociometry warm-ups get group members on their feet, get them moving, and get them talking to each other as they respond to the warm-up directions. The responses to directions help to identify clusters of people with shared experience. It is a way for people to move comfortably toward acknowledging and talking about grief-related difficulties and feelings, and to see that others have similar feelings. Warm-ups are a critical component whereby group members ready themselves to work on a deeper and more authentic level. People move from a thinking center to a feeling center of self, which is where the most difficult grief issues reside. The sociometric warm-ups are useful tools for the facilitator to assess where the group is at collectively, to see particular difficulties for individuals, and for group members to see their own changes over time. We recommend *The Living Stage*, by Tian Dayton (2005), to those wishing for more information on sociometry. Below are some of the warm-ups that have been done in the grief groups.

Line Spectrograms

We suggest that an imaginary line is drawn across the room between pillows, scarves, or some other object to represent each end of the imaginary line. We ask a question, and the ends of the line represent two

Psychodrama and Sociometry   15

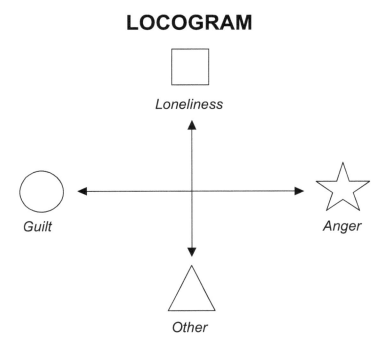

Figure 3.1. Spectrograms and locograms.

extremes (Figure 3.1). We ask group members to simultaneously place themselves where they are on the spectrum. The initial line spectrogram questions are easy questions that don't create any discomfort. This begins conversations with other group members. The questions might be:

How far did you travel to get here? That side of the line represents the longest travel time, the other the shortest travel time. Place yourself on the line spectrum for how long it took you to get to the group. (Group members start talking to each other.)

On this end of the line, you feel like you have no energy and on the other side of the line, you feel like the energizer bunny.

On this side, you have been attending for a while, on the other side you are new to the group.

On that end of the line, you are feeling anxious about being here tonight, on the other end you are feeling completely comfortable.

16 Psychodrama and Sociometry

The facilitator can get to more grief-related prompts after a few questions. Below are examples for a loss of partner/spouse group. The questions can be adapted for groups focused on other types of loss.

Place yourself on the spectrum based on the length of time since the death of your partner or spouse. (Group members can be invited to say the name of their loved one and the date of his or her death.)

Place yourself on the line spectrum of how long you were together.

Place yourself on the spectrum of how prepared you were for your partner's death—for example, whether you had any advance preparation (in the case of illness) or the death was sudden.

Line spectrogram questions are a useful tool to assess how group members are experiencing specific grief issues. Questions can be easily related to the grief topics, such as:

Sadness: I am crying every day vs. I am crying infrequently.
Loneliness: I have difficulty being around others vs. I make the effort and enjoy being around people I care about. Or, I feel very isolated; I have few, if any, friends that I can talk to when I am very sad vs. I have a good social network and feel a lot of support.
Guilt: I sometimes feel I did not do enough to support my spouse or partner vs. I know I did the best I could.
Anger: I feel angry about my partner/spouse's death vs. I feel acceptance because I know there were things that are beyond my control.
Coping strategies: I still feel intense grief vs. I feel I have coping strategies that are helping me.
Meaning: I feel hopeless about the future vs. I feel my life is important; I have purpose and meaning.
Integration of the bittersweet: Memories cause me a lot of pain vs. I can remember happy memories with joy.

The entire group sees that certain grief issues are harder for those who very recently lost a loved one as compared to those who have been living with loss for a longer time. For someone who is in early-stage grief this observation provides hope. Group members who have been attending the group for a while see improvement as they place themselves differently on the line spectrograms over time. They notice their own changes—that certain issues are not as difficult as they were when they first started attending.

Locograms are a variation of line spectrograms in which the group leader designates four spots in the room that are linked with a grief topic and group members choose the spot that most closely represents a topic they are currently struggling with. For example, the facilitator specifies three core grief issues—sadness, loneliness, guilt, or anger—in addition to 'other' (for an issue the facilitator didn't name), assigning a certain spot in the room to that issue. The facilitator asks, "what is the most difficult issue for you today?" Group members move to place themselves in the room related to the issue they are most struggling with. We invite group members to say a few words about why they placed themselves in a specific spot.

This is a useful assessment tool for the facilitator to see whether there is a common issue that is particularly difficult for many in the group. Group members see that, although group members move to various spots, there are also others struggling with the same issue. Group members can also place themselves between two issues that are both most difficult or can stand in the 'other' spot, indicating something that was not named.

Step-in Circle

Group members stand in a circle. One person steps in with a statement "who like me" followed by a statement that is true for the person stepping in. This allows group members to check who has the same or similar experiences. There are inevitable glances of sympathy as group members see other group members share the same or similar experience. The facilitator starts the questions and then group members take over. Many of the questions below were asked by actual group members.

- Who like me did (or did not) have children together with their partner?
- Who like me had difficulty with family members after the death of their partner or spouse?
- Who like me is angry at God?
- Who like me has felt their partner's loving presence?
- Who like me has dreams about their partner?
- Who like me feels especially sad that their partner didn't live to see the family milestones—graduations, marriages, births?
- Who like me has hopes of experiencing love again?

The last question asked by the facilitator is positive. "Who like me has one person that I know is there for me?"

The rest of the session entails sharing what group members felt or noticed during the sociometric exercises.

There is a great deal of research that explores the neurobiological basis of change using experiential action methods, and numerous studies have found that experiential action methods are effective across many settings. It is the treatment of choice in work with trauma because experiential action methods provide a holistic new experience, with new insights—which of course creates changes in the brain. We discuss this in more detail in Appendix II.

Bibliography

Blatner, A. (2004). *Foundations of psychodrama: history, drama, and practice* (4th ed.). New York: Springer.

Dayton, T. (2005). *The living stage: a step by step guide to psychodrama, sociometry, and experiential group therapy*. Deerfield Beach, FL: Health Communications.

Giacomucci, S. (2019). Trauma survivor's inner role atom: a clinical map for posttraumatic growth. *Journal of Psychodrama, Sociometry, and Group Psychotherapy*, 6: 115–129.

Hudgins, K. (2001). *Experiential psychotherapy to treat trauma: the therapeutic spiral model*. New York: Springer.

Hudgins, K., & Toscani, F. (eds.) (2013). *Healing world trauma with the therapeutic spiral model: psychodramatic stories from the frontlines*. London: Jessica Kingsley.

Israel, S. (2019). The therapeutic spiral model: a psychodramatic whole-person approach to working with trauma. In I.A. Serlin, S. Krippner, & K Rockerfeller (eds.), *Integrated care for the traumatized: a whole-person approach* (pp. 91–108). London: Rowan and Littlefield.

CHAPTER 4

THE BEGINNING

Sharing the Story

We suggest that participation in the groups start one month or later after the death of their family member. We have seen group members start attending even decades after the death of a loved one as they finally realize that they need to address their grief.

In the first meeting, standard group ground rules (confidentiality, voluntary participation, no cross-talk, no critique, no comparing) are stated and we ask members to indicate agreement. Group members are then invited to share about their loss in whatever detail they feel comfortable. Some, after recent loss, are in very raw grief, while others, unable to initially work with their grief, find they must unlock the slammed door that has kept their grief unresolved. Why do some wait for a long time to address grief? Putting grief away is a successful short-term coping mechanism that avoids pain and allows people to continue to function and maintain responsibilities. Practically speaking, bereaved with this coping mechanism often hold the 'strong one' position for the family—taking care of others, while they themselves often do not receive the support they also need. Severe depression or substance abuse can develop as problems when grief is not processed.

The first meeting is often the first time bereaved people have been invited to speak fully and honestly about their internal experience. The group facilitators encourage group members to know that the group will be a tender container and that they are not alone with what they are experiencing. Below are several handouts that are appropriate for the first meeting.

Grief and the Heart

Grief is a unique experience for those of us who have it. We may try to put it in some familiar category such as depression or a physical malady, but there are some particular aspects of grief that make it like nothing else.

Someone you love has been taken away from you against your will and maybe also against his/her will. The loss can also be the loss of a job, health, or a former way of life.

Love can be felt all over the body, but the primary place where we experience love and loss is the heart area, in the center of the chest. It can feel like an ache or real pain.

Why the heart? The heart's primary job is to channel love and connection to you and then to others. It does its best job when it is allowed to feel. It feels everything your being experiences every day, and processes those feelings.

Trying to Shut Down Feelings

We may try to shut down all that feeling processing by thinking a lot, keeping busy or distracted, or by denying the feelings. However, the heart will struggle while being ignored and restricted. You might feel more pain later on.

If you let the heart do its job, it will find balance eventually in its own time.

What You Can Do to Help the Heart

The heart loves tenderness and kindness. It loves being recognized for its important role in your life.

- Being in nature or having cut flowers in your house
- Nurturing of any kind, such as bubble baths, massages, manicures/pedicures
- Naps with cats, dogs, or lots of comfy pillows
- Meditation with or without guided imagery
- Soothing foods or drinks such as warm tea
- Learning to listen to your body and your gut feelings
- Colors that you find soothing, such as pink, green, yellow, and so on
- Soothing or uplifting music
- Gentle exercise such as walks in a park with trees and grass
- Spending time with supportive friends who listen
- Spending time with yourself.

© Copyright material from Darrow and Childs (2020), *Experiential Action Methods and Tools for Healing Grief and Loss-Related Trauma*, Routledge.

Grief and Mourning

The death of someone close to us throws us into a sea of chaotic feelings. Sometimes, the waves of emotions seem powerful enough to threaten our very survival; sometimes they feel relentless and never ending; sometimes they quieten down only to arise months or even years later when we least expect them.

Grief is not something we ever really 'get over'. Our loss remains a fact for a lifetime. Nothing about grief's journey is simple; there is no tidy progression of stages and its course is long and circular.

While there is no clear roadmap, there are some features common to almost everyone's experience. Some of the dimensions presented below may ebb and flow within a natural healing process. The walk down grief's road requires time, patience, attention, hard work, and lots of loving care.

Grief is the natural human response to any loss, not only death. An illness, a job change, divorce and separation, unfulfilled dream, a move to a new location, or any other change can bring about a grief response. Grief is not a problem. It is a normal, healthy process of healing.

Shock and Surprise

Even if death is expected, you may feel numb or anesthetized for several weeks afterward. Your actions may be mechanical and you may get things done (for example, handle all the funeral details) but you are not 'all there'. People around you may be saying "Isn't he strong?" or "She's handling this so well." The impact or reality of the death has not fully reached you. This period of shock is your psyche's way of protecting you by allowing reality in slowly. If the loss is sudden, unexpected, or violent, the period of numbness may be longer.

Emotional Release

As the period of shock wears off, reality can be acutely painful. As the full impact gradually dawns on you, conflict may arise about whether to show grief or not to show it. How much and for how long? You might try to keep up a good front or remain strong, even though you may feel like crying or screaming. If people are praising you for being so brave and not 'falling apart', do you dare show them how you really feel? This is a time when emotional release is important and should be encouraged. Concealing painful feelings may prolong the grief process and increase physical and emotional distress. At this point, other mourners can help support your expression of grief.

Loneliness

Sometimes, even before the funeral, the feelings of loneliness, isolation, and depression begin. The funeral is the focus for realizing that your loved one is really gone. Family and friends can be helpful and consoling, but after the funeral the prevailing attitude is "it's all over." The supportive people in your life may disappear. After the funeral, you may suffer a second major loss—everyday contact with your loved one. For some this might mean no home-cooked meals, coming home to an empty house, no welcome-home greeting. For others, it may mean no one to cook for, no one to help with household chores, no one to hold and share the small everyday moments and rituals. If your child has died, there is no one who comes home from school, no one to share your future dreams with or to see grow up. If your loved one has been sick for a long time, you no longer have hospital visits to make. Your entire routine of daily living has been shattered. You are alone, suddenly overcome by an utter sense of depression and despair. It is important at this point to have people in your life who can validate the magnitude of your loss.

Physical Stress with Anxiety

Questions that may come up for you: What am I going to do? What's going to happen to me? How can I get along without her? Will I lose my friends? You may develop the same type of physical symptoms your loved one had. For example, if she had a heart attack, you may now have chest pains. Anxiety and stress may bring with it physical symptoms such as shortness of breath, insomnia, headaches, backaches, or an upset stomach. During the entire grief process, you need to take especially good care of your body; you are vulnerable and may need a lot more rest. You may want to see your physician for a physical examination.

Panic and Disorganization

You may have trouble concentrating on anything but the loss. You may feel something is wrong with you; you may replay thoughts such as: I can't get the images out of my mind, won't they ever stop? Sometimes I think I see her. Sometimes I feel his touch. Sometimes I hear his voice. I've got to do something. I can't sleep. I can't eat. All I do is think about her. Will it ever stop hurting? Will I ever stop dreaming about her? As a bereaved person, you need to know this does not mean you are going crazy. This is a normal part of the grieving process.

Guilt

When faced with real or imagined guilt, you may begin asking questions like: What did I do wrong? What if I'd stayed awake, hadn't gone to work, kissed her, showed I loved him? These questions may indicate guilt, regrets, or unfinished business, which need to be expressed. These feelings can be brought to the surface by sharing with a non-judgmental listener, in a letter, or in a diary. Partial or complete interruption of the grief process at this time can cause severe depression and/or suicidal feelings.

Hostility, Projection, and Anger

In conjunction with or emerging from the feelings of guilt, you may experience hostility. Maybe you are hostile to people whom you perceived contributed to your problem. For example, to the physician: Why didn't he do something? Why didn't he get there in time? Did he do everything he could? You may be experiencing anger at friends who draw away from you or seem to belittle your loss with well-meaning but clumsy remarks. You may be furious with God or fate for taking away your loved one. You may also be angry with your loved one for dying and abandoning you. Anger is a very normal, human emotion and it is important to find ways to release those feelings of "What I'm going through is so unfair." "Why did it have to happen to him? He was a good person." Talking about it and physical activity both help keep anger from burning inside.

Suffering in Silence and Depression

This is a time when you may suffer in silence. You might feel fatigued, worn out, and unable to get started in any activity. Your thought processes are involved with the loss. You may feel emptiness and loneliness but you may no longer want to talk about it. You recognize that others expect you to stop grieving. Your tears, anger, frustrations, or depression are poorly tolerated by others several weeks after the funeral. Except for the initial loss, this stage is the hardest. You, the bereaved person, feel all alone. You may have feelings of "not wanting to go on" and then shock or guilt for having such thoughts. This is a period when you are recreating meaning in life—and it takes time.

The Gradual Overcoming of Grief

Your adjustment to a new status in life gradually occurs with working through this grief period. There can be a noticeable change as early as four weeks to three months, but often it is much longer. By the end of this phase, there may be considerable brightening of mood, more activity, and the beginning of re-establishment with people.

Readjustment to Reality

Because traditional symbols of grief, such as the black veil or clothing or arm band, are out of style, many times it is easy for others to forget you are grieving. You are beginning to restructure your life without the physical presence of your loved one. You will always hold the essence of the person who died. The work of grief is releasing the pain and keeping the love and memories in your heart. You may want to take a vacation or a trip or get involved in a new activity, or take up old activities you used to like. Occasionally, you may feel twinges of guilt as you begin to enjoy yourself or laugh freely again, as though you are somehow betraying the memory of your lost loved one. It is helpful to be aware of guilt feelings that get in the way of readjustment. It is also helpful to recognize that wedding anniversaries, holidays, birthdays, or the anniversary date of the death may cause a temporary flood of feelings or may bring back a very short version of the grief process. This is normal and does not mean that you will be in acute pain forever.

Remember: *Grief is a natural life experience we all go through in healing the reality of loss and change. Each grief journey is unique. Reaching out to others for support and being kind to one's self can enable us to survive the pain.*

© Copyright material from Darrow and Childs (2020), *Experiential Action Methods and Tools for Healing Grief and Loss-Related Trauma*, Routledge.

CHAPTER 5

TOOLS FOR COPING

The second session is geared toward exploring coping strategies to navigate the intensity of feelings. Supportive facilitators provide psychoeducation on the uniqueness of each person's grief process and that there is not a defined time frame at which grief is done. Group members are encouraged to share issues that are most difficult right now. Group members are encouraged to be aware of what they need and to make decisions that honor their own needs. The idea of finding a new normal is introduced and explored. In every meeting, group members are encouraged to be gentle with themselves.

The handouts which follow expand on this topic and include symptoms, feelings, and reactions to grief, ideas for self-care, stress reduction, and ways to ground oneself. The following symptoms worksheet is given to group members for them to circle symptoms they themselves have experienced. Group members are then invited to circle the three or four that are most difficult right now. This worksheet can be provided more than once with instructions to indicate change—which symptoms have become less difficult, are still very difficult, or have increased in intensity? Over time, group member can see their own process of change. Group members then share their own experience with others.

Normal Symptoms, Feelings, and Reactions to Loss of a Loved One

Decreased energy   Headache   Tension   Rapid heartbeat

Loss of sleep   Excessive sleep   Nausea   Forgetfulness

Loss of appetite   Excessive eating   Being distracted   Helplessness

Inability to function at home   Inability to function at work   Exhaustion

Distance from friends   Strained relationships

Sadness   Loneliness   Feeling abandoned   Guilt   Anxiety

Anger   Isolation   Shock, disbelief   Relief   Substance abuse

Depression   Apathy   Numbness   Fear   Flashbacks

Yearning and missing   Out of control   Vulnerability   Loss of belief

Paralysis   Withdrawal   Craziness   Dread   Moodiness

Repeating memories   Stuck in grief   Agitated   Helplessness   Regret

Suicidal thoughts/feelings   Lower short-term memory   Emptiness

Loss of meaning or purpose   Loss of control   Feeling off-balance   Disorganized

Other _____ _____ _____

© Copyright material from Darrow and Childs (2020), *Experiential Action Methods and Tools for Healing Grief and Loss-Related Trauma*, Routledge.

Daily Log: Personal Check-In Process

The daily log is a useful coping tool for the bereaved as well as responders and disaster survivors. The daily log is a tool for grounding, centering, and listening to where people are at on a daily basis. It also illuminates actions to take care of oneself immediately and in the future to survive and build meaning.

The power of the daily log is its regular and clear check-in process. The first questions promote listening, honoring, and paying attention to the body's basic messages. We recommend that people attend to their log at the end of their day. For folks who work night or swing shift, this check-in gives them an ending to their day, whenever that is in chronological time.

Daily log: personal check-in

1. How do I feel right now? Do a body scan. What parts of my body are experiencing sensations? They may include tightness, soreness, heaviness, pain, tingling, lightness, warmth, cold, softness, tenderness, for example.

2. What is the most powerful sensation right now? What does that part of my body want to express? What does it say?

3. What have I eaten today? When did I eat? Where did I eat?

4. What exercise did I get today?

5. What did I do today that felt good? (Just for me)

6. As I sit here quietly, what memories, thoughts, or feelings surface about the day and the day's activities?

7. Do I need to do anything to complete any unfinished interaction or feeling? What do I need right now to feel complete, resolved, and at peace?

8. How can I go about meeting my needs right now? What action steps do I need to do?

9. What are my dreams or daydreams? What message is there for me in these dreams?

10. What is the message for me in this day?

© Copyright material from Darrow and Childs (2020), *Experiential Action Methods and Tools for Healing Grief and Loss-Related Trauma*, Routledge.

Below is a vignette with a mother, Susan, whose son died by suicide—one of the most difficult griefs to experience. She was, in her own words, "totally disconnected from myself and from my world." When we gave her the daily log, she stated that the first question actually brought her to her body.

Susan: I feel tight, and heavy in my chest and abdomen. I feel a little 'spacey'.
Janet: What is the most powerful sensation you feel right now?
Susan (becoming flushed and physically expressive): I am so mad at Brian [her son] for giving up. I tried to save him so many times—from homelessness, from drug addiction behavior, from prison. I never gave up and I don't understand how he could give up. How can I feel this way? I shouldn't be angry.

It is a common experience that those who have lost loved ones do not want to acknowledge anger, because it isn't compassionate or 'spiritual'.

Janet (setting an empty chair): Susan, would you like to talk to your son?
Susan (nodding and crying): I am so angry that you killed yourself. How could you do this? I tried so hard to help you. Do you know what this has done to me? I feel empty every day. Why couldn't I help you and why didn't you take my help?
Janet: I invite you to reverse roles and take the chair of your son Brian and speak from his voice.
Susan (in the role of Brian): I am so sorry, Mom. I thought I would do you a favor because I was such a burden and hadn't taken your help. It was me, I just wasn't able. I knew as soon as I acted, that it was wrong. I regretted what I had done.
Janet: It sounds like you love your mother.
Susan (in the role of Brian): Yes, I will be with you, now that I am not affected by my disease of addiction. I will be your 'angel'.
Janet: Reverse roles and reply to your son.
Susan: Yes, I know you loved me. I know you had a disease. It is good to think that you are now free. I will always love you.

In her own grief process, Susan identified an action step, and began to volunteer at an agency which supports people living with addiction and mental health issues. She became a speaker and a group facilitator for the aftermath of suicide, especially for parents whose children had died by suicide.

The daily log is a powerful tool to help identify what is needed to feel complete and at peace at the end of the day. This daily check-in encourages greater awareness—about what one has done, what he or she needs, and identifying what has given meaning in the day. This boosts the sense of gratitude and facilitates the mind's ability to focus on the message of the day with an eagle's eye view, rather than a myopic perspective of individual events.

Tools for Coping

Here are some tools for coping with the everyday feelings and realities of living when you are experiencing a major loss, illness, death, separation, or any life change.

- Be gentle with your own feeling process. Avoid self-judgment. Do not put "I should have" on yourself.
- Find a supportive person or persons you can trust. Share your honest feelings.
- Give yourself time for healing. The timing of grief cannot be rushed. Plan your time so that you have specific time to focus on your loss, and special time to escape from the pain of what you are facing.
- When you experience fear, anger, helplessness, sorrow, pain, emptiness, isolation, or depression, it can be very confusing. Questions to ask yourself, to focus, are:
  - What is the most difficult right now? (Check body sensations, as well as thoughts and emotions.)
  - What do I need right now? (Focus on immediate, attainable needs.)
  - How can I meet (or get a supportive friend to help me meet) these needs right now?
- Try to maintain as regular a schedule as possible. Avoid unrealistic expectations/goals of yourself.
- Maintain an awareness of your body's need for nutrition and rest. If symptoms arise that are new or unusual, see a physician.
- Listening to your body is critical during this period. Listening is different than doing something for your body. Listening means honoring the message your body is sending you.
  - Words or tears that are unexpressed will cause a lump in our throats.
  - Anger that is held inside can give us an upset stomach, headache, or tight neck and shoulders.
  - Fear can be expressed by wringing hands, shakiness, or queasy stomach.
  - Guilt or resentment can feel like physical burdens we are carrying. (I feel like I weigh a ton.)
  - Sorrow or depression can feel like pressure or 'breaking' in our heart or chest area. Breathing may be labored. We may heave great sighs.
- Often combinations of feelings are felt. It is important to ask the part of the body that is feeling these sensations the following:
  - If you could talk, what would you say?
  - What would you need?
  - What picture or symbol best expresses you right now? What do you look like?
  - What is happening with you right now?
- Writing a letter or drawing a picture about your illness, loss, or grief is a healing way to get your feelings from the inside to the outside. Writing to others with whom you feel incomplete or to your body, or to institutions, the universe, your illness, God, or anybody enables you to process what your body longs to say. It also enables you to release anger, frustration, and isolation and move to a forgiving, life-affirming love for yourself and those who have touched your life.

© Copyright material from Darrow and Childs (2020), *Experiential Action Methods and Tools for Healing Grief and Loss-Related Trauma*, Routledge.

- Record a life evaluation: who and what has been important in my life? Have I done what I wanted in my life? What needs to be done for me to be fulfilled? What activities would give me the most satisfaction right now? Is there anything or anyone with whom I feel incomplete or unfinished at this time? Is there anything I need to do about that—for me?
- Realize the world around you and your daily activities will be filled with landmines—moments of painful realizations of your loss and resentment at a world that marches on, apparently without noticing or caring. Verbalize these feelings. They are normal.
- As a person facing grief or illness, you will be stigmatized. People will not know how to handle you or make you better. They may even be afraid of you, because you represent fear and pain that could come into their lives. Allow yourself to be gently honest about your needs. Focus on taking care of yourself and surrounding yourself with caring people who will accept your process. You do not have to make it better for the world. This is a time to care for you—as you would the most tender, vulnerable child who is hurting.

For you, when you are left with an empty or breaking heart:

- Realize and recognize the loss. Take time for nature's slow, sure, stuttering process of healing.
- Give yourself massive doses of restful relaxation and routine busy-ness.
- Know that powerful, overwhelming feelings will lessen with time.
- Be vulnerable, share your pain, and be humble enough to accept support.
- Surround yourself with life, plants, animals, and friends.
- Use mementos to help your mourning, not to live in the past.
- Avoid rebound relationships, big decisions, and anything addictive.
- Keep a diary and record successes, memories, and struggles.
- Prepare for change, new interests, new friends, solitude, creativity, and growth.
- Know that holidays and anniversaries can bring back the painful feelings you thought you had worked through.
- Recognize that forgiveness (of yourself and others) is a vital part of the healing process and that it cannot be rushed.
- Realize that any new death or loss-related crisis will bring up feelings about past losses.

Grief is a spiral of feelings, seasons, and experiences. It is not a straight line with a beginning and ending. The process of grief is healing the pain of loss and keeping the treasured memories and love within your heart.

Healing Feelings: Tools for Survival

Acknowledge

The first step in dealing with difficult feelings, such as grief, anger, pain, guilt, and sadness, is to acknowledge that you are experiencing them. Listen to your body—and the different sensations and feelings your body is experiencing. Attempt to quieten the rational mind that will sometimes try to convince you that you are fine—that nothing's wrong. Accept your feelings, whatever they are. Try not to judge them (C'mon, you don't have the right to feel that way), transcend them (I'm too nice a person to have these feelings), or feel like you have to act them out (well, if I feel that way, I guess I'll just have to kill myself, or kill someone else). Feelings are irrational—sometimes we may never know why we are feeling a certain way. The important thing to remember is whatever feelings are present, they are OK.

Express

The next step in healing feelings is to get the feelings from inside the body to the outside. An ancient Chinese proverb states, "A feeling held inside increases its strength a thousand times." It can be difficult to find a safe person and place to do this. Talking helps, especially talking about the details of the feelings—the horror, the guilt, the incident, or the aftermath. Letter writing to the person you are having the feelings about also helps, even if this person is dead or far away. Even letter writing to yourself is helpful (the origin of diaries or journals). Drawing, painting, or artwork is a good way to get feelings out, but be sure to make it a free-flowing experience where you are not judging your 'creation'. The healing is the doing, not the finished product. Hitting pillows, banging on phone books with rubber hoses, running, or doing anything physically active is another outlet for feelings. Screaming, yelling, and crying are also healthy releases.

Act

The third step in healing feelings is to do something active to begin the healing process. This can begin by expressing the feelings by lighting a candle, doing a ritual (visiting the grave, planting a tree, having a celebration of life), wearing a ribbon or some other indication that we are in a tender and vulnerable place, or creating a book of memories. Sometimes, we need to burn or bury what we need to let go of as a physical way to release. With guilt, sometimes we need to do some act for atonement to begin the healing. However insignificant or silly it seems, allow your own creativity to tell you what you need to do. You know better than anyone else what would make you feel a little lighter, a little more resolved, a little better.

Reconnect

After the hard work of healing feelings, it is vitally important that we give ourselves a reward. When working with feelings, it is good to focus on them for a limited period, and then give yourself a break.

© Copyright material from Darrow and Childs (2020), *Experiential Action Methods and Tools for Healing Grief and Loss-Related Trauma*, Routledge.

During this break, do something fun and life affirming just for you. You can share time with others or just allow yourself to do something nurturing or 'selfish'. When we deal with feelings, we tap into a special part of us that is very childlike. While we are very capable adults most of the time, it is important to acknowledge and support that little child in our heart, and to move on with the joy and meaning our life can give us. Remember, this does not take hours of therapy—feelings do not last forever if they are allowed to come out. We are not only our feelings, we are complex, multifaceted human beings who have the ability to deal with our feelings in a positive, empowered way.

Self-Care Toolbox

- Call a friend and catch up.
- Light a candle.
- Read your favorite magazine.
- Write poetry.
- Take a walk.
- Go to a local coffee house for a warm, soothing latte.
- Take up a new hobby—knitting, crocheting, cooking, jogging.
- Join a meet-up group.
- Go out for frozen yogurt and get some toppings.
- Join a book club.
- Try a new recipe, one that you have always wanted to make.
- Have a glass of your favorite beverage by the fire.
- Sit in the lobby of a beautiful hotel and people watch.
- Buy a piece of special candy without feeling guilty. (Don't forget to get your sample piece.)
- Buy yourself the cutest stuffed animal you can find. Get one for your inner child.
- Buy yourself a beautiful bouquet of flowers or sniff the aroma of flowers or fruit.
- Plant flowers in the garden.
- Search Pinterest for a new and interesting idea to try.
- Put a beautiful candle in every room of your home.
- Join a gym and begin working out.
- Plan a 'boys' or 'girls' night out.
- Watch old episodes of your favorite TV show.
- Curl up with a warm blanket and watch a movie.
- Lie in bed all day in your pajamas and read.
- Get a massage.
- Take an Epsom salt bath, with a favorite fragrance.
- Go to the make-up counter and get a new look.
- Volunteer for your favorite cause.
- Put together a scrapbook or album of your favorite pictures.
- Go to a yoga, exercise, or dance class.
- Take a class at a local art and/or kitchen store for free.
- Do power walking in the mall in the morning before they open.
- Paint a room or an accent wall a new, cheery color.
- Buy a new perfume, cologne, or scented oil.
- Do a random act of kindness—pay it forward.
- Make a CD mix of your favorite music to support energy, relaxation, empowerment, and a loving heart.
- Play a drum and/or coffee can, plastic bin, or a homemade drum/rhythm instrument.
- Sing karaoke or make up a song or chant.
- Dance.
- Meditate. Join a group praying or meditating for a specific cause or focus.
- Attend a free concert or poetry/book reading.

© Copyright material from Darrow and Childs (2020), *Experiential Action Methods and Tools for Healing Grief and Loss-Related Trauma*, Routledge.

Grounding and Stress Reduction Tools

We think of calming ourselves by taking deep breaths and exercising, which are both wonderful ways of releasing stress. We may have heard of grounding but not know much about it.

Our bodies have an energetic field created by our circulatory and other systems. This is normal. Think of when you get a static shock. However, when we are stressed, we have a lot of excess energy in our bodies with no place for it to go. It can make you feel unsettled, as if you have to do something, but you don't know what, and generally it adds to our stress. A good way to get rid of that excess energy is to 'ground' our bodies. Some ways to ground are to take a walk, wash your hands, do some gardening, or eat a favorite food. If that is not enough, here are some other ideas.

- Epsom salt baths: follow the package directions and put the salts into your bath alone or with bubble bath or with essential oils. Most bath salts do the same thing as Epsom salts—balance your pH by pulling acid out (stress) and raise your pH to a more balanced level between acid and alkaline. This has a grounding effect.
- Sit in a chair and place your feet on the floor. Imagine your spine being full of energy. Imagine your spine is a conduit like a redwood tree or a stretchy tube of light. Let that conduit enter the earth and release all your excess energy. Imagine light from above, any color that feels good to you, coming in and bringing anything you want with it—happiness, calmness, and so on.
- To help you relax before sleep, lie on your back and imagine a conduit of any kind that works for you to connect your back between your hips and your chest to the earth. Let energy release through that conduit. It helps to calm a busy mind.
- Create a positive imprint to replace negative sensory images you may have as a result of the stress. When you complete a positive imprinting, you can utilize this to reground you in the present moment with a lasting imprint that is positive in orientation.
- Take a walk, preferably outside if possible. The connection with nature and the forward-moving action give your body and mind the message that you are taking control and doing something active to respond to the stress. It also reduces the stress hormones in your body and creates endorphin release—more commonly known as a runner's high. This is great to do with a support person, as you are both moving forward, side by side, creating an alliance and a united front to respond to the issue.
- Tap into what is good in your life, whether that be people or pets that you know, or activities that give you energy and happiness, or inner resources that bring you peace.
- Remember to stretch and gently roll your shoulders and neck. Even moving your body a little bit makes a huge difference. It shifts the energy and the mood that you are working in instantaneously. And of course, don't forget your 'tactical breathing'—deep breath in over four seconds, hold for four seconds, exhale over four seconds (or longer), and hold for four seconds. Repeat this pattern.
- Remember you make a difference with what you do and who you are. The fact that you are on the front lines with your presence brings healing and comfort. Even if you cannot make a situation better, your involvement and action create an anchor of support and strength that others will remember for a lifetime.

Emotional trauma is equal to physical injury.

Comfort Anchors, Comfort Tasks

Comfort anchors

Comfort anchors include any object or physical manifestation (such as a place) that provides comfort and grounding—a piece of clothing or jewelry, a stuffed animal, memory reminder (example: a concert ticket) that connects us with what is good in our life, or a symbol of love.

Comfort task

A comfort task is any activity that brings us a feeling of peace and/or a break from the hectic pace of our life—a treat or delight that honors our person and gives us a chance to relax or play.

My comfort anchors

My comfort tasks

The following chapters about specific grief topics are not intended to follow a specific order. The socio-metric warm-ups clearly indicate when there is a theme that is resonating with the group members.

After check-in, the facilitator talks about the topic in a way that normalizes aspects of the particular topic. We have found that it works well to space out grief topics that are difficult to resolve such as guilt, anger, and frozen moments with topics that either do not carry as much charge, or topics that provide the opportunity to honor and remember the person who died. We give out the topic-specific handouts at the end of the meeting. Group members have expressed appreciation for receiving these handouts to read later.

CHAPTER 6

LONELINESS

What Is Loneliness?

Loneliness is one of the most difficult dimensions in grief and can be present with all the other feelings, such as anger, fear, sadness, guilt, and depression. Sometimes, people can be lonely in a crowd or family gathering. Loneliness has nothing to do with the amount of people around us. Loneliness is a universal aspect of the healing grief journey.

- We cannot fix loneliness.
- We lose ourselves in loneliness—we are not who we used to be.
- We lose our sense of personal power.
- We are not in touch with anything good in our lives.

What are some of the feelings associated with loneliness?

- Not able to share or communicate deep feelings
- No one to share with
- Heaviness, physical tightness in chest
- Spiritual bankruptcy. Not able to connect with faith
- Not feeling—numb
- Not able to talk or being unable to tell your truth
- Not loved or lovable
- Not having a friend who understands non-verbal feelings
- Being with a group of people but unable to connect
- Feeling detached, isolated
- Missing something/someone
- Not being heard or acknowledged
- Not getting out or around
- No one to listen to or hug
- Being left behind
- Hopelessness
- Emptiness
- Aching, gnawing pit
- Separation
- Not fitting in
- Emotional wasteland
- Feeling lost
- Feeling rejected.

What we need to ease these feelings of loneliness:

- Someone with whom to talk
- Somewhere to go
- Someone with whom to share feelings
- Someone with whom to share memories.

© Copyright material from Darrow and Childs (2020), *Experiential Action Methods and Tools for Healing Grief and Loss-Related Trauma*, Routledge.

Action Tools in Working with Loneliness

Loneliness is universal after loss. The loneliness comes from the disparity between being able to authentically express feelings and the difficulty this poses for family, friends, and professional network. Bereaved people often choose to isolate themselves rather than pretend all is well. Many grieving people speak of the loss as losing their best friend, the person with whom they were able to share a depth of connection. There is a profound loss of intimate connection. We introduce the following exercise with the hope that identifying and amplifying feelings of being loved, supported, and cared for by others are therapeutic in offsetting loneliness.

The exercise, called the 'social atom', is a sociometric tool which is useful for identifying interpersonal and transpersonal connections. It maps out each person's social network with family, friends, relatives, children, and neighbors with an indication of how close or distant they feel from those people. The social atom is a drawing in which the individual places themselves in the middle of the sheet of paper (with a circle if a female or a triangle if a male). The individual is invited to indicate people in their network (again, with females drawn as circles and males as triangles) at an appropriate distance from the symbol representing themselves (Figure 6.1). Group members are also told that the people they place on their social atom can be living or deceased. Group members choose what closeness or distance may mean; it could be emotional or geographic proximity. They draw solid lines with arrows on both sides of the line for those representing a mutually positive connection. Lines with dashes indicate some trouble in the relationship.

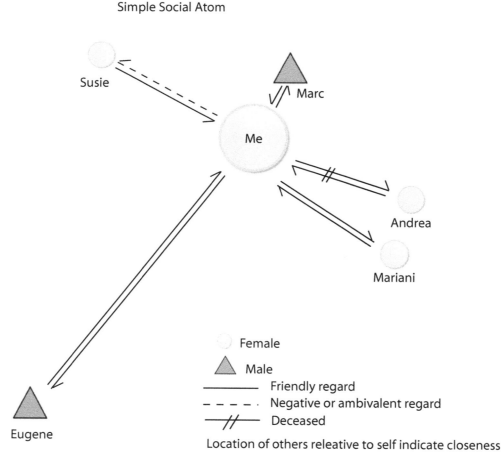

Figure 6.1. Social atom.

Double lines across the connecting lines indicate that the person is deceased. After everyone has finished, group members are invited to share their social atom and then asked to pick one or two people in their social atom who are particularly supportive for them now. They are asked to write a message to or make a request for this supportive person. Alternatively, the group members might be invited to choose a person on their social atom with whom they wish a better relationship—which then moves into action with psychodrama methods.

The following vignettes are accounts of group members exploring relationships with the people on their social atoms. They are invited to have conversations, try out asking for what they need, or to acknowledge and thank people on their social atoms. All names and identifying information have been changed.

Vignettes on Loneliness

Barbara volunteered to work with her social atom. This client had been in a relationship with a man for twenty years. He had never been very expressive towards her; he had never told her he loved her. She ultimately left the relationship, and he died shortly thereafter. Barbara had grief that was complicated by unresolved feelings and guilt. This client chose the man with whom she was currently involved romantically as her most important support person at this time.

> *Lusijah:* Tell me three things about this man. (These questions help the group member sink into feeling the other person, which is important to warm them up to the role of the other.)
>
> *Barbara:* He is kind, he's funny, and he is particular about doing things well.
>
> *Lusijah:* Wonderful. Can we bring him into the room?
>
> *Barbara:* OK.
>
> *Lusijah* (Indicating a place where the boyfriend is to be brought into the room): Barbara, what would you like to say to your boyfriend?
>
> *Barbara:* I want to get better. I want to stop feeling so badly.
>
> *Lusijah:* I would like you to step into his role, now. (The group member actually steps physically to the designated spot when taking on a role.)
>
> *Lusijah:* What is your name?
>
> *Barbara (in the role of boyfriend):* Chuck.
>
> *Lusijah:* How long have you known Barbara?
>
> *Barbara (in the role of boyfriend):* We met shortly after she moved to San Jose, I guess a year ago. We've been together for six months.
>
> *Lusijah:* So, you know that Barbara has been working with her grief at the death of her former boyfriend?
>
> *Barbara (in the role of boyfriend):* Yes, I have encouraged her to do this work. I completely support her.
>
> *Lusijah:* You have been brought here by Barbara as her most important support. What words do you have for her that would be helpful for her to hear right now?
>
> *Barbara (in the role of boyfriend):* You are so beautiful. I love you so much. I want to create a new life with you, to create our own memories and traditions.
>
> *Lusijah to Barbara:* Reverse roles; I would like to for you to hear Chuck's message. Is it OK if I put my hands on your shoulders?
>
> *Barbara:* Yes.
>
> *Lusijah:* I am Chuck. I want you to know that I think you are so beautiful and I love you so much. I want to create a new life with you, to create our own memories and traditions. I want you to feel better.

40 Loneliness

Barbara became emotional while hearing the message. During the sharing, other group members reflected to Barbara that they had noticed her sinking into a more relaxed space while hearing the message of her boyfriend.

It is common for bereaved people to feel disconnected from others. Many experience disruption to their social network, and important connections can be broken and changed in unexpected ways by the death of a loved one. Sometimes, friends and family whom the bereaved person expects to be supportive are not there for them, while people who they would not expect to be supportive turn out to be. Siblings with the same parents can have very different responses in their grieving process. Also, there are changing needs and responsibilities within families after loss. For example, adult children may need to take on more responsibility for caring for the surviving parent. Below is an account of Sally's work with her social atom. Her father had died two years before. After sharing her social atom with the group, we asked her to psychodramatically 'bring in' the two most important people on her social atom to support her.

Sally: I would like to bring in my best friend Jane and my grandmother on my mother's side. She is no longer alive.

Lusijah: Who would you like to be here first?

Sally: Jane, I guess.

Lusijah: Could you please pick someone to play Jane? (Client chose a group member to play this role and the person came to the 'stage' to stand physically in the place designated to be for Jane.)

Lusijah to Sally: Tell me a couple of things about Jane.

Sally: I can be completely honest with Jane and she calls me on my bullshit.

Lusijah: OK, so reverse roles; you are now Jane. (Sally changes places physically with the person she had chosen to play Jane.)

Lusijah: Hi Jane. Tell me what you are wearing. (Early questions are geared to fully situate the group member in the other role.)

Sally (in the role of Jane): I am wearing my running clothes. I run a lot. In fact, this is something Sally and I do a lot together.

Lusijah: What shoes are you wearing? What color are they?

Sally (in the role of Jane): I'm wearing my running shoes; they are grey and blue.

Lusijah: How long have you known Sally?

Sally (in the role of Jane): Gosh, for many years. Our children were together in sports activities, they grew up together, we did a lot together and we came to be friends. She's my best friend now.

Lusijah: I've heard that you call Sally on her bullshit. What does this mean?

Sally (in the role of Jane): Oh, she has pity parties. I try to help her get out of it.

Lusijah: How do you do that?

Sally (in the role of Jane): I am just normal with her; we go out for a coffee or for a run. That usually helps.

Lusijah: Well, you have been brought here tonight as one of Sally's most important supports. I wonder, do you have words that you could say to Sally that might be helpful?

Sally (in the role of Jane): Yes, I was so happy when you started to actively remember your father, rather than not being able to talk about him. It was the elephant in the room that no one could talk about. Now you are talking about him, sharing memories. I think that this has helped everyone. We can all share memories now.

Lusijah: Reverse roles.

Jane (played by the person chosen by Sally to take Jane's role. The person paraphrases what Sally said in the role of Jane): I'm so glad you are remembering your dad now rather than pushing him away. I don't have to be worried about not talking about your dad. Now we can share happy memories about him.

Lusijah (speaking to Sally): Is there anything that Jane can do for you? You can ask her.

Sally (turning to Jane): Just be my friend.

Lusijah: Reverse roles.

Sally (in the role of Jane): I am your friend. I am here for you, Sally.

Lusijah: Reverse roles.

Lusijah: Are there any final words you would like to say to Jane for now?

Sally: (Smiling) Thank you.

Sally was then invited to bring in her grandmother. Sally chose someone to play the role of her grandmother and she came up and stood in the spot designated for Sally's grandmother..

Lusijah (to Sally): Reverse roles. (Sally steps into the role of her grandmother.) What is your name?

Sally (in the role of her grandmother): My name is Ann.

Lusijah: Tell me about yourself.

Sally (in the role of grandmother Ann): Well, I guess I was a little unusual for my time. I went to college back when women didn't go to college. I got married and was widowed. I was left with three children to raise by myself.

Lusijah: Wow, you sound like a very strong woman!

Sally (in the role of grandmother Ann): Well, I was helped by my faith. I was Catholic. Then I got married again and actually had a second life.

Lusijah: Wonderful. I can see why Sally brought you here tonight as an important support for her. You are a very strong woman. Do you have any words that might be helpful to her as she is struggling with her loss?

Sally (in the role of grandmother Ann): You are a strong person. Life is a struggle. Life is not always easy, but you are strong.

Lusijah (speaking to Sally): Now listen to the words of your grandmother. (Sally returns to her own chair as the person she chose to play her grandmother restated grandmother Ann's message.)

Sally: I don't feel very strong.

Lusijah (leaning in towards the client): I am going to make a doubling statement, something you might feel. You can restate it if it's true or change it if not.

Lusijah (as double to Sally): I wish I could be strong.

Sally: Yes, I want to be strong.

Lusijah: What would it look like for you to be strong?

Sally: I need to remember my dad with love. I need to accept that things will not be the way they were. I need to forgive my brother and mother.

Lusijah: Is there a final word you would like to say to your grandmother?

Sally: Thank you.

Lusijah: I would like you to make a body sculpture, that is, place your grandmother and Jane physically and relative to yourself in a way that shows how they support you. (It is important to first check that group members don't mind touching each other.) (Client linked arms with her best friend, Jane, placing her close to her side. The grandmother linked arms 'in spirit' and she was placed on the other side of the room.)

Lusijah: Does this feel complete for now?

Sally: Yes, thank you.

The individual's choice of whom to work with on their social atom varies widely. The exercise is very client-directed once it starts. Some have chosen friends, family, God, as well as the loved one who died. The universal belief that God is loving and compassionate strongly comes into play when group members choose God as an important support. Doing the role reversal with God is felt as a personal message from

42 Loneliness

God. They step away from the experience as having heard and felt God's loving message. "I know it is hard for you. Trust in Me, I am always with you." Or "Make time for Me in your life." It is quite powerful.

Below describes a vignette in which a group member, working with his social atom, chose his wife, who had died suddenly.

Lusijah: Looking at your social atom, who is the most important person right now?

George: My wife.

Lusijah: Hmmm, yes... George, can we invite her into the room?

George: Yes.

Lusijah (sets up an empty chair and gestures to George to sit in the chair): George, step into being your wife as you take this seat. (George switches places, sitting in the chair indicated.) What is your name?

George (in deceased wife's role): Betty.

Lusijah: Hi, Betty. Tell me what are you wearing right now.

George (in deceased wife's role): Oh, I am wearing a beautiful flowered dress.

Lusijah: I'll bet George really loved seeing you dressed up.

George (in deceased wife's role): Yes, I was a beauty pageant winner; he always loved that I am beautiful.

Lusijah: What did you love most about George?

George (in deceased wife's role): George was always so positive and optimistic. He was very good at fixing things. And he really knew how to take care of me.

Lusijah: Wonderful ... You know, George brought you here tonight as his most important support. Do you have anything you would like to say to George that might be helpful to him? Speak to him directly.

George (in deceased wife's role): Yes, I am happy. I love you so much and I always knew how much you loved me. I want you to be happy; I don't want you to be sad. I am fine.

Lusijah: (addressing George as George): So, George, I would like you to be able to hear Betty's message. (Lusijah invited him to return to his own chair and stepped behind George.) Is it OK to touch you on the shoulders?

George: Yes, that's OK.

Lusijah: George, I want you to listen and take in Betty's message now.

Lusijah as Betty (standing behind George, with hands on his shoulders): I'm Betty, George. I want you to know that I am happy. I love you so much and I always knew how much you loved me. I want you to be happy; I don't want you to be sad. I am fine.

George leaned forward, becoming very emotional as he listened to Betty's message. Other group members began to silently weep, clearly touched in witnessing this scene. During the sharing, George spoke about feeling sometimes that his partner was just behind some barrier that he couldn't reach through. George reported that for a moment in this exercise, he felt as though he went through this barrier and actually felt contact with his partner. He expressed gratitude for the experience. He experienced viscerally his wife's message that she is fine, and she wants him to be happy.

The social atom is a powerful tool to connect the group member with their support network. It is a graphic demonstration of the important supportive people they have connections with—alive or deceased. The client experiences the words of support and wisdom in the here and now. Group members do not make descriptive statements about what a support person might say; rather they embody the support person's feelings and care—which comes from the group member's internalized knowing of the support person. This is inevitably a powerful exercise; the final message back to the support person chosen by the client is universally "Thank you." Many people are pleasantly surprised to look at the social network described in their social atom. Group members realize how important their support people are after working with their social atom, and some report making follow-up calls after the group to acknowledge and thank the support person.

A variation on the social atom is to ask if there is someone on their social atom with whom they wish to have a conversation, about asking for what they need or improving their relationship. Then of course jump into action!

Loneliness: Supporting Better Understanding and Communication

Sociodrama explores a theme which is common to many in the group. To explore the thoughts and feelings that contribute to isolation or disconnection, two chairs are placed in front of the group. One chair represents the person who has experienced loss and the other chair represents friends or family of someone who has experienced loss. Group members are invited to come up spontaneously and 'double' or speak from the roles, saying out loud possible thoughts or feelings of the people represented by the chairs. Facilitators and group members participate. The doubling statements below are a sample of the statements made by the group.

Doubling for the Family Member or Friend

- Thank God it wasn't me who lost my spouse!
- I am so afraid that this might happen to me.
- I feel uncomfortable when I see her cry.
- I don't know what to say.
- I feel so helpless.
- I feel so inadequate to support my friend.
- He needs to move on.
- She needs to get back out meeting people and look for another partner.
- I'm dealing with my own sadness; how can I help someone else?

Doubling for the Person Who Is Grieving

- I feel so frozen.
- I don't want to burden others.
- I so want to be able to talk to people about my partner, but feel so embarrassed to be emotional. I am afraid people will see me as weak.
- I wish I could remember my spouse or partner in a happy way without causing discomfort to others.
- It is not helpful to hear about other people's stories of loss right now.
- I desperately miss my husband; he can never be replaced.
- I don't want to hear that I should be trying to meet someone else.

This can be followed by inviting group members to have a conversation with someone who they wish they could communicate with more easily, using an empty chair and role reversals. It is a safe place to try on ways of communicating real feelings and needs with family members or friends (with the benefit of having heard doubling statements from the group on how the family member or friend might feel). The following vignettes demonstrate different aspects of the challenges for communication with friends or family. One

44 Loneliness

exchange with Susan related to her feeling strain with a close friend. We invited Susan to talk to her friend in an empty chair.

> *Susan:* I feel like I burden you when I talk about Jerry. I feel kind of frozen because I'm afraid you are uncomfortable if I share memories or cry.
>
> *Lusijah:* Reverse roles.
>
> *Susan (in role of her friend):* Yes, I don't know what to do. I don't know how to be.
>
> *Lusijah:* Reverse roles. Tell her about what you need and explain how she could be supportive.
>
> *Susan:* Sometimes I have a memory of Jerry, a good memory, and I just wish I could share it. Sometimes I cry after having a good memory, but it's OK, you don't have to worry about me. It is wonderful when someone can just listen—even if I cry.
>
> *Lusijah:* Reverse roles.
>
> *Susan (in role of her friend):* Oh OK. I think I can do that. It helps me to know how I can be supportive.
>
> *Lusijah:* Reverse roles (the client always ends in their own role and has the last statement). Do you have any last words for your friend?
>
> *Susan:* Thank you.

Another group member had an exchange with a friend that included several role reversals in which the topic of loss was ignored. After the end of the role play the group member stated that he experienced that speaking of loss with this particular friend was a painful reminder to the friend of his own many losses. He expressed acceptance of where his friend was at instead of feeling disconnected from the friend.

An older group member, Rose, had an exchange with her son. Rose had lost her husband decades before and started coming to the group when she became depressed after finding a box of her husband's letters. She did not feel supported by her son. In the role play, there was no resolution in the exchange on how she could be supported. The exchange indicated emotional distance—the son couldn't understand what his mother was experiencing. I suggested a plausible different reality (surplus reality) of inviting the son, who normally has a hard time expressing feelings, into the scene—but this time able to express his feelings. Another group member spontaneously came into the exchange. He sat in the chair of the son.

> *Other group member (playing role of son):* You know, Mom, I am just not very good at expressing deeper feelings but I do feel them. I am committed to being here for you, being family for you.
>
> *Rose* (nodding and softening): Yes, I know this is true.

As group members come to know each other, it is quite wonderful to see them connecting with each other and their shared human experience. Psychodrama methods give others a vehicle to sensitively offer an alternate and very plausible feeling that may not have been expressed in the role reversals. They become agents of each other's healing.

CHAPTER 7

FEAR

Dimensions of Fear

Fear is a common emotion and state of being that we, as human beings, experience in the face of change, loss, and transition. From low-level anxiety to full-blown panic, fear can take over our bodies and our lives. Below is information about how fear operates and some tips to enable us to work with the energy of fear in ourselves and others.

1. Fear is a primitive physiological and emotional state that has enabled humans to survive the dangers of a harsh physical environment. Although contemporary life is generally a less dangerous physical environment, it is still an emotionally stressful environment, and these primitive reactions are still operating.
2. Fear is oriented toward the future or focused on issues of the past. It is a feeling of being uncomfortable with repercussions from what has been or what will be. The best way to work with someone in fear is to bring them into the here and now. By focusing on the present moment, we can determine what the most frightening issue is right now, and where the feeling of fear is sitting in the body right now. Then it becomes easier to act on that particular issue in a positive, action-oriented way, moving from a place of fear to a place of empowerment.
3. Fear is directly connected to control and the need for human beings to control their daily lives—their routines, their surroundings, and other significant people in their world. Fear is an emotion experienced by the 'inner child'. The adult part, who wants to maintain control, usually attempts to stifle the fear with a rigid, dominating attitude. People who need to maintain control generally build a wall around the vulnerable parts of their hearts and are unable to receive positive or negative feedback. As a result, when criticism, real or imagined, is experienced, the person will most often respond in a defensive way.
4. People often form a pattern of behavior in early childhood that becomes an automatic, unconscious reaction to any threatening feeling inside or outside a situation.
5. The best way to deal with fear is to talk directly to the rational mind in a very logical manner. By coming from a calm, grounded place in the present moment, the rational mind, which is so afraid of losing control, can be acknowledged and given power.
6. In working with the overwhelming waves of feelings in grief, it is helpful to know that when there are difficult feelings—pain, anger, guilt, helplessness, and so forth—the feelings will eventually wind down in the body and resolve naturally. Sometimes this only takes a few moments. There is a fear that, once we start crying, or expressing rage, or some other very powerful emotion, it will never stop. We wonder if the pain will become bigger and more overwhelming. Feelings will pass if given space for expression.
7. Remember, fear is not bad or negative. It is an integral part of our survival mechanism. Fear can be damaging to emotional well-being when it runs one's life and controls every move, or when it becomes an unconscious, automatic response to any threatening situation. Fear is helpful when it serves as a warning to be aware of a particular situation, or to encourage listening to inner intuition about a person or event.
8. When people work with their fear and the emotional energy that is so potent and present, fear is transformed into courage and the ability to stand up for their truth in a clear, non-defensive way. As people contact and become aware of their own individual fears and how the fear operates in their life, they become more sensitive to others' fear and have more compassion with themselves and their fellow human beings.
9. Remember, it's a jungle out there, although the wild animals might be emotional, instead of physical.

© Copyright material from Darrow and Childs (2020), *Experiential Action Methods and Tools for Healing Grief and Loss-Related Trauma*, Routledge.

Action Methods for Working with Fear

Connecting with personal strengths and resources helps counterbalance fear. We use the practice first developed by psychologist Kate Hudgins (discussed in Chapter 3) to identify and amplify strengths that can serve as internal allies as clients explore fears. Kate Hudgins developed the 'circles of strengths'—a physical and visual representation of the many strengths of individuals in the group that become a metaphorical container of safety and strength in which to do further work.

Group members are seated in a large circle around cards that have been placed on the floor from a therapeutic card collection. (We have used The Masks We Wear, The Faces We Put On, by Mario Cossa or Soul Cards 2 by Deborah Koff-Chapin. Both have evocative images.) We invite group members to get up, wander around examining the cards, and pick up one or more cards that represent strengths. In explanation, we say that a strength or resource can be interpersonal—someone who knows them and wants the best for them. They can also choose an intrapsychic strength, an internal personal quality that is personally important, which helps them in their life. Examples are persistence, intelligence, sense of humor, and so on. The third strength category is a transpersonal strength, something greater than themselves which might be guardian angel, God, or someone who is no longer in embodied physical form. After choosing one or more cards to represent strengths, each group member briefly shares the cards they have chosen, and the specific strength, and puts the cards at their feet, creating a physical and visual circle of strengths.

Next, we invite group members to make a list of things they are afraid about. After completing the task, group members are invited to share their list of fears, and are then invited to do further work, in action. Below is a vignette of a member whose father had died. She was estranged from most of her nuclear family and had entered an intensive outpatient group after a suicide attempt.

Lusijah: Choose one of the fears on your list and let's explore this fear. Pick a scarf that would represent that fear. (Client chose a scarf.) Tell me about this fear.

Sandy: This represents a fear that I will have a break from an old friendship.

Lusijah: OK. Put the scarf on and step into that role. You are now the voice of this fear speaking to yourself. What is the message from this fear?

Sandy (playing the role of fear): You will no longer be interested in her. You have been in such a period of growth and change that she will not be able to relate to what you've been through. She does not have the depth to really understand you. This friendship will be over.

Lusijah: All right (giving a time-out signal). Now I am speaking to Sandy. Take the scarf off and just put it on the floor. (Pointing to her strength scarves) Look at your resources and invite the one in who can help you with this.

Sandy walks over to the scarf representing her strength: That would be my connection to spirit.

Lusijah: OK, pick up that scarf and put it on and speak from this strength to that message from fear.

Sandy (visibly changing body posture and facial expression while taking the role of her transpersonal strength): Oh no, we love each other, have known each other for years and years. We will continue to love each other.

Lusijah: Where does this voice reside in Sandy?

Sandy (in the role of her strength): Right here (as she points to her chest). In my heart.

Lusijah: Reverse roles and put the voice-of-fear scarf back on. Where does this voice reside in Sandy?

Sandy (in the role of fear): (After a pause) That voice is up here, in my head (pointing to her head and smiling). This is just a story that's in my head.

Lusijah: OK (smiling). Let's put that scarf down now. Look at your list again and see if there is another fear that needs help.

We continued with a few more fears that included fear of being able to take care of herself, fear of being stuck and unable to work towards her goals. These fears are common after loss as there is often a change in one's social network and perceived loss of personal power. After role reversal into each message of fear, the client was able to choose allies from her strengths and speak from that role, and successfully challenge that message.

CHAPTER 8

SADNESS

My sorrow is my love looking for a way to express itself.

(A young man whose wife died suddenly)

Dimensions of Sorrow

Sadness is an expression of ineffable love absorbing loss of unimaginable magnitude. In many cultures, the sadness of grief is acknowledged. Permission is granted to feel, show, and share sorrow, pain, and grief. In certain traditions, there are professional mourners whose role at funerals or memorial ceremonies is to kick start the free flow of tears. By example, they create a safe environment to allow the expression of sadness. Sorrow is recognized as a normal and natural reaction to grief.

Western cultures emphasize the 'rightness' of maintaining a stoic façade, of 'being strong', of carrying on with a stiff upper lip. There is implied virtue in 'getting it together' and 'moving on'. Some mourners in the West feel compelled to act, at least in public, as though nothing has happened. In fact, with a pervasive discomfort around grief, many feel they must appear happy and carefree, so as not to make others uncomfortable. Permission for tears, helplessness, withdrawal, depression, pain, and other very real manifestations of coping with loss is denied. This tradition of denying grief is taught and reinforced from cradle to grave.

In the U.S., our modern model for grief was President Kennedy's family following the assassination. Showing minimal emotion, his family was deemed brave and dignified. Images of his widow and small children became icons for public reaction to tragedy. His mother, who had already outlived two of her children, appeared the embodiment of the assumption that one is never subjected to more sorrow than one can bear. His brothers carried on his legacy in public office and countless others assumed decades later that his son would likewise follow a dutiful path.

Just take a look at the language often used to describe strong emotions:

He's a crybaby.
She lost it.
They fell apart.
Can you believe how out of control she is?
I think he's going crazy.
You've got to admit they're acting a little flaky.

And when in the midst of sorrow, what does one hear?

You've got to get a hold of yourself.
You're bumming everyone out.
C'mon, it's been long enough; you need to get over this.
I'm worried about you.
You're taking too long to move on.
What you need is to concentrate on work and put all this other stuff out of your mind.
Think about getting out there to meet someone (in the case of loss of spouse or partner).

And so bereaved individuals endure a secondary trauma in the aftermath of grief—the weight of internal and external stigmas. At a time when people most need to acknowledge their pain, to express vulnerability, to accept tender emotions, and ultimately to celebrate their treasure trove of memories, they are admonished to shut down. This tug-o-war of public expectation with private pain is truly traumatic.

© Copyright material from Darrow and Childs (2020), *Experiential Action Methods and Tools for Healing Grief and Loss-Related Trauma*, Routledge.

A body full of sorrow will express itself physically—with or without permission. The body feels. Empty arms long to hold and touch. Eyes strain with unshed tears. The stomach churns in fear and loneliness. Muscles clench with tension, anger, unfinished business, and shame.

Sadness exudes an energy that, even though it is invisible, is as real as the earth beneath our feet. It is the testimony to the depth of our love. Through the cleansing release of tears, the burden of pain lightens. A griever needs to give permission to oneself and to each other for expression of sadness.

The feeling of sadness is so huge and overwhelming, there are often no words for it. People cannot articulate the depth and magnitude. Caregivers must be patient and supportive, listening to repetitive details and reinterpretations. It is possible to plant seeds of hope for healing and even joy with time, and that memories are a recognition of the enduring power of love.

Some Gentle Reminders

- Allow yourself some quiet, introverted time.
- We live in a culture that places great emphasis on being happy—or acting happy even when we do not feel good. Be aware of outside pressure upon you to move forward and be cheerful.
- Be conscious of making choices for yourself that reflect your inner needs and moods, rather than the dictates of others.
- Because this is a time of increased isolation, plan ways of being with others that feel comfortable with your needs. Surround yourself with friends who will understand your changing feelings and reactions without expectations. Even a simple act, such as watching TV with a cup of hot chocolate with someone else, is comforting.
- Make a list of activities that nurture you. Be aware of time frames, particularly when you invite others, or when they invite you to events. It may be healing to spend a couple of hours shopping, but not an entire day at the mall.
- This is a time of inner evaluation and contemplation. Keep a journal. Write down your thoughts, feelings, and dreams. Be particularly aware of your body's sensations and chronicle your feelings and events of the day.
- Give yourself quiet time to read a book—perhaps an inspiring story of courage, a romantic novel, or a humorous story. You do not have to focus on death, loss, or grief.
- Meals can be challenging to get together. Make a big batch of your favorite dish and freeze meal-sized portions to re-heat when you don't feel like cooking. Go to a restaurant for a change of pace.
- Plan an outing to a favorite nature spot. The beach or the mountains can be comforting, because your environment will speak to your inner feelings and offer serenity and peace. This is healing, even if just for an afternoon.
- Be aware that the daily routine of work can be draining. It may be supportive to throw your energies and focus into work, but after a while, level of functioning diminishes. Lack of concentration, lack of focus, disorientation, and lowered attention span are all normal reactions one week to several months after the loss. It may be difficult to be around other people in a work mode because of the difference in mood between you and your work colleagues.

- Particularly at work, focus on one task at a time. It is easy to become scattered, overwhelmed, and ineffective. Make a list of priorities that absolutely need to be accomplished. As you complete each task, mark it off your list. You will visually see progress and also get the worry lists out of your mind.
- Sometimes it helps to plan and put special effort into a pet project at work or home. As long as the activity excites and sustains you, and does not give you more burdens or pressures, it can be a positive way to channel your energies.
- Be honest about how you are feeling, and about the limits of your capabilities at this time. Let those around you know how they can support you in a concrete way. Become a part of support groups or organizations in your community where people in your same situation meet. This can lessen the isolation and detachment you feel with the world.
- Make a donation of time or money to a favorite cause or organization. This will lessen the feelings of helplessness and bring about healing to others in your human family. You will be touching others—and acknowledging life again.
- Hold on to hope: you will survive and rebuild your life.
- Accept and flow with your feelings and needs. Be open to the individual story of your journey of healing as it unfolds. Appreciate the depth and beauty of your pain without judgment. The more loving you can be with yourself, the faster and more completely you will heal.

Remember:

Tears are the unspeakable expression of the depth of our love.
Booker T. Washington

Action Methods for Working with Sadness

When clients express sadness, missing, and yearning, they can be invited to dialogue with their loved one, either with role play or letter writing. Below is a vignette from an individual session.

A client, Debbie, who had recently lost her father was tearfully talking about missing her father as well as feeling that he was still around. She had told him before he died that he couldn't leave her, and she worried that maybe she was keeping his spirit around.

Lusijah: Would you like to have a conversation with your dad? (Client nods agreement and a chair is pulled out.) Choose a scarf that can hold the place of your dad. (Client chooses two scarves and shares why she chose the two scarves.) Go ahead and place the scarves over the chair. Talk to your dad.

Debbie (tearfully): I miss you, Dad. I miss the talks we used to have. I miss being able to talk to you, to ask your opinions. Are you OK? I want to know that you are OK.

Lusijah: Reverse roles and as you sit down in the chair take the role and voice of your father. (Client sits down.) I would like to ask you some questions. Tell me your name. (The purpose of asking questions when the client is role-reversed is to assist them to feel in the role they are taking. When the client exhibits a different facial expression and energy, this indicates that the client has been able to connect with the essence and voice of the role, which is a critical part of healing.)

Debbie (in the role of her father): Peter. Pete.

Lusijah: Tell me about yourself.

Debbie (in the role of her father): I had an interesting life. I was a competitive athlete, a cyclist. I loved sports. (Client continued to talk about her father's life.)

Lusijah: Tell me about your relationship with your daughter, Debbie.

Debbie (in the role of her father): Debbie, ahhh… (smiling) We are so much alike. I used to call her Tiger. I loved going to her track meets. She has so much spunk, I guess like me. She got in trouble when she was younger, just like me. She is so strong and I am so proud of her. I love her.

Lusijah: She misses you very much. You heard what she said. Do you have any helpful words?

Debbie (in the role of her father): I love you so much. I am so proud of you; I want you to be happy. I didn't want to leave you. But I want you to know I am OK, I really am OK. I am with our dogs. You will be OK, you are strong. And you can talk to me any time.

Lusijah: So, reverse roles again, take your own seat again. I would like to ask your permission to take the role of your father physically, so that you can hear his words. Is that OK? (Client nods affirmatively.)

Lusijah (in the role of Debbie's father): I didn't want to leave you. I am OK, I am with our dogs. You are strong and I want you to be happy. May I give you a hug? (It is important to ask permission for physical contact.)

Debbie immediately came out of her seat and had the visceral experience of giving her father a long embrace, as I spoke her father's words, "you will be OK, you are strong, you can talk to me any time." This was an emotional experience. The grounding tool of the 'body double' (developed by Kate Hudgins and discussed in Chapter 3) was used to bring Debbie back to the present and in her own body.

The 'body double' speaks as the client in the first person, saying, "I can feel my feet on the floor, I can feel my body on the chair, I can feel my breath (and breathing with client)." Be patient as the client returns to the present. The client will indicate when he or she is back naturally. Debbie expressed gratitude at the end of the session. She came into the following session, reporting she had had a good day and for the first time was able to talk about her father without tears. Of course, there will be more tears, but this represents a first experience toward the slow building of a new relationship that connects with the internalized loved one, without crushing sadness.

Bibliography

Didion, J. (2007). *A year of magical thinking*. New York: Vintage Books.

Grollman, E. (1995). *Living when a loved one has died*. Boston, MA: Beacon Press.

Lewis, C.S. (2001). *A grief observed*. New York: HarperOne.

Moffat, M.J. (ed.) (1992). *In the midst of winter: selections from the literature of mourning*. New York: Vintage Books.

Zuba, T. (2014). *Permission to mourn: a new way to do grief*. Rockford, IL: Bish Press.

CHAPTER 9

ANGER

Anger is often part of the grieving process. When events impact our life and put us in a state of being out of control, feelings can be like a runaway train. Many times, we can layer events, reactions, and internal experiences into a cycle that builds in intensity, perpetuating the feelings and reactions.

Targets of anger may include doctors who were not able to save the family member or were insensitive, other family members who were perceived as not supportive, God for taking their loved one, or just anger at the world in general. There is sometimes anger at the person who died—which creates guilt for even having these feelings (Figure 9.1).

In this week, group members are invited to share feelings of anger they may have. Hearing that others are angry allows group members to accept this difficult feeling as a normal part of grief. Below is a handout given during the session that works on the topic of anger.

Figure 9.1. Guilty–angry.

Managing Anger

Anger is an emotion that can be extremely difficult to express or even acknowledge. For people who have lived through loss and change, anger can become a very real part of their daily lives.

Focusing on the past (regrets, unfinished business, and guilt) or the future (projecting what could happen, what might go wrong, catastrophizing) means we are not in the present—dealing with one moment and one issue at a time. Angry feelings that arise from being in the past or future are not based on the reality of the present moment—and are most often not helpful.

Anger is a force that can move us into fear, guilt, or even self-destruction. On the other hand, anger has the potential to give us great power, clarity, and a healing of our helplessness.

To recognize, acknowledge, express, and accept our anger gives us access to the power behind the anger, and can open the doorway to more safely feel and express deeper fear, pain, and love.

We live in a society that encourages us to hide our anger. Anger is seen as 'bad'—and to be a 'nice' person, one is told he/she should never feel anger. Anger often starts as frustration, irritation, or annoyance at minor issues that one may try to cover over or ignore. Some may fear expression of anger because of past consequences. The symptoms of repressed anger include:

- Procrastination in the completion of tasks
- Perpetual or habitual lateness
- A liking for sadistic or ironic humor
- Sarcasm, cynicism, or flippancy in conversation
- Over-politeness, constant cheerfulness
- Frequent sighing
- Smiling while hurting—'grin and bear it'
- Frequent disturbing or frightening dreams
- Over-controlled monotonous speaking voice
- Difficulty in getting to sleep or the inability to sleep through the night
- Boredom, apathy, loss of interest in things you are usually enthusiastic about
- Slowing down of movements
- Getting tired more easily than usual
- Getting drowsy at inappropriate times
- Excessive irritability over trifles
- Sleeping more than usual—maybe twelve to fourteen hours a day
- Waking up tired rather than rested and refreshed, even though you have had enough hours of sleep
- Clenched jaw, especially while sleeping
- Grinding of teeth, especially while sleeping
- Chronic stiff or sore neck
- Chronic depression, extended periods of feeling down for no reason
- Stomach ulcers
- Tightness in muscles, tightness and churning in stomach
- Constipation and/or diarrhea.

© Copyright material from Darrow and Childs (2020), *Experiential Action Methods and Tools for Healing Grief and Loss-Related Trauma*, Routledge.

Anger is a physical sensation experienced in our bodies, so it is healing to do something concrete with the angry energy, instead of just thinking about the anger or 'figuring it out'. It really doesn't matter why one is angry. The fact is, one feels angry.

Steps for Processing Anger

Step One: Recognize It

Everyone has his/her own bodily signals that indicate anger. Learn yours and listen to your body, as well as to feedback from others who might be able to recognize symptoms before you do. When you find yourself depressed or down, take a look at the past twenty-four hours. Has anything occurred or has anyone made you angry? Tune in and listen to your intuitive gut response. Again, don't just listen to your mind.

Step Two: Own It

Your anger is yours. No one can make you feel anything. Acknowledge that you have a human right to be angry and accept that feeling, without attempting to justify reasons behind it. Try not to blame others for your anger, as this is another way of avoiding dealing directly with the anger.

Step Three: Release It

Find a way to express your anger in a non-damaging way. It is usually best to express the anger in a physical, concrete way, so you are able to experience physical release. Suggestions:

- Repeatedly say aloud: "I'm not angry at _____." See how long you can say it before it turns into, "I am angry at _____." This is very good for anger that is difficult to acknowledge.
- Write an 'unfinished business' letter to the person with whom or thing with which you are angry. Write down every feeling you have, especially when the feelings contradict each other.
- Dialogue with the person with whom you are angry. Say out loud every thought, feeling, and image you have kept inside. Let yourself talk until it is all out. Then, sit in silence for a moment and breathe in the relief and freshness of releasing the resentment that was inside of you.
- Tear up an old magazine, page by page. Start slowly, crumpling each page. Then begin to move more quickly. As you tear up the pages faster, put words to what you are destroying. Trust whatever comes from your mouth. Afterwards, throw the pages away or burn them.
- Scream in your car, in the shower, or anywhere safe, where you can make the loudest sound you need to make. Get the anger and pent-up frustration from the inside of your body to the outside.
- Pound on a pillow. Again, put words or at least sounds to what your fists are pounding.
- Do any intense physical activity, such as running, racquetball, tennis, martial arts, cleaning the house, and so forth, that allows your body to actively express the angry energy.

© Copyright material from Darrow and Childs (2020), *Experiential Action Methods and Tools for Healing Grief and Loss-Related Trauma*, Routledge.

- Share with a safe, supportive person about your anger. Ask them to just listen and acknowledge your feelings, without giving you a ton of advice or judging you.
- Free-form drawing on large pieces of paper in bold colors is also very powerful. Don't try to draw anything specific—just let your arms and hands move freely over the paper. Large felt-tip pens are very good tools for this, as they give us a sense of power and expression that is more immediate than crayons.

Most importantly, do what feels right and comfortable for you. We all may feel somewhat silly when we first begin any of these exercises, but as time passes, the embarrassment melts away to our deeper feelings, and we have the opportunity to release one more piece of our burden.

Anger is an emotion that generally covers up three deeper underlying emotions: hurt, fear, and pain. Don't be surprised if these deeper emotions surface as you release your anger. Remember, above all, flow with your own feeling process and be very gentle and loving with yourself.

Earl Grollman (2011) writes: "Resentment is a natural part of the grieving process and helps to express anguish and frustration at the curtailment of a life so precious. Bottling up anger causes greater stress and leads to depression."

Action Methods to Work with Anger

Anger is a common component of the grief process and is one of the very most difficult grief issues. Anger is challenging because it can topple beliefs or assumptions that provided a life structure in the past. Anger follows a felt sense of betrayal by God, the doctor, family, friends, and even possibly the person who died. This following activity works in individual sessions and in groups.

We invite individuals or group members to write a letter to someone they feel anger toward as a warm-up. After writing the letters, group members are invited to work further with the letter they have written. Below is a vignette with Claire, who chose to work on her anger toward her father, who had not been supportive of her after the death of her mother. Claire's parents had been divorced when she was a child, and her mother had been diagnosed as bipolar many years after their divorce. The client had complex grief issues. Two chairs were set up facing each other.

Lusijah to Claire (who was seated in one of the chairs): What do you need to say to your father?

Claire: It was so hard after Mom died. I felt so lost, adrift. I feel angry that you were not more helpful, and that you were so distant and uninvolved.

Lusijah: Reverse roles.

Claire (in role as her father): (Claire sat silently staring other at the empty chair.) I don't know what to say.

Lusijah (stepped over to take a position to the side of Claire): I am going to make a doubling statement. If it seems correct, you can repeat it or change it if it feels wrong.

Claire (in role as her father): (nodded OK.)

Lusijah making doubling statement: I feel frozen.

Claire (in role of father): Yes, I feel frozen. I don't know what to do. I don't know how to support you.

Lusijah: Reverse roles. Tell your father what you need.

Claire: I need you to talk to me. I want to hear you talk about Mom. I feel confusion. I loved Mom but there are memories that are difficult. I need to have someone to talk to.

Lusijah: Reverse roles.

Claire (in role as her father): OK, I understand. I will try to be there for you.

Lusijah: Reverse roles.

Claire: Thank you, Dad.

The 'aha' moment for Claire in this drama was the father's statement of being frozen. The following week Claire shared thoughts and feelings that had come up after her drama. Claire stated that it had been very helpful, that she really felt the truth of her father's sense of helplessness—of being frozen. Claire commented that it had been a good experience to have practiced saying what she would like to say to him, to say what she needed from him, and that it seemed less scary now. Claire noticed that being able to sit in the other's role was quite helpful. She shared that when she felt anger in the past, she had not been able to empathize like this with the other person.

The drama touched another group member, Sara, whose father was hit by a car driven by someone on drugs. Sara had written a letter to the man responsible for her father's death. She was very upset that she would never have the chance to have a conversation with this man, as he died just before the completion of a trial about his role in her father's death. He never apologized to her family for having killed her father. Lusijah set out a chair representing the role of the person who killed her father. Sara was not asked to take that role (because it is not helpful for clients to take the role of a perpetrator of violence); rather others were invited to make doubling statements to the role of the perpetrator.

60 Anger

Lusijah: Talk to the man who killed your father.

Sarah: I am so angry. You killed my father, driving while you were drugged out. Then you fucking died before you received justice. You never apologized to us.

A group member offering a doubling statement: I'm sorry I didn't say I was sorry to you and your family. I felt so bad, I just couldn't face you and your family.

Sara: Bullshit! I don't accept that.

Another doubling statement: I'm sorry, I had just taken my painkillers before I left the hospital. I was so doped out, I just didn't know what I was doing. I didn't mean to hit your dad.

Sara: No, I don't buy that! It was your fault. You should never have gotten behind the wheel.

Sara then stated as an aside, "This man has no remorse, has no soul, he will go to hell." I invited feedback from the group. One person stated that she couldn't imagine the kind of horror he must have gone through prior to his death, with having known that he had killed somebody. Sara was still very angry.

Lusijah: This man is a piece of shit.

Sara: Yes, he is.

Lusijah: He deserves to go to hell.

Sara: Yes.

Lusijah (as an aside, gently to Sara): How long does he get to dominate your life?

Sara: (This hit a resonance for Sara, who nodded but remained silent.)

This was a moment that was relevant for everybody in the group. To what extent will their future be defined by anger about their loss? Sara, who had been filled with rage since the beginning of attending the group, softened for the first time, saying she had started to consider that she needed to be less angry.

In another vignette with Sara, working with anger toward her aunt, she stated she felt her aunt had abandoned the family. Sara did a role play with her aunt that was unproductive. Sara was not giving an inch as she did role reversals. Finally, I doubled Sara, amplifying her position, stating, "I am mad now and I will be mad for the rest of my life." This doubling statement caused Sara to come out of role, an indicator of an "aha" moment. The entrenchment of her anger had not allowed for her to feel empathy in the other role. With Sara, amplifying the anger with more force helped her to see this as an observer rather than being caught up in the anger.

The following vignettes are from the Loss of Partner/Spouse group after writing the anger letter. Group members were invited to explore the feelings expressed in their letters more fully in action. The first volunteer was very activated, saying he had written his letter to God.

Lusijah (setting up a chair first): Here is God, John. Talk to God.

John: I am so angry at you. I had counted on spending the rest of my life with Deedee. We only had five years together. We had so many plans. We knew from our first day together that we were perfect for each other. She was such a good person. Why did you let her die?

Lusijah: Reverse roles.

John (in role as God): (John seemed initially dumbstruck at stepping into the role of God.) I know this is very hard for you. I am sorry you are so sad.

Lusijah (speaking to John in the role of God): Yes, but John wants to know why you let her die.

John (in role as God): I can't give you an answer now. I am sorry you are hurting so much.

Lusijah: Reverse roles.

John: I want to know whether I will understand some day. Will I get the answer to this after I die?

Lusijah: Reverse roles.

John (in role as God): Yes, you will get your answer some day.

Lusijah: Reverse roles. John, I would like to ask you if you have some last words for God for now.

John: I want to have answers to my questions.

It was unclear how helpful this exchange was to the group member, although other group members stated that they noticed a moment of softening. This particular exchange demonstrated John being able to connect with his own deeply held belief that God is loving and compassionate. While playing the role of God, it seemed that he experienced God's sorrow that John was suffering, which had the effect of softening his anger.

Another group member, Patty, had written a letter to her husband's doctor, angry at the insensitivity of his care. Patty had spoken to the doctor after her husband's death, accusing him of insensitivity. His response had been unsympathetic, saying, "I am a doctor. I gave your husband the best care that I could, and I was honest about my opinion."

Lusijah (placing a chair for the doctor): Here is the doctor. Talk to him.

Patty: I am so angry at what you said to my husband. It was as if you announced that you were giving up, that my husband was not worth your concern or efforts. You were so insensitive.

Lusijah: Reverse roles.

Patty (in the role of the doctor): Yes, I know you feel this.

Lusijah (standing to the side of the client): I am going to make a doubling statement. You can repeat it if you agree or change it if it seems wrong. It is hard for me to be treating patients day after day who are very ill. I can't be feeling the pain of all of my patients and their family members. I wish your husband had not died.

Patty (in the role of doctor): I am sorry that I said things that were insensitive. I am sorry that I wasn't able to tell you this after your husband died. I wish your husband had not died.

Lusijah: Reverse roles.

Patty (Tearful): It was so hard to feel you had given up. Thank you for listening and understanding my feelings.

This particular exchange was very short. This is a good example of how doubling can present a different and plausible point of view from the doctor (surplus reality)—stating a self-protective mechanism that is common among people who work with very ill patients, and his wish that her husband had not died. Patty, in role reversal, connected with that message, and was then able to speak from a more conciliatory place. Back in her own role, she was also softer.

Bibliography

Grollman, E.A. (2011). *Talking about death: a dialogue between parent and child.* Boston, MA: Beacon Press.

CHAPTER 10

UNFINISHED BUSINESS

Unfinished business is the stuff that hangs on. It is often resentment about unresolved issues in the relationship with the loved one but can also be persistent anger or guilt. These come up, for example, when the one who died had mental illness or substance abuse, or was abusive. In the case of a deceased parent, perhaps that parent failed to protect the client from abuse. Working with unfinished business entails helping group members find a way to remove the heavy rocks in their psychic backpack. In this process we explore the meaning of forgiveness, suggesting that it is not about excusing harmful behavior. Forgiveness is an important aspect of working with unfinished business. It's a way to move into the future unencumbered by anger and resentment.

What Is 'Unfinished Business'?

Unfinished business describes any unresolved feelings, issues, or acts related to changes or losses in our life. Life is full of constant movement and change—even positive change can bring about a feeling of loose ends and incompleteness. It is important to bring closure to what is left undone, to move forward with energy and commitment.

When unfinished business is not addressed, the feelings will take physical form in the body. Many body symptoms and illnesses are related to unresolved emotional issues—not because the pain is 'all in your head', but because it actually manifests as a physical response. When people are not able to let go of unfinished business, they also can lose the ability to be close to others, or to form lasting, intimate relationships.

What Is 'Finishing'?

Finishing is a process that may be ongoing, as individuals remove petals of a flower to reveal deeper feelings. Here are tips to actively resolve the feelings of guilt, anger, resentment, regret, sadness, and helplessness that often are the result of unfinished business.

Tools for Finishing Our Unfinished Business

- First ask yourself, "Do I want to finish_____right now?"
- If the answer is yes, find a safe, comfortable place, and sit down facing an empty chair. Sit quietly, relax, and breathe deeply for a few moments. Now, imagine the person, object, experience, memory, or whatever is seated in the chair opposite you. Focus your thoughts and feelings on the person or issue at hand. State your feelings aloud in the form of an 'I' statement.
  - "I'm still angry with you for dying."
  - "I miss you."
  - "I wish I could tell you how much you mean to me."
- Your feeling may rush forward after the first statement. If not, continue verbalizing statements, trying them several times, just to feel if they have any impact on your body. Continue this process until you have shared all of the feelings inside. It is a natural winding-down process.
- After sharing your feelings, particularly in a death-related situation, it is helpful, in your own time, to say, "I know I will never see you again. I know you are dead. I will always keep my love for you and my memories in my heart. I say goodbye to what was. I let go of you as I once knew you. I wish you well. I will begin to build my life without your physical presence here with me."
- In completing, it is necessary to point out what you have lost. What, in detail, do you miss about the everyday contact you had? What are the qualities you most yearn for, and what are the special memories that only the two of you shared?
- Doing this expression in a letter form, or using color and drawing, is another avenue to approach completing unfinished business. These methods may be less threatening for some people.

© Copyright material from Darrow and Childs (2020), *Experiential Action Methods and Tools for Healing Grief and Loss-Related Trauma*, Routledge.

- Unfinished business also incorporates all of the wishes, dreams, and hopes for the future. All of the "I wish_____" statements need to be expressed.
- Then, if it feels right, write a response letter from the person or situation to whom you addressed your letter. This provides an opportunity for full-circle expression.
- Rituals of leave taking, ceremonies of saying goodbye, celebrations of a new-found love and hope, and random acts of kindness are concrete actions we can do to heal unfinished business.
- If the answer is no to the question of motivation around finishing, give yourself permission to wait until the time is right for you to actively address those issues, actions, or concerns that remain unfinished. As with all aspects of grief, the timing is absolutely your own. Just as there is no right or wrong way to grieve, there is no timeline that is right for everyone. The prioritization and path to finishing are uniquely your own.

And Just When Are We 'Finished'?

Unfinished business issues are often entwined with each other. It is vital to work with one issue at a time. Otherwise, we are overwhelmed by too many feelings and experiences at once.

Usually, we experience an emotional release and/or change of attitude. Trust your body. There are levels of release, and sometimes it takes working on the same issue more than one time for complete resolution. Be gentle and patient with your own process.

Finishing can be the turning point where we transform our life in a powerful, expanding, healing way.

Remember:

Grief is a life-altering experience—not a checklist or project plan.
Life is full of unfinished business.
And while in the midst of grief, finishing is sometimes an unattainable goal.
Take on what you can, when you can, without disturbing your hard-won sense of equilibrium.

Unfinished Business Meditation

Allow yourself to ease into a relaxed state of being. Let go of the cares and worries of the external world. Feel all of your obligations and responsibilities fall away from your body, mind, heart, and spirit. For these next few moments, you have no burdens you need to respond to. There is no issue or person you need to worry about. This time is for you and your process of healing and releasing.

Give yourself this gift by first gently becoming aware of your breathing. Notice the ebb and flow of air as it enters your nose and/or mouth, travels down to your lungs, is pumped by your heart through your veins and arteries, bringing nourishment and sustenance to every cell in your body. Close your eyes, if that feels comfortable. Allow your breathing to continue. No need to change or alter it at all. It is automatically doing its job of supporting your life, in this body, on this planet, at this time.

Now go to a beautiful place in your imagination. It might be a place in nature or a special place only you know about. This can be a real place or an imaginary place. Allow your five senses to drink in the wonder and loveliness of this special place. All of the sights, colors, sounds, aromas, and textures fill your being with the most amazing sense of safety, comfort, familiarity, and deep belonging. This is your place, sacred to you, and especially designed for you.

After you have had an opportunity to drink in fully the healing power of your special place, notice that there is a person walking toward you, gently and steadily. This is someone with whom you have some unfinished business, some unresolved interaction, or an unspoken sentiment. It may be guilt, regret, anger, abandonment, rejection, or perhaps an unspoken appreciation or an "I love you" that was never expressed. Know that now, in this sacred place, he or she has come to you, well and healthy, fully open and aware that he or she has come to witness what you have to say. The person is willing to hear what it is that you wish to tell them. It may be a long-forgotten or hidden feeling that perhaps never could be said in the past. This is the time to express your truth in an uncensored way. Allow yourself this time and space to say anything and everything you never got the chance to say.

Notice that the person receives what you say with acceptance and respect. Allow this reality to sink into your awareness. When you are complete with your expression, thank the person for coming into your special place and honoring what you have shared.

Then, become aware that he or she has something to share with you in response. This is an affirming and uplifting statement that his or her heart wishes to say to you. Notice, also, that he or she has a symbolic gift to give to you, a gesture validating the difficult and fruitful work you have done with each other in this healing process.

Receive the gift now, and take it into your heart and being. This is the symbol of the ability you have to heal painful wounds from the past and create a new dynamic in your relationship. It does not matter if this person has gone, or died, or still may physically be a part of your life. This moment you can claim for your own healing—a step on the road to deeper joy, freedom, and peace.

When you feel complete, say goodbye to the person and gradually, in your own timing, begin your journey back to the present time. Take a deep breath and, with every moment of breathing, find yourself connected to your body in the now. Stretch your body, your neck and shoulders, and arms and legs if you wish. Allow each breath to bring you back to this moment, to this place. Allow yourself to sigh. Become aware of your surroundings. Gently open your eyes.

And if you wish, have a pen and paper ready by your side. You can now begin writing your thoughts in a letter form to the person you spoke with in this meditation. Take as much time as you need.

Be aware that by doing the work of releasing and resolving a piece of your unfinished business, you also create the energy for others to do the same. It is truly a way we bring healing into our world and open the doorway to transforming the seed of pain into the fruit of meaning, and perhaps even love.

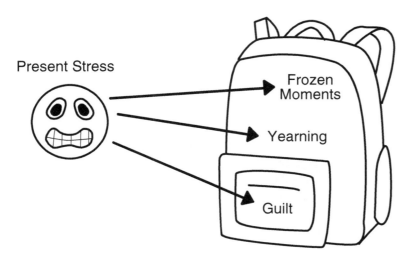

Figure 10.1. Unfinished business backpack.

Action Methods: Unfinished Business with Metaphorical Rocks

This first exercise can be done with individuals and groups. The following describes an individual session with a client who had been ordered to do grief counseling as part of a rehab program. The session started outside, and the client was asked to walk to the stop sign around one hundred feet away carrying a bag of rocks and then repeat the walk without the rocks. Of course, the client noticed how much easier it is to walk without rocks!

We talked about metaphorical rocks the client is carrying that she would like to stop carrying. While listening to meditative music, we provided paint and large smooth rocks to the client for her to explore her personal 'rocks'. The client painted a big rock with 'guilt', then others with 'anger', 'hatred', and 'selfishness'. The client was tearful throughout the session as she came in touch with the grief issues around her brother's and father's death, and her history of substance abuse. The client was somewhat surprised to hear that she was going to take these rocks with her and keep them in her bag. We asked her to notice the weight of these rocks and to consider how it would be to not carry these rocks around. We asked her to stay aware of the weight of the rocks and how it would be to be less burdened by these metaphorical rocks. We asked her to consider her readiness to take these rocks out of her psychic backpack.

The heaviest rock was guilt that she didn't take her brother's calls when he was in rehab, because she herself was not sober. He was killed shortly thereafter in a public park—a random bystander to gang violence. The client felt enormous guilt that she had not been a good mother to her children because of her drinking and believed she would have been a disappointment to her father. Heavy rocks indeed! We invited the client to consider what intention and symbolic action she could take if she felt a readiness to let go of some of these metaphorical rocks. Would it be helpful to leave the rocks in a personally meaningful place or to throw them away with or without witnesses?

The following week, the client came into the session excited to talk about the rocks. The client kept up a journal about the process of her willingness to let go of the rocks, labeled selfishness, hate, anger, and guilt. She had been able to take the symbolic action of throwing the rock into a pond near where she was living. She said that she had only been able to get rid of the guilt rock the day before. The client shared her thoughtful and touching journaling which reflected personal pain related to self-esteem. A visualization was done with the most difficult 'rock'—the guilt vis-à-vis her father. The visualization called into presence the aspect of her wise and loving father, asking the client in the visualization to ask her father to help her with her guilt and then to listen to his reply. After the visualization, the client was given art materials for her to capture some aspects of what she felt during the visualization. As she was drawing, the client said she had felt during the visualization the unconditional love of her father and his encouragement to let go of her guilt.

The following is an account from the Loss of Parent group. The issues are different with loss of a parent versus loss of a spouse. The reality is that no parent is perfect, many far from it given their own issues. Many adult children have ambivalence about parents who have died. This is particularly true when a parent had addiction issues or serious mental health problems, as the surviving adult child tries to make sense of anger at the poor parenting they received alongside awareness of the parent's illness. The anger toward a parent who has died is then compounded by feelings of guilt for the anger. This complexity and ambivalence often involve the surviving spouse of the parent who has died.

Group members were given a drawing of an empty backpack and coloring materials to draw unresolved issues in their 'backpack' (Figure 10.1).

These could relate to core issues that had been previously explored—anger, guilt, loneliness, sadness, and so on. After group members finished the drawing, we dumped a bag of rocks into the middle of the floor. We asked the group members to pick rocks that seemed related to the weightiness of the items in their backpack. Each group member explored a rock of their choice and were asked questions such as:

- What does this rock represent?
- Does this burden represented by the rock help you in any way?
- What do you need to help you with this unfinished business?
- Is there some internal belief that might keep you attached to this burden, such as, if I put this down, then I will either forget or be disloyal to my parent?
- How willing or able are you to take this rock out of your psychic backpack?
- Are there any obstacles that are making it difficult to let go of this particular unfinished business?

The first group member had chosen the biggest rock available, representing anger at her mother for failing to protect her from a step parent. She was thoughtful with the questions, expressing that she was not at the point of being able to take that rock out of her backpack. We asked her to go ahead and put the rock in her purse and take it home. This resulted in a moment of comic relief as everyone else looked surprised and quickly tried to replace the larger rocks they had chosen by smaller rocks. We discussed the process of feeling the weight of the burdens of unfinished business, and we encouraged group members to live with their rocks, feel the physical weight of them as a metaphor, and to be curious about what feelings arose in the next week. Group members were invited to do some ceremonial or symbolic act of releasing their rocks if they felt ready to take rocks out of their backpacks.

The following week, one of the group members spoke about her process with the rocks. The client had taken many rocks home with her that represented different pieces of unfinished business. The client spoke of her ambivalence about her mother's behavior after her father's death. The client had felt that she had been left having to take care of everything. Very often, the adult child who holds the position of the strong one in the family shows up in the groups. In the process of caring for others, they face a vacuum of support for themselves. The client reported going on an outing to a bridge over a stream where her parent's ashes were to be scattered in the future. The client reported making an intention to let go of her resentment of her mother by the symbolic act of throwing the rock into the stream. The client also shared a rock that had represented her anger with her brother because he had not been an equal partner in assisting with their mother's issues after their father's death. The client shared that she had not been able to get rid of this rock but had been able to spend some contemplative time alone with it in an outdoors setting. The client described the metaphor of being able to leave the larger rock and find a smaller rock to exchange. At the

68 Unfinished Business

following meeting, the client walked into the group, took a rock out of her bag, and announced that she was "leaving this rock here." When asked about the meaning of this rock, the client stated "self-judgment."

This following account took place in the Loss of Partner/Spouse group.

One person volunteered to explore her picture of her backpack. Her unfinished business was not knowing what to do with her husband's clothes, a very common experience. The client spoke about keeping all of his clothes in dressers and the closet and that she had no space to put her own clothes. She was unemotional as she described spending forty minutes just looking at his socks and underwear. Action methods are spontaneous and client-directed. A suitable prop was found—a box of tissues!

> *Lusijah:* Here is the drawer of your husband's clothes. Start taking them out and talk to the them as you take them out.
>
> *Andie* (who became instantly extremely emotional, sobbing): I love you so much. (Taking a tissue) Here are the socks you used to wear going to the gym. (Taking another tissue) Here's your shirt that we got when we were in Hawaii. Oh, we used to have such a good time together traveling...

All group members were strongly affected. Most also began to cry in witnessing the scene, including one fairly long-time member who had never cried in the group. The client continued to talk about the memories that the items of clothing held for her.

> *Lusijah, gently to Andie:* If I were a piece of clothing, I might be saying, "I help you remember Jack."
>
> *Andie:* I just can't bear to get rid of the clothing yet. I know there are family members and friends who would enjoy receiving a piece of clothing belonging to Jack.
>
> *Lusijah:* Yes, it is really hard to get rid of Jack's clothing. Can we bring Jack into the room and hear what words he says to you?
>
> *Andie:* Oh, he would think...
>
> *Lusijah (immediately vacating the seat next to her):* Here is Jack's seat, take his seat and let's hear what he has to say.
>
> *Andie (in the role of Jack):* I love you, I am with you, I am not the clothes.
>
> *Lusijah:* Is it a problem for you if Andie gets rid of your clothes.
>
> *Andie (in the role of Jack):* No! I would like my friends and family members to have something to remember me by. (Client was still fairly emotional in playing the role of Jack, but was able to be in his role.)
>
> *Lusijah:* Reverse roles and I would like you to hear Jack's message. May I touch you?
>
> *Andie:* Yes.
>
> *Lusijah* (going behind the client and putting both hands on her over her heart): I am Jack. I love you, Andie. I am always with you in your heart. I am not the clothes. (Client continued to be very emotional and Lusijah stayed in Jack's role.) Can you feel my presence and my love?
>
> *Andie:* Yes.
>
> *Lusijah:* Stay with this knowing. (After a few minutes) Begin to take slow breaths. (Client started to breathe and calm down.) Are there some last words that you would like to say to Jack?
>
> *Andie:* Yes, I love you Jack.

The person doing the work is encouraged to just stay in that place, not worry about sharing anything now, but can do so if he or she wishes. We invite other group members to share how the work has touched them, without comment or evaluation of the person doing the work. This type of sharing is powerful in giving the client the experience of feeling supported and less alone in their pain. It is important to be gently insistent that other group members refrain from commenting specifically on the group member's work, rather encouraging the others to stay in their own experience—that reflects what came up for them in witnessing the work.

In this instance, all spoke about the meaningfulness of having pieces of clothing. One group member, a twenty-one-year-old woman, said that she had been quite moved and realized how powerful it was to witness another's work. She related it to her own experience, having kept a sweater that had belonged to her boyfriend who had died. She shared that she felt very connected to the other group members who were two or three times her age.

It is a good practice to check in with a client after an especially intense session. Action methods start a process that continues to evolve. The following week, Andie shared her processing of her experience. She said she had spoken of the experience with a good friend at work, and that this friend had offered to be with her if she decided she was ready to start going through Jack's clothing, which she did start doing shortly thereafter. This seemed a turning point for Andie. At the beginning of her attendance at the group, she could hardly speak through her tears. After this session, Andie never expressed the same intensity of grief.

This client was the sort of group member group leaders feel lucky to have. She was fearless in her willingness to work through her own grief issues. The true success of a group leader is when a member clearly has gotten better at holding both the bitterness of loss and the sweetness of positive memories and knowing that their loved one lives on within themselves. A group member's departure from the group is an indicator of therapeutic success, and yet as facilitators, we often feel sad to know that the incredible privilege of walking alongside the hard part of another person's life—the witnessing of true human courage and wish to grow—has come to an end with this person.

CHAPTER 11

FROZEN MOMENTS

What Are Frozen Moments?

Frozen moments are a consequence of solidifying the experience of trauma through the five senses, that get stored into our brains. People are especially vulnerable to this phenomenon when the trauma is unresolved. A good example of this is when a loved one dies traumatically and the bereaved was unable to say goodbye, or speak final words of appreciation or gratitude. What is imprinted through the five senses is that last moment of trauma, which overshadows the good memories and positive influences of this individual in the survivor's life. In other words, the trauma is preventing the bereaved from access to the love and goodness, the special memories, experiences, and life impact that were shared with the loved one. Processing frozen moments helps bereaved people to reconnect with the totality and richness of the relationship.

Effective interventions to respond to 'frozen moments' include:

- Encouraging the expression about the details of that traumatic moment. Remind the survivor that the victim has moved on from his or her trauma (if he or she has died) and is no longer living in that moment of pain. After expressing details of the trauma, lead a guided meditation for the survivor to ask for help of the loved one to release the trauma. This reconnects the bereaved with the loved one and gets them out of that past 'frozen moment'.
- An excellent way to connect is to bring a photo of this person when they were well and happy, and to dialogue with them.
- Play a piece of music that is a reminder of the loved one, to elicit that person's energy or presence.
- Claiming the gifts of the energy, qualities, and memories creates a positive link to building a relationship in the present time. Write, draw, or in some way express the gifts and qualities of the person that sustained your relationship together.
- Dialoging, letter writing, role play, and guided imagery are all good ways to connect with the feeling and essence of the deceased.
- Write a list of all the qualities (positive and negative) of your loved one. Claim the qualities you would like to keep. Then, write a list of your feelings, thoughts, and judgments about that person. Match the qualities that will help you process the frozen moment.

Moving from the negative frozen moment to the positive qualities of love, beauty, and goodness helps people reclaim the essence of the relationship in present time. Although the loss of the person physically cannot be replaced, the ties of relationship can be kept forever. This gives energy and resources to building a new normal with optimism and strength.

Working with Frozen Moments: Day of Death in Action

Frozen moments show up sometimes as dreams with a recurring theme. One client described her frozen moment as a black hole sucking any light into itself. Facing and talking about this frozen moment are often experienced with fear and anxiety and a question of why go there—ever?

From Lusijah

I faced my own frozen moment in a so-called 'trauma drama' at a psychodrama training workshop on trauma which is described below. Before starting the drama, group members were invited to choose a card representing the observing part of self from the therapeutic card collection The Masks We Wear, The Faces We Put On, created by Mario Cossa, the group facilitator. The observing ego concept was developed as a psychodramatic safety structure by Kate Hudgins and Francesca Toscani in the Therapeutic Spiral Model (discussed in Chapter 3). Each group member role-reversed into his or her observing ego role and asked to state the how this internal role could be in service as a resource. Each person placed his or her card somewhere visible in the room. Messages of the observing ego cards included, "I can keep breathing," "I can witness what is happening," and "I can feel my feet on the ground." I volunteered to work on my trauma at the death of my partner.

> *Mario:* Tell me about the trauma you would like to work on.
>
> *Lusijah (tearfully):* I have a stored feeling of anxiety I felt when my partner was in the last moments of his life, feelings of being helpless and frozen. This was not the death I had wished for him—that he would die peacefully.
>
> *Mario:* Tell me what happened.
>
> *Lusijah:* Husain woke up around 5 a.m. He was in a great deal of pain and gasping for breath, going in and out of consciousness. I was scurrying to give him his prescribed pain medication, increase the oxygen level, holding him as he sat to prevent him from falling over. Against his wishes for no medical intervention, I asked if I could call 911 and he agreed. He had stated earlier that he did not want to die in a hospital and I still have confusion about whether calling 911 was the right thing to have done. The paramedics came and worked on him as I stood frozen. As he lost consciousness, I followed an impulse to get his phone and play a selection of song-based prayers. The paramedics took him to the hospital and he never regained consciousness. I think listening to those prayers helped him let go.
>
> *Mario:* OK, let's set the scene. (Lusijah used scarves and pillows to set up the scene.)
>
> *Mario:* Please choose someone to play the role of Husain. (After Lusijah chose someone) Let's go ahead and enact the scene, focusing on from the time Husain woke up until he lost consciousness.
>
>   Scene is enacted.
>
> *Mario:* Lusijah, come out of the scene. Tell me anything you noticed.
>
> *Lusijah (tearfully):* That was pretty much how it happened.
>
> *Mario:* Role reverse into observing ego. (After role reversal) Tell me, is Lusijah able to continue this work right now?
>
> *Lusijah (as observing ego):* Yes, she is able to.
>
> *Mario:* How will you support Lusijah?
>
> *Lusijah (as observing ego):* I will stay with Lusijah. I will remind her to breathe and to stay in touch with her spiritual core. I will remind her to just notice.
>
> *Mario:* Lusijah, I would like you to witness what happened with someone else playing your role. Choose someone who can play your role. (After choosing a group member to play Lusijah's role) Lusijah, let's watch again.

Scene is enacted, Lusijah watches in tears.

Mario: I would like you to go in and double yourself as we play the scene again.

Scene is enacted as Mario encouraged Lusijah to make doubling statements with the help of observing ego.

Lusijah (as double/observing ego): I can keep breathing. I am here with you, Husain. I love you.

Mario (asking Lusijah as double/observing ego): Did Lusijah do the right thing to call 911?

Lusijah (as double/observing ego): Yes, she did the right thing.

Mario (after scene is enacted): Come on out of the scene again, Lusijah. How are you doing?

Lusijah (no longer tearful, peaceful): I am doing all right.

Mario: Can we play this scene one more time with you again playing yourself?

Lusijah: OK.

Mario (after scene is enacted): Can we bring Husain into the scene, to get his words from being on the other side? (After an affirmative nod from Lusijah) Shall we let the same person play Husain from the other side? (After an affirmative nod, the person playing dying Husain gets up and goes to another place in the room.)

Mario: Reverse roles (indicating Lusijah to take the role of Husain on the other side).

Mario: Hello, Husain. How are you now?

Lusijah (in the role of Husain): I'm fine, I'm great. I feel free. I am great.

Mario: Do you have anything to say to Lusijah? She has been struggling with the memory of how it was when you died.

Lusijah (in the role of Husain): Ah, Lusijah, I love you. I will always be with you, surrounding you, loving you. I am fine. You took very good care of me. I knew you were totally there with me. You were with me. I was happy when I died.

Mario: Reverse roles. Lusijah, listen now to Husain's message.

Group member playing Husain relays message as Lusijah quietly nods with tears in her eyes while hearing the message.

Mario: Do you have anything you would like to say to Husain?

Lusijah: Thank you. I know you are with me. I will always love you. I miss you.

Mario: Would you like to give Husain a hug?

Lusijah: Yes (Lusijah gets up, gives the person playing the role of Husain a hug.)

Mario: Does this feel complete for now?

Lusijah Yes.

Mario: Step out of the scene. (Lusijah walks to where Mario is standing.) Is there anything you would like to share?

Lusijah: Yes. In watching the scene played again and again, I realized that Husain was not panicked or anxious. It was me who felt anxiety. I saw how much love was in the room, how loving I was of Husain. There was love.

The drama was a powerful and personally transformative experience in working with my own trauma. I experienced the process of transforming my frozen moment trauma. In watching and playing the scene many times, I noticed something. I saw how loving and supportive I had been when my partner was dying. This was a new dimension to how I stored that memory. It was a new and fuller story that became hardwired alongside the traumatic memory. I also noticed that my partner, Husain, was not anxious when he died. Since that time, when I go to that previously frozen moment memory, the anxiety and fear are much diminished because I experienced the more compelling reality of the loving support I gave to my partner.

On a professional level, the experience was evidence of how the frozen moments can be approached in action. The process is for the protagonist, the person whose story is unfolding, to go through several

74 Frozen Moments

steps: first, to tell the story, set the scene, enact the scene—not once but many times. The protagonist first plays him- or herself in the drama, then chooses someone else to take his or her role while observing the scene, and then the protagonist can go and double him- or herself to add any unsaid words or to remind the protagonist to breathe and to notice as an observer. The spouse can be brought into the drama as well, in the same way that has been discussed earlier though role reversal. The director of the drama is monitoring the state of the protagonist. Emotions must be somewhat activated, but not so much so that the person becomes flooded and immobilized.

To approach frozen moments in precisely this manner is beyond the possibility of a group that lasts for ninety minutes, but I understood from the enactment experience I had that frozen moments can be transformed.

Vignettes on Frozen Moments

Group members were invited to work with their frozen moments. Tom in the Loss of Partner/Spouse group volunteered to work with his frozen moment.

> *Lusijah:* Tell us about your frozen moment.
>
> *Tom:* I know I was supportive and loving to Jill. The whole family was in the hospital room with Jill. The thing that is very hard for me is that I stepped out of the room to use the restroom and Jill died while I was out of the room. (Tom had become tearful.)
>
> *Lusijah:* I would like you to go inward within yourself, to imagine who you might be able to ask for help with this memory. Maybe it's your guardian angel, maybe God, maybe your partner. Imagine asking for their help with this painful memory. (After a moment, I asked Tom who could help him.)
>
> *Tom:* My wife Jill can help me.
>
> *Lusijah (setting out a chair):* OK, here is a chair for your wife. Sit here and take her role. Speak from her role and voice.
>
> *Tom (in the role of Jill):* You know, we had such a wonderful life together. I love you and our sons. I am so proud of our four wonderful sons. I don't want you to be sad. I want you to be happy in your life.
>
> *Lusijah (standing next to Tom, offering a doubling statement for the role of Jill):* Tom, don't feel bad that you left the room. It was hard for me to let go with so much love in the room. I needed you to leave the room so that I could let go. (Tom neither accepted nor rejected the double statement.)
>
> *Lusijah:* Tom, I would like you to be able to hear Jill's message. Pick someone who can take the role of Jill.
>
> *Tom:* Can you take the role, Joan? (Joan agreed.)
>
> *Lusijah:* Go ahead and sit in your own seat. I want you to be able to fully take in Jill's message. Is it OK if Joan puts her hands on your shoulders?
>
> *Tom:* Yes.
>
> *Joan (playing the role of Jill):* You know, we had such a wonderful life together. I love you so much and I love our sons. We have such wonderful sons and I am so proud of them. I don't want you to be sad, I want you to be happy in your life. (Tom openly wept as he heard Jill's message.)
>
> *Lusijah:* Tom, do you have some last words for now, to Jill?
>
> *Tom:* Thank you. I love you.

After this ended, we spoke about how frequently it happens that a loved one dies when a spouse or family member steps out of the room and we speculated that it is hard for the loved one to let go when the spouse is in the room. Tom didn't say too much about the experience that night, but he came back the next week reporting how powerful and important his wife's message was to him—that she wants him to be happy. This group member had expressed earlier that he had met someone whom he was growing to love. His family was not supportive. Hearing this message from Jill, that she wants him to be happy, was an important and helpful message for him. As is often the case, the person doing the work touches other group members who have personally experienced similar feelings. Experiencing love again is something that most people who have lost a spouse think about. Tom's vignette created a natural space for group members to share on this topic.

There was another group member, Virginia, who said audibly when the topic was announced that she could not do this and was close to walking out of the group. The group member sitting next to her urged her to stay a bit. Seeing the process, Virginia was the second volunteer to work with her frozen moment—right after Tom.

Lusijah: Tell us, Virginia, about your frozen moment.

Virginia (immediately crying as she told the story): It was after lunch. Bob had gone to lay down and I noticed there was a funny sound to his breathing. I went to help him sit up so he would be able to breathe better. That didn't help and so I tried to stand him up, but then he was like dead weight and he slipped through my arms and fell on the floor, hitting his head. I think I may have injured him. Then I called 911. He died on the way to the hospital.

Lusijah: That sounds like a very painful frozen moment. (A moment of silence.) Virginia, I would like you to go inward within yourself, to imagine who you might be able to ask for help with this memory. Maybe it's your guardian angel, maybe God, maybe your partner. Imagine asking for their help with this painful memory. (After a moment) Who can help you with this memory, Virginia?

Virginia: Bob can help me.

Lusijah (indicating a chair that was set up): OK, I want you to step into Bob's role, speak in his voice. (Virginia sat in the chair, taking Bob's role.) So, Bob, you have been brought here to help Virginia with a difficult memory.

Virginia (in the role of Bob): I didn't suffer. I know Virginia loved me. (Virginia was clearly in role, as evidenced by the emotional shift—the tears had stopped and there was certainty as she spoke in the voice of Bob.)

Lusijah: Virginia is worried that she hurt you…

Virginia (in the role of Bob): No, she didn't. There is nothing that she did that hurt me and there is nothing she could have done to change things. I know that Virginia was doing the best she knew what to do. She wanted to help me.

Lusijah (addressing Virginia): I would like you to hear Bob's message. Choose someone in the group who can take his role.

Virginia: Joan, could you take Bob's role? (Joan agreed.)

Joan: May I put my hands on your shoulders?

Virginia: Yes.

Joan: I'm Bob, Virginia. I didn't suffer. I know you loved me. There is nothing that you did that hurt me and there is nothing you could have done to change things. I know that you were doing the best you knew what to do. I know you wanted to help me.

Lusijah: Virginia, are there any final words you would like to say to Bob for now?

Virginia: I love you. Thank you.

When Virginia sat and heard Bob's message, she experienced an immediate shift in how she held the frozen moment, stating she was very grateful for the experience, and that she was so glad that she had stayed. The following week, Virginia spoke about her experience when she went to bed after the group. She described that frozen image as a dark hole, black without any light, a place she couldn't go near. She shared an image that came to her before bed. The black hole that had been her frozen moment was now gray; it was not as opaque, and there was some light that was now part of that image. Virginia expressed gratitude for the exercise.

Although group members are working on their individual stories, the group feels cohesive and close after sessions with high intensity. It takes enormous courage by group members to share and deeply work with these searingly painful memories, that can also embody deep feelings of shame. Painful memories are transformed in the process of telling the story of the traumatic frozen moment, experiencing the deep witnessing and tender holding of the story by others, and feeling and hearing the truth from the loving and compassionate voice of the loved one. At the end of the session on frozen moments, a group member spoke. "We all need to be kind to ourselves and try to be happy, because all of our partners want this."

Self-Compassion and What I Did Right

The anxiety and avoidance that occur when thinking about frozen moments mean there is little room for acknowledgment of what the bereaved person did right. Below are a couple of ways that groups are can be invited to consider this. The vignettes below use commercially available Soulcards 2, by Deborah Koff-Chapin (available on Amazon).

This work begins with group members being asked to pick a Soulcard that represents their frozen memory and a card representing self-compassion. Group members share the cards they have chosen. We amplify feelings of self-compassion by inviting the group member to take the role and the voice of self-compassion. The facilitator interviews the person in the role of self-compassion, asking questions about what they did right, what was the effect or benefit of what they did, and if the person in the role has important and helpful words for the group member. After the role of self-compassion provides helpful words, the group member role reverses back to him or herself. The group member then listens to the helpful words (restated by the facilitator or another chosen by the group member) and can say any last words back to self-compassion. After everyone has worked with their card, we invite group members to notice common themes from the voice of self-compassion. These are common themes that emerge from the voice of self-compassion:

- You did the best you could.
- You need to be less hard on yourself.
- You know your parent (or spouse) knew you loved them.
- No matter what you did, it wouldn't have changed the outcome.

Here's another exercise focusing on what was done right. Invite group members to write about things they did that they feel good about during the last part of their parent's or spouse's life. Group members are asked to write legibly. After the writing is complete, invite them to pass the piece of paper to the left or right with the instructions that the people receiving the paper should look it over and then share it in paraphrased form with the group, making it into a story. This exercise allows group members to write about what they felt really good about, and it allows them to have this witnessed by the group. This is a powerfully positive activity.

CHAPTER 12

GUILT

Guilt Is …

a state of being affecting our physical, emotional, and spiritual selves.

a way of responding to an event, memory, or action (or inaction).

a natural human response that needs to be expressed.

a legitimate feeling, like blame or resentment, that helps us make sense of bizarre, chaotic acts and/or experiences.

an act of placing blame/responsibility on oneself, as opposed to anger or hostility which transfers the responsibility/blame to someone or something else.

Guilt Occurs When …

perfection is a goal—because we always will fall short and fail.

we do/feel/say something that we regret.

we don't do/feel/say something that we wish we had done.

we hurt someone else.

we sin (whatever our definition of sin is).

we are stuck and unable to make an important decision.

we violate our conscience, our beliefs, our moral system.

Feelings of Guilt

Guilt is not necessarily rational. But the feeling of guilt is very real and needs to be validated. Guilt may serve us in some way, so we keep guilt around. It's not necessarily a negative experience. Many creative, positive, honest, life-affirming acts are born out of guilt, and the need to resolve guilt.

Feelings of guilt are often manifested in the body:

- Taking on the symptoms of someone we love who is ill or who has died, e.g., chest pains related to heart attack,
- Stomachaches, headaches, loss of appetite, diarrhea, constipation, panic attacks. uncontrollable shaking, backaches, or poor posture
- Poor self-image, helplessness, hopelessness, lowered functioning
- Depression and panic can mask feelings of guilt.

The Process of Resolving Guilt

Acknowledge feelings and details about the issue. What specifically is the cause of the guilt?

- Act of atonement: a creative action we do to heal our self of guilt.
- Talk with the person with whom we feel guilty.
- Write a letter to the person or situation or thing we feel guilty about.

© Copyright material from Darrow and Childs (2020), *Experiential Action Methods and Tools for Healing Grief and Loss-Related Trauma*, Routledge.

- Perform a ritual act—rosary, Kaddish, planting a tree, doing volunteer work, baking bread, celebration of life, and so on.
- Forgive our self, acknowledge "to err is human" and that failures and shortcomings are ways to grow into deeper understanding and acceptance of self and others.
- Allow others to forgive in their own time and way and accept the healing balm of their love.

Guilt Exercise

We've found that one of the most powerful tools for healing guilt is to write a letter to the person you feel guilty about, so tonight we are going to do a letter-writing exercise.

It's best to write the letter to that person, whether that's someone who has died or is dying in your life, or someone who is far away, or perhaps someone who lives with you.

When you have identified the person you wish to address, begin your letter. Date the letter and then write Dear _____ to whomever you are writing. We ask that you complete three sentences in this letter. Allow the feelings to come; let the tears flow, if that feels right. You are not going to have to read any part of this letter to anyone; it is just between you and the person you are writing to.

> The first sentence to complete:
> I feel guilty because …
> The second sentence:
> Please forgive me for …
> The third sentence:
> I forgive myself for …
> The fourth sentence:
> My action step is …

Then, sign the letter, and mail it to yourself. You can burn the letter when you get it back or bury it. Do whatever feels right in the moment to honor your feelings and do the action step in your letter.

Check in with yourself, and note the feelings and thoughts that surface. Reach out for support or just connect with others after you have completed this exercise.

The Guilt Reality List

This exercise is designed for the rational mind to do a reality check regarding feelings of guilt. In the first column, make a list of everything you feel guilty about. Be specific and clear. In the second column, put a star by items that you had some control over or could have changed. In the third column, star the items over which you had no control. Then, examine the third column, and determine what guilt can be released. After that, go back to the second column and explore action steps that can support you in bringing atonement to the guilt issues.

Softening Guilt with Action Methods

Guilt is one of the most painful grief issues. It is usually tied to a specific memory. It can be about something said or done in frustration that is regretted later or something the client wishes they had said or done but didn't. For example, someone who is trying to support and care for their spouse who is ill or physically or mentally disabled might remember frustrated feelings, words, and reactions with shame and anguish. Many bereaved people expressed a painful wondering about whether they had told their spouse "I love you" the day they died. Others who experienced the loss of their spouse unexpectedly agonize that they may have had a disagreement as part of the last interaction with their spouse. The following vignettes demonstrate use of action methods while working with guilt.

The client speaks to her husband in an empty chair. The client may have difficulty with role reversal around the topic of guilt. An alternative is to invite others in the group to 'double' the position of the spouse, that is, to make statements about what the spouse might plausibly say. These double statements are offerings and can be rejected by the client. Below is a vignette from the Loss of Spouse group.

Della: I am so sorry that I was not at the hospital when you were so sick. I had just had surgery and I went home. I didn't feel very well, but I had no idea that you were so sick. I am so guilty that I wasn't there with you.

Doubling statements for the husband made by other group members included:

"That's OK, I knew you were not well yourself."
"I know you loved me even if you weren't there."
"I am so sorry I couldn't be there for you."

The last message created the 'aha' moment. Della nodded when she heard this, saying yes, that is what he would have said. This exercise was very powerful to her; she experienced an important insight addressing her guilt, that they both would have wished to fully support each other. In this case, insight came through plausible possibilities offered by other group members rather than through role reversal. The internal shift of the client's guilt proved to be transformative and stayed with the client.

Group members have expressed guilt about not insisting on a better diet or medical care. Another client felt guilty wishing she had been more forceful about her concern regarding her husband's smoking. A doubling statement for the empty chair position of her husband saying, "I loved to smoke, this was my decision," seemed to create a moment of insight, letting her off the hook for responsibility for his choices.

Guilt that is associated with loss is heightened because there is no last chapter in their mutual story to resolve the guilt. These exercises are intense for group members. The pain that is expressed is like the tip of an iceberg. In practice, group members take the experience home and continue to work with it emotionally during the week. It is music to our ears to hear the client's check-in the following week, demonstrating that the work has become integrated, and there has been an internal shift with how the anguish of guilt is held.

An alternative to role reversal is the guilt letter explained earlier in this chapter. This can be followed by a short visualization that invites the loving and compassionate presence of the spouse or parent who has died into the room. We ask group members to remember the feeling of being loved and cared for, times when they heard trustworthy wisdom given, and to remember the love they feel for the deceased. We ask them to feel the essence of their loved one and bring it into the room. After this short visualization, the group members are asked to turn the piece of paper over and to write a reply from the voice of the loving and compassionate spouse or parent. After finishing, group members are invited to share. One very touching exchange is detailed below.

One male client started attending the Loss of Parent group after becoming depressed and suicidal. He had been attending the group regularly for around four months and had never displayed emotion in the group. The client's mother had been murdered when the client was six years old. His mother had taken the younger children upstairs to bed. He had continued watching television downstairs, so he did not go with his mother and younger siblings. Later, when he went upstairs, he was the first to discover his mother's body. As he told his story, it became clear that he subsequently became the caretaker for the family, feeling he had to be strong for his father, who had fallen apart emotionally. This client described his sense of guilt because he had not gone upstairs with his mother, and that he had always believed that if he had been there, he could have prevented her death. The client's voice broke in the first display of emotion in the group as he shared that the letter written back from the role of his mother stated, "there is nothing you could have done" and that he felt his mother's forgiveness.

This is a poignant story of a child's horror and his assumed blame. These feelings were carried into adulthood, showing up as depression, suicidality, anxiety, and severe sleep problems. He finally realized that he needed to work with his grief—over twenty years after his mother's death.

Although this is not psychodrama with role reversals, it uses the same aspect of stepping into and speaking from another role. It is powerful and transformative because the bereaved becomes the voice of the compassionate spouse or parent and he or she feels the genuine sentiment of that voice. That voice becomes a profound gift of healing to the one who has been left behind.

CHAPTER 13

MEMENTOS

The Power of Action Steps in the Aftermath of Loss

Throughout the history of our civilization, mementos have been transformative tools to heal grief, and to celebrate and honor loved ones who have died. When we keep a memento, it is a physical grounding of memories, emotions, and thoughts that have occurred in the past, or perhaps what we promise will happen in the future.

In wedding vows, the rings become a memento of the promises made on that day. In Victorian times, a mourning locket often had a photo or a lock of hair from the deceased person, to constantly keep them near the heart.

Meaningful objects as grounding points are supportive and comforting. Here are some examples:

- The Healing Heart program serves families who have experienced loss. Family members meet by age groups, separately and simultaneously. Each child receives a stuffed animal which they keep throughout the group, and then take home. It becomes a healing anchor in their expression of grief.
- Memory boxes are another tool for grounding memories by keeping physical objects in a box that is decorated by the grieving person.
- Group members are invited to share mementos. They get to share the essence of their loved one. Fellow group members bear witness to the memories.
- Balloon releases are a powerful way to process unfinished business and convey unspoken I love yous. Environmentally safe balloons can be sent up with a message attached, which allows for the release of painful feelings and the rebuilding of the connection to the love.
- Create a heart hotel. One of our clients stated that everyone she loved had a room in her heart hotel. When he or she died, no one else took their room. The deceased person keeps their room forever. The client stated that she adds new rooms in her heart hotel as there are new people to love. As an art project, the bereaved can collage each room with the symbols, memories, and qualities of the person who has died.
- A message in a bottle is a time-honored way to send a note to the person who has died.
- Tattoos are another permanent way to memorialize someone, and to honor one's grief.
- Jewelry is another form of memorializing people who have died. Jewelry can even be made from the cremains of the person.
- Planting a flower, bush, or tree is another way to honor a person who has died.
- Headstones and gravesites are other ways to hold a place marker for memories and actual physical remains of the person who has died.
- Writing a card or letter to the deceased and having them write you a letter back from their most spiritual and aware place is also a great memento. A client reported that he kept his wife's response letter in his shirt pocket and looked at it whenever he felt sad.

- Doing an action step in honor of the person who has died is a great way to perpetuate their memory. One firefighter created a program called Random Acts of Kindness, in honor of the dead babies he had tried to save.
- Creating a collection of sayings the person has shared over their life is another way to bring forward his or her wisdom and insight. These may be sayings the deceased actually spoke, or quotes that were favorites.
- Raising money by participating in a fundraiser for the person's favorite cause, or maybe in acknowledgment of how he or she died (for example: events and organizations that fund research to cure disease) is a great way to keep their memory alive.
- Creating a piece of art, dance, or theater is yet another way to perpetuate the person's memory. The Taj Mahal was built by a prince to honor his beloved wife after her death.
- We can also call upon our ancestors to support us in moving forward in our life. There are many cultural traditions that honor the special connection we hold with our ancestors. Some include lighting of candles (novena), pouring libation for the ancestors, the Obon Festival, and Día de los Muertos (Day of the Dead).
- Our Centre for Living with Dying program holds an annual Light of Lights ceremony for our community, that is attended by hundreds of people. We light candles for our responders and caregivers on the front lines, and individual candles for those who have died. It is a powerful ceremony which brings together the community in a healing and meaningful way. Many people say they feel lighter after having attended this ceremony. Their grief seems a bit more manageable, and they do not feel as alone—rather, held together by a community of grieving and healing people.
- Some people use sensory mementos to connect with the person who has died. These include a favorite perfume or aftershave, an article of clothing, favorite song or piece of music, or a favorite meal or food.
- Wearing jewelry that belonged to the loved one helps some people feel connected with them as well.

CHAPTER 14

UNIQUE ISSUES AFTER VIOLENT DEATH AND SUICIDE

Over the years, the Centre for Living with Dying (CLWD) has worked with thousands of incidents, from major trauma, such as 9/11, war, and community incidents (shootings, natural disasters, violent deaths, riots, suicides, as well as individual and family tragedies). The thread that is woven through each of these events is the need for immediate, intermediate, and long-term support.

As caregiving professionals, addressing the nuances of complicated grief created by sudden and/or traumatic death, we break the conspiracy of silence and enable individuals, families, communities, and nations to heal.

We supported a mother, Rosa, whose son Ramón, had been brutally murdered in a gang-related incident. She described an unusual phenomenon. When she looked at the photograph of her son, she felt his eyes following her across the room when she moved. The photograph, rather than being a source of comfort, became painful and frightening. We invited her to bring the photo into the next appointment and call upon her son's essence to help her understand the situation. It became a three-way dialog between the photo of her son, Ramón, Ramón's essence, and herself. She was invited to move spontaneously among the roles.

Rosa: Why do your eyes follow me around the room?
Photo of Ramón: I am not at rest.
Ramón's essence: Please help my mom understand. She is scared.
Photo of Ramón: There is something still unknown about my death.
Rosa: How can I find out what it is?
Photo of Ramón: Go to where I died—there is something there.
Rosa: The police did not find it?
Photo of Ramón: No.
Ramón's essence: Can you not scare my mom? Allow her some peace.
Photo of Ramón: I just wanted to let you know. I will be calm now.
Rosa: Thank you so much. I need you to give me comfort and be a reminder of my beautiful son.

After this dialogue, Rosa discussed her concerns with the police and they actually did find a piece of evidence which helped to convict the murderer. As people explore the details of their experience with trauma, they are able to delve deeper into meaning and sometimes unexplained intuitive awareness. In death, grief, and loss in general, it can be difficult to hold multiple valid truths instead of choosing either/or. It is even more challenging in sudden, unexpected loss. There is a loss of mooring to reality. Nothing feels safe, no one feels safe, and some express that they feel as though they are going crazy. It takes longer for reality to set in after a violent loss.

The first task when working with those faced with sudden trauma is to create safety—physical, mental, emotional, as well as spiritual. Before people can connect with the new normal of life, they need a waystation to gather personal resources. We use an adaption of Maslow's needs hierarchy:

- Survival (food, clothing, and shelter)
- Safety
- Emotional connection (awareness—relationships—giving and receiving)
- Building the new normal, identifying meaningful action steps
- Self-realization/transformation (integration of new insights).

It is built like a pyramid, with survival and safety being the first foundation structures to secure in place. Below are examples of the progression—starting with creating safety and progressing through the strengthening of relationships, taking action steps, and finding new meaning.

Creating a Safe Space

When we worked with a family whose father/husband had died by suicide, we prepared the room, so family members could choose their seating. We brought water and cups, as well as tissues, and placed them on the table. We then offered them a candle we had made for their lost loved one, as well as handouts on grief, suicide, and trauma at the end of our first session. The goal was to create survival and safety first, and then to slowly empower the family to be the best support for and with each other. We became their 'backup singer', holding the space so they could acknowledge the varying reactions to their pain, to reconnect with each other by hearing and honoring each other's thoughts and feelings, and begin to rebuild their lives without the physical presence of their family member who had died.

Several years ago, we were asked to respond to a workplace shooting, where several employees had been shot and killed. Many of the employees felt the need for support as they reentered their workplace. We did a ceremony of cleansing and survival as we brought them back to their office, walking beside them as they put the puzzle pieces back together. This included discussing with each other what happened, where it happened, and then, as a group, they reclaimed the safety of their workplace together, bringing in a spiritual and emotional energy of protection and healing.

Issues and Dynamics around Suicide

The death of anyone we care about causes intense feelings of loss and grief. Loss through suicide, however, is particularly devastating to those close to the individual. Suicide is the deliberate ending of one's own life and, as such, it contradicts all of our assumptions about the human will to survive.

The first question normally asked is "Why did this person do it?" Generally, people die by suicide because their problems and pain seem overwhelming. They may feel there is no solution or change in sight, and earlier attempts to deal with problems failed or backfired.

Causes of Suicide

Leading causes of suicide include:

- Depression: this may be brought on by personal loss, heredity, or body chemistry. Life seems unbearable; the person may lose interest in all activities and withdraw.
- Crisis/impulse: major life changes such as loss of an important person, job, and so forth, can result in overwhelming anger and frustration.
- Old age/disease: the prospect of increasing pain and suffering, as well as loss of independence, income, and dignity is frightening. Suicide may seem to be the only alternative.
- Drugs/alcohol: drug or alcohol abuse can weaken a person's self-control and lead to suicide attempts and other self-destructive behaviors.
- Mental illness: a biochemical imbalance in the body can affect emotional, mental, and social functioning.

Any combination of these situations is particularly dangerous.

An especially difficult question for those associated with a suicide victim is "Could I have done anything to help avoid this?" Feelings of guilt and helplessness are common, and the answer to the question, unfortunately, is one of the hardest things to accept—we will never really know.

We do know that victims of suicide have usually thought about the event and sometimes even rehearsed it for a long period of time. Crisis counselors who work with suicidal clients report that, while in many cases they are able to provide the necessary support to help the person through a destructive episode, in other situations the client will succeed in spite of the fact that every conceivable support was in place.

It is important to encourage clients to be gentle with their grief process when these thoughts and questions repeat themselves. The person who dies by suicide leaves many victims behind. Survivors need to stay in the present, honor their feelings, and begin the journey through the grief process.

Survivors of suicide commonly share feelings such as the following:

- Shock and dismay: I can't believe s/he would do this!
- Guilt: I should have done something
- Fear related to a sense of loss of control, abandonment, or inability to relate to the event
- Anger at feeling rejected or abandoned
- Horror and/or terror

© Copyright material from Darrow and Childs (2020), *Experiential Action Methods and Tools for Healing Grief and Loss-Related Trauma*, Routledge.

- Physical sensations of grief
- Nightmares and flashbacks
- Feeling crazy and/or unable to function. These may be delayed, as well as immediate, responses
- 'Landmines', such as sensory (sight, smell, sound, textures) or memory triggers may bring back trauma and loss
- Anniversaries are also difficult. Grievers may have a reaction two to three days before the date of death, birth, special day, or holiday.

These feelings are normal and healthy reactions. They can best be dealt with by:

- Talking openly and honestly with others in a supportive environment
- Crying, which relieves emotional and physical tension. This applies to both men and women
  - Reading literature about loss and the grief process
  - Completing any unfinished business or unresolved feelings using ceremony, letter writing, or sharing.

Unresolved feelings and grief can be stored in the body and psyche and emerge later in detrimental ways. Therefore, it is important to stay with the feelings and obtain support.

The length of time it will take to recover from this loss will vary with the degree of involvement with the person. It may take from a few weeks to several years to never. Encourage survivors to trust the healing process. They will emerge from this experience and they will be changed by it. Eventually, for some survivors, memories may bring feelings of acceptance. For some, the relationship to that special person will not have died; it will have changed its form. The good times will eventually be remembered and treasured.

For other survivors, suicide is experienced as the ultimate act of rejection, and acceptance and/or forgiveness will come slowly, if at all. Self-esteem may be completely destroyed. Guilt and anger may be deep and long-lasting. It may never be possible to totally understand the tragedy. Lives are complicated and no one person or one single factor is responsible for a person dying by suicide. Patience and consistent, non-judgmental support can provide the context needed to allow these individuals to work through their pain and gradually find healing.

On Violence

When violence becomes a personal reality, we become acutely aware of violence endemic to the society and culture. Events that once were distant and removed now affect a survivor's feelings in a profound way.

The horror of sudden tragedy (9/11, natural disasters such as earthquakes, volcanos, floods, fire, hurricanes, murder, suicide, assassinations, kidnappings, hijackings, molestations, abuse, etc.) reverberates through our bodies. These events are a reminder of all the violence that has been witnessed or been a part of earlier life experience. It is important to acknowledge this response to violence.

For victims, survivors, witnesses, and caretakers, trauma weaves an invisible link between personal experience and disasters throughout the world—no matter how random or dissimilar to our own. Something happens somewhere else in the world and, while the mind rationalizes—"I'm in no immediate danger" or "What happened to me has no relationship to what's happening elsewhere"—the body disagrees. Pulse rates rise. Heads throb. Stomachs knot up. Chests tighten. All the demons return to ignite fears and self-doubt. Events—distant and seemingly removed from our lives—headlines, sound bites, social media become trigger points to raw, personal emotion. Disaster takes on a human face—the face of one we love, or the face in the mirror.

When people face trauma, every part of their being is affected—body, mind, and soul—physically, mentally, psychologically. Common reactions include trembling throughout the body, loss of body sensations, uncontrollable crying, numbness, detachment, disbelief, angry, hostile, belligerent behavior, lightheadedness or dizziness, nausea and/or a bad taste in the mouth, sleeplessness/excessive sleep/exhaustion, sudden or cumulative weight loss or gain, unidentified fear or panic, inability to concentrate or stay on task, desire for dramatic life changes—move, change jobs, begin or end relationships—overly risky behavior, false bravado, or frequent colds/flu/headaches/digestive ills.

This is the power of trauma. It's important to be aware of the short-term and cumulative impact on the lives of those affected. It is vital to allow the expression of reaction to violent news. Others' stories of violence will trigger hidden feelings in relation to one's own violent losses. When individuals have personally experienced the gut-wrenching isolation of violence, it is natural and easy to empathize with others who are presently experiencing similar life trauma. Those who have experienced violence know that it no longer just happens to the 'other person'. The reality is that violence can strike anyone, anywhere, any time. Violence carries with it a unique energy. Because this energy dynamic is different than what people are accustomed to coping with, it can be frightening. Violence can activate the primitive survival instinct—there may be rage that is beyond normal anger. Some may also experience physical strength beyond normal capabilities. It is common to feel drained and exhausted, because the impact of physical or emotional violence depletes energy. Because perceived safety has been shattered, people feel a systemic state of anxiety, tension, and fear. There is hypervigilance in finding any safe, peaceful place that feels secure, in addition to fear for loved ones and for oneself.

Deep in the unconscious, below the rational mind, violence and the memories of violence can affect dreams, ability to sleep, ability to be close to others, or even to relate to others (even in the most casual contacts, such as a grocery store clerk). The ability to do even the simplest activities of daily living is affected. People may suffer from sleeplessness or a paralyzing fear that prevents them from accomplishing basic tasks. An overwhelming need to protect loved ones from any harm is common.

Many people have shared that they have seen, felt, heard, or somehow experienced the presence of the loved one who has died, or of a frightening 'negative presence' (almost like violence, horror, or death personified). Children are especially sensitive to this experience, and while they may not share spontaneously, when asked, many young people will reveal these hidden fears or visions. It is common to be afraid to be near the place where the violent act occurred, and yet feel inextricably drawn to it. It is a way to make

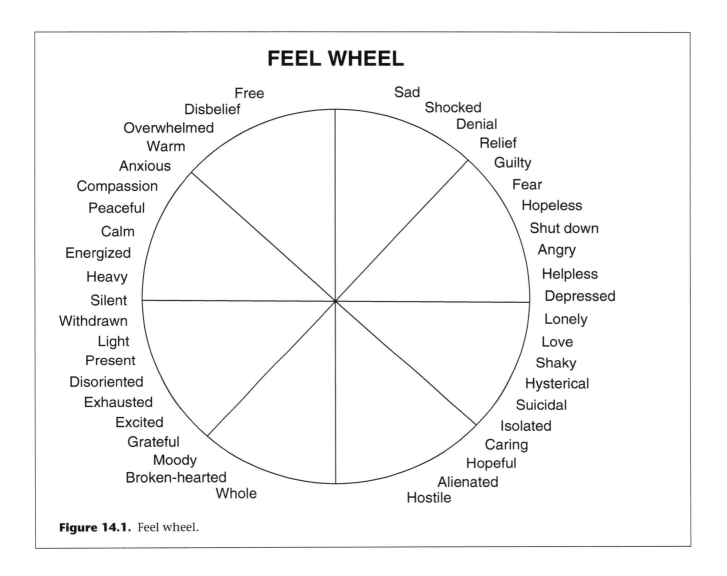

Figure 14.1. Feel wheel.

90 Violent Death and Suicide

what happened real. When something as bizarre as rape, murder, suicide, or accident occurs, it is hard to believe. It is a slow healing process to realize the effect of the violent act on the survivor, and to begin to reclaim personal power in life.

We encourage people to acknowledge the magnitude of their horror and loss, as well as the tremendous impact violence has on them. We ask them to share the details with someone with whom they feel safe. We encourage them to express every detail of the fantasies, visions, and feelings, including the visual, auditory, olfactory, gustatory, and kinesthetic elements. Below is an example with the feel wheel to assist clients to identify difficult feelings (Figure 14.1). Clients can utilize the words around the feel wheel or create their own words to write into the segments. This also can be combined with other art: coloring, drawing symbols, and so on.

A thirteen-year-old client, Roberto, had just survived the murder of his father and his uncle. His culture did not allow him to discuss his ambivalent feelings about their deaths, and he felt shut down.

Janet: What is hardest for you right now?

Roberto: There are too many feelings and ideas in my head and in my heart. They have no voice.

Janet: Look at this feel wheel. It has different feelings in each pie slice. (Roberto looks at the feel wheel.) There is an arrow and you can point to what is most up for you.

Roberto first moved the arrow to 'blame' and then after a few moments moved the arrow to 'relief'.

Janet: Let's give 'blame' a voice. What does blame say?

Roberto: I warned my dad and uncle to stay clear of gangs, and to lie low. I had a dream that my dad and uncle were going to die. They didn't listen. I blame them that they ignored me and now I feel so sad.

Janet: You sound angry, also.

Roberto (crying): Yes, I am angry. Now they are gone. My dad is gone.

Janet: I would like you to write a letter to your dad and uncle, telling them how you feel.

He then wrote a letter to his dad and uncle, expressing his anger, blame, love, and sorrow at their deaths.

Janet: Bring to mind that part of your dad that cared about you and loved you. Feel this for a moment. Now turn the letter over and write his reply.

Roberto was willing to share the message.

Roberto: He said I was not responsible for his well-being. That was his responsibility. And he said I did not have the power to protect them.

Janet: Let's now listen to 'relief'. What does the word 'relief' say?

Roberto (speaking in the voice of relief): I don't have to worry any more. I am no longer responsible for my dad's and uncle's safety.

Janet: Yes. And, your message to your dad was right. He didn't listen, but it was right.

Roberto: Yes, my warnings were right.

Janet: So can you trust yourself and your feelings?

Roberto: Yes, I can trust my feelings and pay attention to my dreams. And I can share what I think and feel, even if others don't take it seriously.

Janet: Thank you for letting us hear the message from 'relief'. This message is a gift to all of us.

As a final action step, Roberto took his dad's bandana to the gravesites of his uncle and father. Placing it at their sites, he released his ancestral connection to the gangs, and the guilt that he felt over his relatives' deaths.

We provide the following handout to those who have been affected by violent death.

Surviving Violent Death

Sound, smell, taste, touch, sensory experiences, the presence of your loved one, the details of the trauma, how you would like to kill or maim the perpetrator are all important aspects to release. Many of the feelings that arise in coping with violence are not culturally 'acceptable'. It is like being thrust into another dimension of reality where we don't know the rules.

The most valuable gift we can give our self and each other is the gift of gentle acceptance. When judgment or criticism creeps in, remind yourself that your life has been turned upside down and inside out. It will take time and patience to build the foundations again.

For protection, and to reclaim our power, there comes a time to actively create a sense of safety and comfort around our self: body, mind, emotions, and spirit.

- Create a comfortable physical environment which gives you a sense of control over your immediate surroundings.
- Change room arrangements, furniture, color schemes, pictures, even the bedroom where you normally sleep.
- Choose foods that are appealing and easy to prepare. Listen to what your body needs for nourishment.
- Create a support system of friends, family, and associates to call or visit if you need not to be alone.
- Cut back on demanding activities and focus on what makes you feel good.
- Ask for spiritual protection, using whatever faith or belief you have to call upon a 'higher power' to watch over you and protect you from harm. If this isn't appropriate for you, imagine the love and comfort from your friends and loved ones wrapping around you like a blanket of healing.
- Treat yourself well—rest, work out, eat right.
- Learn deep-breathing and relaxation techniques.
- Treat yourself with the same degree of kindness and care you show loved ones.

Avoid impulsive decisions over major or life-changing events during the immediate aftermath of trauma. Changing jobs, moving to another city, ending/beginning relationships may appeal to a need to regain a sense of control. Such decisions are stressful and potentially tumultuous. Later, such changes may indeed be exactly what you need—when the time and circumstances are right.

Ask for and accept assistance whenever and however you need it. Asking for help is not a sign of weakness. Accepting a helping hand is not an admission of dependence. Seeking or accepting help from others may feel awkward or uncomfortable. This may challenge your sense of independence, autonomy, or privacy. We have found however that those who do ask and allow others to help develop inner strength, resilience, and self-sufficiency. They can develop, in fact, a capacity for giving back to their community more effectively.

The nature of sudden, violent separation, loss, or death of a loved one can leave survivors feeling violated, like a piece of one's heart has been torn out. This is made worse without normal closure. If people are unable to see the deceased's body or a part of the body, the process of saying goodbye is harder.

Questions arise: "How much did my loved one suffer? How long was she/he in pain? Could I have done anything differently to protect him/her?" These are normal. When they come up, it is necessary to gather all the information from the coroner's report and other sources to establish what happened. This is a natural need, but not everyone will have this urge at the same time. Listen to your own needs and timing.

© Copyright material from Darrow and Childs (2020), *Experiential Action Methods and Tools for Healing Grief and Loss-Related Trauma*, Routledge.

Some people feel comfortable in directly asking their loved ones how it was for them. Talking with our loved ones who have died is a healing tool that aids resolution of what is unknown, incomplete, and unfinished. Writing letters to that special person is another form of communication that can free us from the burdens of guilt, pain, and unanswered questions. Again, it is important to honor whatever feels appropriate or comfortable for you in any given moment.

Expect a delayed and/or recurrent reaction. Sometimes memories surface when least expected. In the midst of emergency, we tend to operate on automatic pilot, responding with core strength and skills to act decisively. In the aftermath of trauma, as shock wears off and reality sinks in, we are especially vulnerable to delayed reactions.

Intense reactions are normal. Trauma is, by nature, devastating. Although survivors don't feel normal, their reactions are normal. It is an unexpected event or series of events for which there is no means to adequately prepare oneself. We convey this message to people affected by trauma.

Everything feels crazy because it is! Life has turned upside down, but your feelings are a natural response. Your feelings are your body's means of absorbing shock, your mind's means of gaining eventual acceptance, your soul's means of searching for balance, healing, and meaning. You are normal, but your life, at present, is not—and you need to take care of yourself right now moment by moment, day by day.

Remember: The violent event only happened once and the victims only experienced that event once.

Questions to Explore in the Midst of Trauma

- Who should I tell? Who can I trust?
- What is going to hurt or be difficult?
- Where can I go to feel safe and secure again?
- When will this pain go away?
- Why do I feel so alone?
- How do I survive this grief?
- Who wants to be around me, to hear me whine?
- What's going to happen now?
- Where can I regain control in my life?
- When will everyone just leave me alone?
- Why can't I make myself feel better? What can I do to help myself feel better?
- How can I support those I love in grief?

Exploration of these questions can provide a solid foundation for a survival plan. We encourage people to use the wisdom of their special people—alive or dead—to support them with answers, at least for now. Using role play and role reversal, writing down random thoughts and impressions, asking for your dreams to reveal clues, as well as approaching support people, will help to identify tools and action steps.

Informing others about one's situation and building support systems early help others understand and support the process of healing. This helps shield survivors from the devastation of isolation.

Remember: Grief is not a problem to be solved, but a process to go through—step by step, day by day, to healing.

CHAPTER 15

GRIEF WORK BEYOND THE ACUTE STAGE

Grief doesn't end after eight weeks. Universal aspects of acute grief are a part of the eight-week program, but as the initial shock and intense feelings become softer, there are many issues that remain as people journey toward healing and finding a new normal. It is common that bereaved people make progress and then later uncover deeper layers that are still unresolved and difficult. Acute grief topics can be worked on more than once. Sociometric tools such as spectrograms and locograms (described in Chapter 3) provide an effective way to assess how group members are progressing with acute issues, for them to see their progress, and to get a sense of what other issues are arising and possibly common to the group. Below are second-stage grief topics that come up and ways to work with these issues.

Working with Dreams in Action

After a sociometry warm-up indicated that many have a hard time with frozen images, Bonnie, in the Loss of Parent group, stated that she has had a difficult recurring dream. Bonnie was asked if she wanted to work with her dream and she agreed. We asked her to set a scene with scarves and pillows to represent her bed and to lay down and enter into the story and feeling of this difficult dream. When she had recaptured the dream, she could indicate this by putting up a finger, which she did.

Lusijah: So, tell us, Bonnie about your dream.

Bonnie: I am some place with my mother, my aunt (mother's sister), and my sisters and their children. My mother is going around saying goodbye to family members. I am just observing what's going on. When my mother says goodbye to my sisters, they are sitting on the couch watching television and they hardly break their concentration. They only respond casually. Then my mother goes to my aunt, telling her that she is afraid, and wants my aunt to come with her. The aunt responds saying that she can't go with her. Then my mother approaches her grandchildren and they all say goodbye. (As Bonnie is telling the story, she is emotional, but not overwhelmed.)

Lusijah: Bonnie, I would like you to choose other group members to play the different people in your dream. (Bonnie chooses other group members to play roles.) I would like you to play yourself and let other people re-enact your dream.

Lusijah (after the enactment of the dream): What are you feeling as you watch your mother try to say goodbye?

Bonnie: I feel helpless, frustrated, and angry.

Lusijah: Now please pick someone to play you, and you will stand outside and watch as the dream is enacted again.

Lusijah (after witnessing the dream): How do you feel watching, now standing outside of the dream?

Bonnie: I feel the same thing, frustrated and angry.

Lusijah: OK, you are going to get to redo this dream. Please go back to your bed and redream the dream as you wish it could have been. Redream the dream you want; you can change anything. (Client went back to her bed, to dream the dream she wanted, indicating with a raised finger that she had completed the redo.) Tell us about the dream now.

Bonnie: All of the family members are loving and responsive to my mother. My mother is able to recognize that my aunt can't go with her.

Lusijah: What is different about what you do in the dream?

Bonnie: I make sure that everyone is listening! I hug my mother and tell her I love her.

Lusijah: OK, so let's run the dream again. (Client then played herself in re-enacting the new dream, hugging her mother at the end.) Does this feel complete for now?

Bonnie: Yes, thank you.

The witnessing of re-enactment is powerful for other group members, bringing up their own regrets and frozen memories. It is important to let other group members share about how they were touched watching the work. They should not comment about the person doing the work—in any way—because the person who has done the work is wide open emotionally. To hear that his or her work has touched or reminded others of their own stories makes the protagonist feel safely connected to the group.

This next vignette occurred in an individual session with a grief client whose toddler son had been sexually abused and killed. Fiona came into the session saying she had not been doing very well, that she been having a lot of troubling dreams.

Lusijah: Tell me, Fiona, about your most recent dream. Tell me about the dream as if it is happening right now.

Fiona: I had this dream last night. I have gone into a house and am trying to get upstairs. The stairs keep flattening. The upstairs is where my room is in my mother's house. I leave the house and the building starts to fall apart with debris falling on me. I have been having dreams with a similar theme of buildings falling, with earthquakes, debris falling on me.

Lusijah: Hmm, wow, thank you for sharing the dream. Let me just talk a little about dreams. This is your dream and only you can make sense of any meaning. Very often in dreams a house is like a metaphor for the space we live in. Many people who do a lot of work with dreams believe repeated dreams and nightmares insist on the dreamer's attention and are believed to be helpful to the dreamer. These repeating difficult dreams are a message for the dreamer to pay attention. I could comment on the dreams if this was my dream.

Fiona: OK, I would like to hear this.

Lusijah (speaking from first person, in present tense): I am trying to get upstairs to a higher place out of the painful situation that exists for me right now. I can't do it, everything is falling apart. When I leave, the house falls down, the debris of the falling house (maybe symbolic of the situation I am in), it threatens to hurt or kill me.

Fiona: That sounds right.

Therapist: I would like for you to expand on this dream if you are willing. I would like to take your arm as we walk around the room. You can close your eyes and I will make sure you don't run into anything. Just allow more of the dream to come into your mind's eye.

Fiona (nodding her willingness): The lower part of the house is beige, there are two people in the house of Caucasian ethnicity who I don't know. They are neither kind nor unkind. As I go up the stairs I see the doorframe at the top of the stairs is made out of cracked concrete and it's crumbling. The stairs are like escalator stairs, they just flatten out and I can't get upstairs. The house and stairs do not look nice, and the house is dirty. After I leave, the house debris is falling on me. I don't mind being killed.

Lusijah (knowing Fiona's strong religious beliefs): But you are still alive and I know that God has a plan for you.

Fiona: Yes, I know. But I wouldn't mind if my life ended sometimes.

Lusijah (nods in acknowledgment): I would like you to sit down now and close your eyes and recreate the dream as you might like it. You can start with walking into the house, trying to get upstairs, but this dream will have a different ending. Let me know when you feel you have recreated the dream. (Client sat quietly with her eyes closed.)

Fiona: OK, I have recreated the dream.

Lusijah: Good, tell me about the dream.

Fiona (smiling): OK. The house is very colorful, my mother and brothers are in the house and are very happy to see me. They are very loving as I enter the house. The house is very clean and in good shape. When I see the stairs, I can see that I can get upstairs. As I walk into the upstairs room, there are big windows and I can see the forest and sugarcane fields. The sun is coming into the windows; it is a beautifully sunny day.

Lusijah: OK, so now we are going to walk around the room again, with me holding your arm, with your eyes closed, and I will retell the dream. Allow yourself to fully see this in your mind's eye. (Both get up and begin to walk around the room.)

Lusijah: I am walking into my mother's house. It is so beautiful and colorful. There are my mother and brothers. My mother is giving me a hug (I give Fiona a hug). She says, "Welcome Fiona, it is so wonderful that you are here, come in." I feel so happy to be here. I feel safe. Now I am going upstairs to my room. Everything looks so nice, everything is clean. I look out the windows in my room and see forest and sugarcane. The room has so much light, the sun feels good.

Lusijah: Fiona, I want to soak in this feeling of being in a safe and loving place. You are now in your room in your mother's house. Stay with this feeling for a while.

Fiona (after a few minutes): Thank you so much.

Repeating nightmares are associated with trauma and exhibit a frozen sense of horror and usually helplessness. Full exploration of the dream sheds light on fears that are still stuck. A father who lost his young child to murder had recurring dreams of seeing young children who were in various situations in which they would die. In the dream, he was frozen and couldn't intervene to help save the children. The repeating aspect of the dream put a spotlight on his feeling of powerlessness to have prevented his son's death. We suggested that, before going to sleep every night, the client visualize himself being physically empowered, and 'see' himself successfully intervening to save the children. A few weeks later, he reported that he had intervened and saved children in a dream.

Finding New Meaning

Creating a new normal and establishing life meaning is a second-stage aspect of processing grief. Below are several ways this topic was explored with clients.

Envisioning the Future

There is a psychodramatic concept of the different roles people have in their lives—that roles change, as some become obsolete and new roles arise. This activity encourages clients to consider the future they want. Clients are invited to look at a therapeutic card collection that is spread out on the floor. Clients are invited to pick one card to represent their grief, another card to represent a future projection of where they would like to be, and a third card to represent a personal strength or resource that will help them move towards their future projection. The personal strength is the client's choice, but can be a good friend or family member who loves them (alive or not), someone who wants the best for them, or it can be inner guide, guardian angel, or God. Group members are invited to share their cards and do further exploration in action.

Lusijah: I want to honor the place and importance of your grief and wonder if you are willing to place the grief card somewhere offstage for now, wherever you feel it needs to be for now.

Cindy: OK. (Cindy took the card and placed it under the cushion of the couch.)

Lusijah: Let's work with your card that represents you some time in the future. Will you show me the card? (After looking at the card) How much in the future is this?

Cindy: This is two years in the future.

Lusijah: Go ahead and step into your future self. Stand over here to take this role.

Lusijah: Hello, future Cindy. What are you wearing?

Cindy: Let's see, I am wearing a dress that is very colorful.

Lusijah: What about your shoes?

Cindy: They are sandals with block heels.

Lusijah: Show me how you walk now, wearing these clothes. (Client starts walking.) Tell me what you are feeling in your body as you walk.

Cindy: I feel great. I have energy.

Lusijah: What do you notice about how you are breathing? What do you feel in your stomach, back, hands?

Cindy: I feel like I am standing up straight, my hands are swinging. They feel relaxed.

Lusijah: Great. Just walk around a bit, stay with that feeling. (After a brief moment.) What are you doing these days?

Cindy: I am working. I changed jobs and am happy with my job. I am planning my wedding.

Lusijah: Wonderful! (Cindy nods and smiles.) So, let's change now and look at the card you chose that represents a strength or resource. Show me the card you chose and what it represents to you.

Cindy: This card stands for my fiancé.

Lusijah: OK, so go ahead and step into his role. (Cindy physically moves to another spot.) What is your name?

Cindy (as fiancé): Brad.

Lusijah: Congratulations, you and Cindy are going to get married soon. How long have you known each other?

Cindy (as fiancé): Two years.

Lusijah: What do you most love or respect about Cindy?

Cindy (as fiancé): We laugh so much together. She is not what you call a wallflower. She is spunky, smart, talented.

Lusijah: Yes, I know what you mean (smiling). Cindy has brought you here today as her most important strength. You know of course that her father died recently. What words might you say that would be supportive and helpful to Cindy?

Cindy (as fiancé): You are so strong. This has been really hard for you to have lost your dad, but I want you to know that I love you, I know you will get through this. You've got to believe in your strength and what you are good at. We have a happy life in front of us.

Lusijah (to present-day Cindy): I would like to let your strength and future self have a conversation. Step in the role of future Cindy now. Do you have anything you would like to ask or say to your strength?

98 Grief Work beyond the Acute Stage

Cindy (as future self): I try to be strong, but I am sad sometimes. You always help me when I am sad. Please keep helping me.

Lusijah: Tell him how he helps you.

Cindy (as future self): You are kind and you bring me back to normal. You suggest that we do something, go to the store or go to a movie. This helps me.

Lusijah: Reverse roles.

Cindy (as Brad): I can do this. Thank you for telling me how I can help you.

Lusijah: So, I would like you to step into your present-day self. I am putting your future self at the other end of the room. Look at this pile of scarves. I would like you to do a symbolic walk towards your future self. Consider now as you look at the scarves. Pick some scarves that represent thoughts, feelings, or activities that you would like to release and other scarves representing thoughts, strengths, feelings, or activities that you may need to make bigger or more prominent as you move toward your future self.

Cindy (after thoughtfully choosing scarves and taking small steps towards the card representing her future self): I want to keep the memories of my dad and want to keep the love I have for dad.

Lusijah: So, go ahead and put the scarf around your neck and shoulders, maybe give it a hug (smiling).

Cindy: I want to hope and believe I will get better. I want to embrace my future life with Brad. (Cindy puts the scarf around her shoulders.)

Cindy: I want to release guilt that I didn't do enough. (Drops scarf.) I know I cannot get rid of my sadness, so I can't drop it, but I don't want it to be so big.

Lusijah: Where would you like to put it?

Cindy: I'll fold it up and put it in my pocket, I can take it out sometimes, but it is not always with me.

Lusijah (nodding): In your present self, do you have some final words to your future self, your strength, and your grief? (The cards are now placed on the floor so that Cindy can face each card with a last message.)

Cindy: OK, future self. I really want to get to where you are. To Brad, my strength. I am so glad you are with me and so thankful for your support. OK, to my grief. Wow, that card looks so ugly. OK, you will always be with me, but maybe just back up a little, so that you are not so big in my life.

Another variation on this activity is to invite the client to set up a sculpture of the future using other group members to take the roles, and to place the other group members, scarves, and cards in proximity to him- or herself to represent prominence or importance of these elements. Suggest that the client might want to take a picture of the sculpture.

This next exercise uses the psychodramatic concept of surplus reality. Tell group members that in twenty years they are to be honored at a meeting because of their accomplishments or contributions in their work. A good friend who knows and respects them is going to introduce them to a meeting. The introduction will include talk about their strengths, how they have transformed their own grief experience, how their accomplishments have been influenced by their loved one, what they are doing that would make their loved one proud. Group members are given a piece of paper in which to plan out the speech the friend is going to make to introduce them. After writing the speech, each gets up to take the role of their friend who is to do the introduction, standing next to where they had been seated. The group member is then interviewed in the role of their friend, being asked their name and how they know the group member. This is a powerful and affirming experience for groups. The exercise allows group members to speak without resistance to naming personal strengths and to step into a whimsical exploration of how these personal strengths might play into future life meaning and satisfaction. It is wonderful to hear group members mention the activity the following week as having stayed with them. They have gotten a taste of a future with meaning.

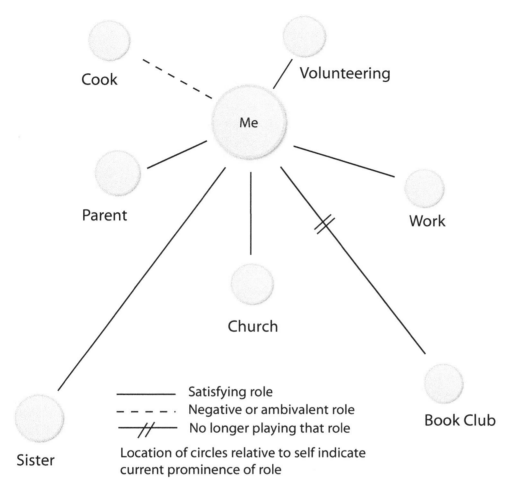

Figure 15.1. Life-meaning atom.

Because grief disrupts interests and activities that were enjoyable or meaningful, we normalize the difficulty of seeing a future while still newly or intensely in the grieving process. These (forward projection) psychodrama sessions are a snapshot of what is happening right now; we encourage the client to be non-judgmentally curious. When clients stay in the group for a while, the topic can be revisited, and group members see that they are in a different place.

This activity highlights current activity that clients find meaningful, using an adaptation of the psychodramatic tool called the 'social atom' (discussed in Chapter 6). We call this adaptation the 'life-meaning atom' (Figure 15.1). Group members start with a blank piece of paper designating themselves with a symbol in the middle of the sheet of paper and fill in the rest of the paper with activities they are currently engaged in. The activities can be both helpful and activities that take them away from what they'd rather be doing. Group members are invited to share their drawings and to pick three of the most important activities. Below is a vignette with Stella, who volunteered to explore her life-meaning atom.

Lusijah: Could you hold up your life-meaning atom and tell us about the three most important activities on it?
Stella: I chose going to church, water-color painting, and baking.

Lusijah: Great. Which one shall we explore first?

Stella: Going to church.

Lusijah: So, I am going to ask you to step into the role of church-going Stella. (Stella takes a step away from where she was standing.) Tell me, Stella, about what you do when you are involved with the church.

Church-going Stella: Of course, I go to church every Sunday. I also volunteer with other women on a committee that plans social activities and fundraising activities. I can be much more involved than I used to be because I have more time. When my husband was alive I couldn't leave him alone.

Lusijah: How is church-going Stella helpful to Stella? What does she do for Stella?

Church-going Stella: I help Stella a lot. I am with people, and it feels like work that is useful. I like being able to spend time with other women.

Lusijah: So, it feels useful, and it helps with getting together with other women. Does that help Stella with feeling less lonely?

Church-going Stella: Definitely.

Lusijah: Are there any downsides?

Church-going Stella: No, I don't think so.

Lusijah: OK, Stella, let's explore another activity in your life-meaning atom. Which one next?

Stella: How about the water-color painting?

Lusijah: Great, so step into the role of artistic Stella. (Stella takes a step away from where she was standing.) Stella, tell me about your painting.

Artistic Stella: I attend a water-color painting class. My husband was a wonderful artist and I started painting when he was alive. He used to always give me such good feedback.

Lusijah: Is it hard now, not having his feedback?

Artistic Stella: It was at first. In fact, I almost stopped painting because it was so painful to think that I couldn't get his feedback. But I decided I was going to continue to paint. The most amazing thing happened. I would do a painting and I could still hear his feedback! I could hear in my head just what he would say.

Lusijah: Wow, that is wonderful! We contain our loved ones on a cellular level, because we do know what they would say and how they would say it. What does artist Stella do for Stella?

Artist Stella: I provide creativity in her life. It is also a way that I remember my husband.

Lusijah: To keep a part of him close to you.

Artist Stella: Yes.

Lusijah: Stella, let's explore the last part of your life-meaning atom. The one who bakes. So, could you step into the role of the baker Stella. (Stella moves physically to stand in a place slightly to the right of where she was standing.) Tell me about your baking.

Baking Stella: I am a good cook and I make very good baked desserts. At some point, I couldn't eat what I made for health reasons, so I would give what I baked away to neighbors. My husband loved my baking.

Lusijah: Lucky for your neighbors! What does baking Stella do for Stella?

Baking Stella: She sure makes good friends! The neighbors enjoy getting what I bake. I like to bake what my husband loved. It is nice to still make his favorites and have other people enjoy them.

Lusijah: Yes, the group has certainly enjoyed it when you have brought in one of your husband's favorite desserts. Stella, I would like you to take your own position and choose people in the group to play each of the roles. (Stella chose group members to play the roles.) Now Stella, I would like you to listen as each role talks about what they do for you and for others.

Each role spoke of their importance for Stella.

Stella: I really enjoyed this. It makes me realize the value of these activities and that they are nice ways I remember my husband.

People see their current activities as vehicles to engage with others, ways to use different parts of self (intellect, artistic, caring), and to see that they derive positive regard and respect from others. Sometimes the activities are a positive way to connect with the memory of their loved one. One eighty-three-year old group member spoke about her horticulture work, splitting off new plants that she gives away, her bridge groups in which she uses her intellect and where she is highly respected, and her practice of sending cards to those who need support. She cried as she received the messages from group members who took the roles of her important activities, acknowledging that these activities create positive self-esteem.

As a variation on the life-meaning atom, group members can specify activities that are currently meaningful, were meaningful in the past, and activities that they are reaching for in the future. Here are four questions we ask after the completion of the drawings:

1. Do you see new activity additions or an activity that has recently had a more prominent place in your life?
2. Is there an activity that gave meaning to your life earlier that you would like to bring to more prominence again?
3. Are there activities you want to engage in more?
4. Are there activities you feel ambivalent about or want to drop?

Expressing Gratitude

Acknowledging and feeling gratitude for the gifts received from the relationship with the person who has died is meaningful. We have noticed that, when clients are in a space of remembering positive experiences, they smile. We suggest the following activities to promote gratitude and honoring of the loved one.

1. Make a collage from magazine pictures to remember how the deceased impacted their life, and how their loved one is still part of their life. Group members then share the collage.
2. Dialogue with the loved one on special days (Mother's Day, Father's Day, anniversaries) to express gratitude. Invite clients to speak in their mother tongue to express heartfelt feelings. As an example, see the vignette below with Maria. She was the youngest of ten children and had been the caretaker for her elderly parents until their death. Maria had done incredibly courageous work to find the life she wanted, having gone back to school and having found work. This individual session occurred around the time of Mother's Day.

Lusijah: Would you like to talk to your mom? (Maria nods affirmative, Lusijah pulls out a chair.) Here she is; talk to her, Maria.

Maria: I am so grateful for all you did for me and for being such a wonderful example of a woman staying close to faith.

Lusijah: Reverse roles.

Maria (as mother): I am so proud of how you are living your life.

Lusijah: Do you have some words that Maria needs to hear?

From here until the end, the client spoke in Spanish, the language her mother would have used. The translation was that Maria's mother's voice encouraged the client to live her own life and to not take on the responsibility of care for other family members.

Maria (crying as she had the final word to her mother): Thank you, mama. I love you so much.

3. Write a love letter to one's spouse expressing gratitude. After the letter, do a brief visualization, calling that part of the spouse or partner who loved and respected them into the room. Invite group members to turn the letter over and write their partner's reply. This is a powerful experience. This is especially important if the client did not have a chance to say these words to their loved one.

Reparative Work with Surplus Reality

Surplus reality is another tool that comes out of psychodrama, in which a client experiences what might have been. This can create a reparative experience and/or insight with unresolved issues, ambivalence, anger, and guilt. It results in new perspectives about events or relationships. This tool is especially helpful when the deceased had difficult issues, such as addiction, mental health problems, or medical issues. To imagine that the deceased is unencumbered from these issues and can express love or remorse is healing. Surplus reality creates a felt sense of receiving love, support, and caring that was not received in life, often along with a softened feeling and acceptance that this support was not available for the deceased to give when they were alive.

In an individual session, Bella stated that her father had died from alcohol-related causes when she was fifteen years old, after multiple attempts at treatment. The rehabilitation center sent him home saying there was nothing further they could do. The family knew he was dying from cirrhosis of the liver. She said that the family felt relief after his death. Bella cried as she shared that she had no good memories of her father, but did have a frozen memory of her father speaking kindly to her the day before he died, as well as her mean response. Bella tearfully said he was abusive to her and her siblings. Knowing the importance of the client's religious/spiritual feelings, the client was reminded that God is merciful. The client was asked to close her eyes, imagining that her father is no longer suffering from his illness, and that he has been given God's grace and healing. The client sat quietly with her eyes closed.

> *Lusijah:* From this place, what might your father say to you? Speak from your father's voice, from the voice of your father who has been healed.
>
> *Bella (speaking as father):* I love you, I love all of you because you are my family. I am so sorry.
>
> *Lusijah:* I would like you to listen to his message now (asking permission to touch her on the shoulders). I love you, I love all of you because you are my family. I am so sorry.
>
> I repeated the message softly several times, adding, "I hope you can forgive me."
>
> Bella cried as she heard her father's message, nodding her head when she heard her father asking for forgiveness. She was deeply in the experience.
>
> *Lusijah:* Stay with what you are feeling. (Client remained with the experience with her eyes closed for several minutes.)
>
> *Bella (opening her eyes):* Thank you so much. I really felt his message. Thank you so much. My father's birthday is in two days and it has always been hard. I think it will be different this year.

These short scenes often seem quite simple. It is unnecessary to get full explanation or statement about what Bella's father is sorry about. Bella knows. To try to elicit an explanation will put the client in their thinking center rather than their heart.

We checked in with Bella a couple of days later because of the intensity of the session. She reported that she was fine and expressed gratitude again, saying she had felt her father's love, adding that "I have waited for a long time to feel this."

CHAPTER 16

FAITH AND THE GRIEVING PROCESS

People experience the same acute grief issues irrespective of whether or not they have a spiritual or religious practice; however there are unique grief reactions that relate to the survivor's beliefs or lack of beliefs. We explore these unique issues below and provide tools, exercises, and strategies that are healing for varied individual orientations around faith.

Those who do not have a religious or spiritual practice are additionally faced with an existential crisis about the meaning of their loved one's life and their own mortality. If death means ceasing to exist, what was the point of life? Existential meaning can be addressed with role play with survivors taking the role of the deceased and being interviewed about accomplishments, successes, how the deceased impacted and shaped the survivor's life and the lives of others. Maybe there are inherited traits that would be noted. Their life made a difference and the essence of the deceased continues to exist in some expression.

There are ways to support people without a religious or spiritual practice with use of sensitive language. Religiously charged terms like 'soul' can be called 'essence'— the felt knowing of the core of who the loved one was—much in the same way that people are sensed as kind, lighthearted, prickly, and so on. The felt knowing can be elicited through visualizations to help heal grief. Below is a visualization that was done that worked well for clients with or without a strong religious or spiritual orientation.

Relax into your chair and feel the support of your feet on the ground. You can either close your eyes or have soft eyes for now, however you feel most comfortable. Take three breaths, feel your lungs fill as you breathe in, and feel the air coming through your lips as you exhale.

Think of a beautiful place that you and your loved one enjoyed visiting together. Maybe it was the beach, or a forest, or near a lake or river. Take a moment to breathe in the fresh air and feel the warmth of the sun on your skin and a slight breeze on your cheeks. As you are walking, you sense something that cannot be described, which you know to be the presence of your loved one. As you walk closer, feel in your heart this is the essence of your loved one. Take a moment to remember how it felt in happy moments. Imagine how they smiled; remember times that he or she supported and showed love to you. This essence is regarding you with love and compassion. It feels like the best memory of being loved. Notice how his or her image shows up for you and how this makes you feel.

You now have a chance to ask your loved one for the help you need. Go ahead and ask this essence of your loved one for the help you most need. It could be asking why you have been left behind or asking for help with how you will be able to move on with your life, whatever you need from your loved one.

Listen to his or her reply

When you have heard his or her reply, find a way to thank him or her, maybe in words or an embrace. Say goodbye for now and turn around and walk back from where you came. Notice your breathing, notice a feeling of fullness in having felt their loving message. Take a few more breaths and, when you are ready, rejoin the room, gently opening your eyes.

This visualization can be specifically adapted to a client in individual work. In a visualization with a client whose young child had been killed, we suggested that the client was in a dream going up high into the sky and meeting her child, who was very excited to show her and tell her about where he lives now. We asked her to notice the colors and lighting, what the child looked like, what he was showing her. We suggested that her child had a message for her, and for her to listen to the message. This was transformative, as the client deeply experienced that he was OK, creating a new narrative that was comforting and very different from the repeating frozen image of his death.

Many great works of art and literature have been created about loss and grief. *A Grief Observed*, by C.S. Lewis (2009), *When Bad Things Happen to Good People*, by Rabbi Harold Kirshner (1980), and *The Sunflower*, by Simon Wiesenthal (2008) examine powerful issues such as loss of faith, change in relationship to a creator or higher power, and belief structures about life and love. The issues of guilt, forgiveness, reconciliation, and redemption are primary and essential to creating/reclaiming a strong base for resilient survival. Religious leaders and practitioners have tackled these issues, because they are the basis of our individual and communal understanding of life, illness, loss, and death. A more recent book, *Cops, Cons and Grace*, by Brian Cahill (2018), addresses issues of faith, and the struggle to determine the reframed normal of one's outlook on life and the world in the aftermath of traumatic death.

Death of a loved one touches the core of our spiritual (not necessarily religious) foundation. A crisis of faith involves personal/religious beliefs that are fractured or shattered by loss of a loved one. Therapeutic tools facilitate a deep exploration of the survivor's thoughts, feelings, and beliefs that supports restructuring of a 'new normal'. It is important to include cultural and familial overlays, and how they impact the development of the foundation of beliefs, as well as how to use these cultural roots in an affirmative way to strengthen sense of ownership and the claiming of a newly transformed belief structure.

When community can underpin and strengthen this journey, there can be exponential results. For example, cultural traditions around the world are almost always based upon acknowledging life changes, whether positive or challenging. In assisting clients/grieving people, or those facing traumatic change, it is important to create meaningful ceremonies of leave taking, including action steps to say goodbye. A wellspring of emotional and spiritual resources supports this process, both internally and externally. Highlighting resources and courage building for clients bridges the chasm between past and future and supports the reframing of the perception of their truth.

We have done this at the Centre for Living with Dying program for thirty-eight years, through our community Light of Lights ceremony. We hold this ceremony every year on the second Wednesday of December, deliberately in the middle of winter holidays for many cultures around the world. It can be an excruciating time for people in grief, as memories flood back, and even simple preparations become overwhelmingly painfully difficult. We gather people together to light candles for those they wish to honor or for particular causes which are dear to them. We have a bank of community candles, honoring special issues such as suicide, homicide, life-threatening illness, homelessness, earth/ecological grief, and responders/caregivers on the front lines (first/emergency responders, social workers, community workers, healthcare professionals, and clergy). This brings the community together to support and honor each other's role in our survival and resilience. It is also an action step to honor loss and celebrate the love that never dies. This type of community gathering fosters healing, builds connection, and creates a deepening of peace and understanding—a global environment that supports and sustains people in grief and trauma.

We have coined a term—cultural humility. Culture and beliefs—and the struggle to find meaning—are ever intertwined. Those who work with grief can never be fully culturally competent. Rather we attempt to be culturally sensitive by becoming culturally humble and willing to open our heart and mind to honor the cultural truth of the people we support.

The following example demonstrates cultural differences. Through a crisis response program at the hospital, we were supporting a grieving mother whose son had been brought to the hospital.

"Ms. Green, we lost your son," the doctor stated.

"Well, then, find him. He just came in," she replied emphatically.

"Your son is gone," the doctor continued.

"He could not have gone too far," she exclaimed.

Finally, the doctor expressed, "Your son has died. I am sorry."

To which, Ms. Green retorted, "Why should I believe you now? You lied to me before."

We spent time with Ms. Green after the doctor left. In her cultural tradition, which was Creole, originating from the New Orleans area, it was customary to wail and tear at one's clothing to express acute grief. She began her grief ritual by screaming, crying, and ripping her clothing, saying her son's name over and over. The doctor returned to the waiting room and sedated her, due to his discomfort with her traditions. I stated I would care for her, but he was adamant. As a result, her grief became buried and delayed. After several months of supporting her, it became clear that she needed to complete the grief tradition in the hospital in order to put her son's spirit to rest and peace.

With the help of the emergency department staff, we were able to recreate the scene in the emergency room, putting her son's shirt on a pillow and placing it in the treatment room where her son had been. Ms. Green was then able to take the time to wail, tear her clothing, and complete her honoring of her son's death of his body, while building her new relationship to his essence in her heart and life.

In daily life, cultural traditions are sometimes minimized or even abandoned when grief or trauma occurs. However, many people are drawn back to those filaments of light that connect them to ancestors and roots of their cultural tree. The key in supporting clients, friends, and families in these situations is to help them in identifying action steps to engender hope and connection that include and honor the religious or cultural context of the client. It might be a hybrid of methods at different places and times. The truth is, beliefs and life meaning are always changing and evolving. The grief journey deepens appreciation of life when grieving people actively claim what they need at any given time.

A social worker, Mari, had survived the death of two babies in a three-year period. In her culture, it was taboo to discuss or grieve babies who had died. Her husband did not even wish to acknowledge the losses. After much individual grief work, in which Mari was able to write letters to each of her babies, as well as have letters written to her from her babies, she felt ready to approach her husband about doing an action step. They had an amazing backyard garden. Mari asked her husband to plant a small tree in honor of each of their dead babies. Her husband agreed to this action step, which gave them both a way of coming together as parents to acknowledge the (albeit short) life of their children.

Ceremonies of Leave Taking

Ceremonies of leave taking—rituals created to help say goodbye—are a major component of acting upon beliefs, faith, and the challenges that come with confronting a major loss or change.

Ceremony supports the healing processes of change and loss. If commonly practiced rituals (such as funerals) have lost their meaning, grieving people have the power to create their own unique rituals that fulfill the need to say goodbye in a personally more meaningful way. Ritual is an acknowledgment of loss and a vehicle for individual, family, and community healing.

Human beings feel the need to say goodbye to people who have died or to situations that are no longer a part of their life. Across time and geography, cultures have created ceremony to process life passages. Bereaved people need to take what works from their traditions and develop individual observances that hold meaning for the specific issue. We encourage clients to organize a ritual of leave taking that focuses on what they need to do to say goodbye. Some may appreciate help in organizing a personal ritual.

106 Faith and the Grieving Process

Keep in mind when planning a ceremony:

- Purpose
- People
- Symbols
- Action steps
- Mementos
- Traditions that have meaning.

There is no right or wrong way to create a ritual of leave taking. We suggest grieving people explore with a creative mind and heart—what feels right. No matter how elaborate or how simple, the power of ceremony is directly related to the personal meaning it has for the grieving person.

There is a general flow to creating a ceremony full circle:

- Acknowledge the loss.
- Express the pain of that loss/change.
- Release the burden of the loss and any unfinished business.
- Perform a physical action to memorialize the healing/memories of the loss.
- Honor the love and meaning gathered from the loss.
- Celebrate life and reconnect to what is good in present time.

In supporting bereaved people as they organize a ritual of leave taking, focus on what each individual needs to do to say goodbye. When working with families or groups, it is important to compromise and to create enough space for everyone to get many of their individual wishes honored, while weaving it all into the group's collective wisdom and purpose.

Steps in formulating a ritual of leave taking include the following:

1. Establish what the group would like to do and what feels comfortable for them:
   A. Who else do they want to participate (other family members, friends, minister, musician, etc.)? How will they participate?
   B. Where do they want to have it (indoors, outdoors, park, church, home, grave site, special place)?
   C. When do they want to do it (date, time of day, anniversary, holiday, special day)?
   D. What memorabilia should be part of the ritual (candles, photographs, etc.)?
2. Components of ritual:
   A. State purpose of gathering
   B. Allow for expression of feelings about the loved one:
      1. Unfinished business: what they want or wanted to say or do
      2. Memories
      3. Moments of missing that person and moments they would like to share now
      4. All feelings related to the person
   C. Speaking directly to the person:
      1. Say the person's name and share:
         a. What the deceased has given them
         b. What they give to the deceased now
         c. Anything they want the deceased to know
      2. Say goodbye to the person directly. This is where the group can use candles, music, flowers—whatever has meaning and feels appropriate to them

D. Wrap-up and celebration:
1. Give the group time to wind down and share relaxing time together
2. Complete any physical rituals, i.e., planting a tree, lighting a candle, painting a picture, creating a card, etc.

Remember that anniversaries, holidays, and any special days spent with the deceased may be especially painful. Grieving people need to be aware of what they need to do to create a safe environment to acknowledge their feelings and decide if they need to do any further ritual.

Examples of Rituals

1. A widow went down to her late husband's favorite bar and ordered a round of drinks for everyone in memory of her husband. People were able to talk about her husband, and each person gave him a farewell toast. She did this after her husband's funeral, which had felt impersonal to the memory of her husband. The clergy did not even pronounce her husband's name correctly. This was a more fitting and meaningful action step of honoring his life, and his unique and funny personality.
2. A husband whose wife died suddenly baked bread for his wife and shared it with friends in a bread-breaking ceremony with wine. This action step was created after the husband spoke with the essence of his wife, asking her for help. She stated to him, "Bake me one of those beautiful loaves of bread you make so well." He knew in an instant this would give him meaning and resolution.
2. A mother whose son died by suicide held a party in which she invited friends and family to share memories of the child: funny, sad, mischievous, and so on. She displayed some of his belongings and talked about each one of them and what they meant. Then, they gathered in a circle and sang a goodbye lullaby. After the party, his clothing was made into pillows for everyone to keep as a memento.
3. A young woman, a singer and musician, died in an automobile accident. All of her friends gathered on a hill top covered with wild flowers. Each person picked a flower, offering it as a gift to the young woman with a spontaneously composed song, in which each person created a lyric. Then they gathered in a circle, singing and dancing in celebration of her life.
4. Friends of a boy who killed himself gathered at a beach to sing his favorite songs and light candles to say goodbye. Some brought recordings of songs, while others actually sang. Each person could participate in whatever way that worked for him or her.
5. A mother who had a stillborn child went to the hospital months later to visit the delivery room. She took a pillow off the empty bed and sat in a chair, rocking and crying. She was able to give her stillborn a name. When the stillbirth happened, she was in a medical crisis, so she was taken into surgery. She had never had the chance to say goodbye to her baby.
6. A young student died suddenly, and the entire school gathered together outside in the quad to release ecologically correct helium balloons in honor of their friend, and to share their sorrow and love. They attached messages to the balloons for him and watched as the ascending balloons disappeared into the sun and clouds.
7. A young man died of AIDS. In addition to making a quilt panel for the Names project, several family members and friends combined a church service with a candlelight vigil, followed by a celebration of his life done in a party atmosphere.

Another tool invites us to have a dialogue with our faith, with our questions, with our ancestors, with our spiritual guides or mentors, or even with death, the afterlife, or the end of life. We can do this through action methods or letter writing. Before opening the dialogue, we call upon our deepest wisdom beneath the fear, pain, anger, betrayal, or isolation.

108 Faith and the Grieving Process

Ten-year-old foster child, Ricky, who had been physically and sexually abused, was responding to the death of his grandmother, who died of a massive stroke. She had been his one pillar of support. He railed against God for taking his grandmother. He stated that he didn't believe in anything, and he wanted to die as well. Nothing mattered. We explored with him his grandmother's deep belief in God, and how that had given him comfort when she was alive. Now things had changed. In an inviting way, we offered for him to write a letter to this God. Using quite colorful language, he expressed his lack of faith and belief in this 'God' that would take his Mamaw away. After a couple of letters, we asked him to write a letter from God to him in response. This is where the magic happened. 'God' wrote back to him, saying "You are right. I had no right to take away your Grandmother. I am sorry. I am sad too. But your love for your grandma keeps her alive in your heart. You will never forget her and neither will I."

These redemptive moments do not take away the pain of the loss, but they do give a way to actively explore what meaning and what healing we can derive from the loss through surviving it. The key is to ask the difficult questions, to share the unfairness and betrayal arising from formerly held faith structures and beliefs. In rebuilding a new belief structure—that is born of the fires of our heart's testing—there is deepened faith and acceptance of the unknowable and indefinable Creator.

Many times, in the grief journey, people will seek a 'spiritual' connection or message from their loved ones. This can be a comfort if the message is affirming. Teresa Caputo, a well-known medium in the U.S. (known as the Long Island Medium) has written a book, *Good Grief* (2017). She describes some of her experiences, and the philosophy that our loved ones live on in a spiritual way and can give us messages of hope and healing. While this is not for everyone, it can be a useful resource for people looking for that further connection.

The concept of forgiveness is another issue that arises in relation to faith, belief, and spiritual orientation. What is forgiveness? What does it mean to forgive, or be forgiven? This is a delicate subject, and one that is often misunderstood. Working with forgiveness can bring a great deal of healing and relief. When addressing this issue, it is important to attend to where clients are, what their background beliefs say about forgiveness, and what they are willing to explore. Using action methods, as well as our four components to healing (acknowledge, express, act, reconnect) can facilitate the process of forgiveness— of self, and perhaps of others. This should not be rushed. If grieving people can consciously identify the goal, the results are cleaner and more fulfilling. It is important to remember that acceptance does not mean agreement. We do not forgive for the other person; we forgive because it gives us a sense of completion and release. A powerful book, *The Sunflower* (2008) by Simon Wiesenthal is a great book that explores forgiveness—and our beliefs and feelings about it. *Forgive for Good* (2002) by Fred Luskin is also a helpful book to recommend to clients for exploration of forgiveness. Clients need to be met in the present moment to address their own specific issues about forgiveness and what needs to be processed. The starting point is defining the term 'forgiveness'. Depending upon people's background and spiritual beliefs, that definition can be quite specific and unique. Then what is the process of forgiveness—of self, of other, of the world, of a greater power or consciousness? And what are the benefits of forgiveness? We explore this more later in the book.

Remember: If something takes more energy than it gives, consider not doing it. If something gives you more energy than it takes, consider doing it. It will free the energy for deeper, richer loving and living.

Bibliography

Cahill, B. (2018). *Cops, cons and grace: a father's journey through his son's suicide*. Eugene, OR: Wipf and Stock.

Caputo, T. (2017). *Good grief*. New York: Atria Books.

Kirshner, H. (1980). *When bad things happen to good people*. New York: Random House.

Lewis, C.S. (2009). *A grief observed*. San Francisco, CA: HarperOne.

Luskin, F. (2002). *Forgive for good: a proven prescription for health and happiness*. New York: HarperCollins.

Wiesenthal, S. (2008). *The sunflower*. New York: Schocken.

CHAPTER 17

CREATIVE EXPRESSION ACTIVITIES FOR LARGER GROUPS AND DAY-LONG RETREATS

The Creative Process in Grief, Loss, and Change

The tools of creativity are immensely helpful in processing loss, trauma, and grief. The activities we present in this chapter might be used with community groups, in schools, or workplaces that have experienced a traumatic event. They are also useful for groups of people facing similar life-threatening circumstances or illnesses (HIV, suicide, cancer). They are especially powerful with larger groups with a longer period of time to process. Art, music, writing, poetry, movement, and creative ritual/ceremony create a container of safety for free expression. Many of the exercises in this chapter demonstrate creative activities as tools that are particularly helpful and supportive for individuals who do not flourish in talk therapy. Art is a change agent in bringing survivors from out of control to in control. There are many books using creative arts with grief. We list some our favorites at the end of this chapter for further reading.

Using Music with Grief

When working with children and youth ask them to bring a piece of music that best describes their grief—where they are right now. Clients use art to explore very difficult emotions. If the piece chosen by a youth is a vocal piece, invite them to add their own lyrics to personalize their expression.

One youth brought Beethoven's fifth symphony as a description of his journey of trauma and grief. As we went through each movement, he was able to articulate how the music related to his grief journey. As we listened for a second time, we invited him to draw a road, with the people and activities that showed up on his journey. He drew two-legged and four-legged beings that he had lost, either to death or abandonment, as well as the people who were supporting him and who had become his allies. With the music, as well as his drawing, the youth was able to ground in his resources, while moving forward, step by step, into his new life in the present time. He exclaimed, after this process, "I finally see and feel the living in the dying. When I was bullied, and when my father moved out of state, and when my grandmother was killed by her boyfriend, I saw only pain and the dead end of death. Now I find life and joy in the smallest moments of beauty, in the brief connections with others. I feel alive even through the pain."

In larger groups, invite participants to form a circle, and to close their eyes and put their hand to their heart to feel their heartbeat. With every breath, encourage them to experience their own rhythm. Then invite them to pick a rhythm instrument, or to just use their body as an instrument to express their unique rhythm. Each person slowly starts to create their rhythm expression. We find that the group gradually moves into a harmonious blend that is amplified by the individual/ group experience. It is powerful and transformative. The rhythm of their bodies, hearts, and souls brings a unity that is amazing. We have also

Larger Groups and Day-Long Retreats **111**

utilized the music of Gabrielle Roth, a pioneer of Ecstatic Dance and the Five Rhythms in longer retreats to find their own body/mind/soul connection with movement.

Explore Where Trauma Is Stored in the Body

The following activity works well with individuals as well as groups, for all ages. Invite clients to outline their body on a large piece of heavy-weight paper. Inside the outline, ask them to draw or write descriptions of their grief experience and place where it is in the body. Invite clients to role play the different parts, each having a distinct and specific voice.

One young woman, Jesse, whose parents had died in a car crash, stated that her heart felt like it was on fire. When Jesse's heart spoke, it declared, "I am burning with guilt that I did not stop my parents from going home that night. It was a long journey and I knew they were tired." Once that realization came forth, we invited Jesse to speak in the role of her hands (her drawing had an image of her mom on one hand, her father on the other). Her hands gently spoke, "It was our decision. It was not your fault. And we want to give you a rose for your heart, to soothe the sorrow and guilt. We love you and are always with you." This revelation brought forth comfort and healing for Jesse by integrating the different messages within her body.

Poetry with Grief

Poetry is a powerful tool to distill and amplify feelings, hopes, and beliefs in the aftermath of loss, and can help identify key healing tools. We have employed many ideas from *Poetic Medicine* by John Fox (2002). We often start with a prompt. It can be a line from a poem already written or a phrase, such as "my grief is…" When group members are finished writing, we invite volunteers to read their poem, usually twice so that we can bear witness to it and the poet can hear the resonance of his or her words. Then, other group members offer, with permission, a line or word that particularly touched the listeners. At no time is the poem critiqued.

My Grief is, by Janet Childs
    My grief is
        shards of frozen, windswept days
    They cleanse the acrid guilt
        build a box for memories
        that live beyond the tears
    My grief is
        wisps of clouds
        deep, pungent roots
    Caught in my throat, and eyes
        when I whisper choke your name
    My grief is
        my hope
        my gentle letting go
        my love
        looking for home

Writing and reading this poem in a group setting gave me the capacity to hold and honor contradicting aspects of my grief experience.

Circle of Meaning

This activity is a powerful activity for larger groups and day-long retreats and is also relevant for work with secondary grief.

1. Draw a large circle that fills the page.
2. Within the circle, write or draw symbols for everything and everyone that gives you meaning in your life: activities, occupation, family, friends, pets, associates, hobbies, beliefs, possessions, hopes and dreams—in essence, all internal and external sources of meaning. It does not matter if the items are positive or negative. Most items will be a combination of both.
3. Place a star beside the most important person or thing in your life right now. This focus may change two seconds from now. Simply go with your gut feeling and do not think too much about your choice.
4. On the back of your circle, make two lists: (1) What you get from the most important person/thing in your life; and (2) What you give to that most important part of your life. Put down everything—even the negative aspects of what you give and receive.
5. Go back to the circle and imagine for a moment that the starred person or thing was no longer a part of your life. Perhaps they died, or moved away, or you lost them.
6. Now, checkmark every aspect of your circle affected in any way by the loss of this part of your circle. Some areas will literally be changed, others will be affected by your views, attitudes, and feelings in the aftermath of the loss.
7. Now, look at your circle, and the checkmarks. Notice who and what is affected. In the grief process, when we refer to the 'magnitude of loss', this is what we mean. When you lose one part of your life, it is not just one piece of the pie that is gone. The entire pie is changed and altered irrevocably. This is why the grief journey heals slowly and in cycles, dealing with one loss at a time.
8. Look back at the give/receive lists. This can be another dimension of your loss. Not only do we yearn for what we no longer receive—but also what we can no longer give. One young man said it very well, "Sorrow is my love looking for a way to express itself." And another comment many people in grief say is, "Oh, how my arms ache to hold my loved one." We can even miss some of the habits and behaviors that were previously annoying or frustrating. "I wish I could hear my spouse snore one more time."
9. As you gaze at your circle, take this exercise a step further and ask yourself: who and what is important in my life? Am I spending quality time with who and what gives me meaning? If I were to die tomorrow, would I feel complete with my life? What do I need to do to increase the 'meaning quotient' in my life at this time? In other words, how can I live my life to the fullest today? Take a look and notice if you have any unfinished business or unresolved issues with anyone in the circle. Listen to your intuition and trust yourself if a name pops out of the page. What do you have to do to complete any unfinished business? Do you need to share any appreciations, or say any "I love yous"? Or is there another issue to clear, such as, "I'm sorry," or "I'm sad, angry, lonely." Sometimes, writing a letter to that person can be very helpful in acknowledging the issues and feelings you are processing. Then, you can send, burn, bury, or keep the letter.
10. Repeat this exercise every six months. Just see how it shifts—and how you change in the continuing journey of balancing life and loss, love, and healing.

© Copyright material from Darrow and Childs (2020), *Experiential Action Methods and Tools for Healing Grief and Loss-Related Trauma*, Routledge.

When using the circle of meaning in groups, sociometric methods (described in Chapter 3) can be used to create connections and validate shared feelings. For example: invite the group to share by a show of hands or verbal disclosure responses to these questions:

- How many of you put your health in the circle?
- How many of you put pets in the circle?
- How many of you put possessions in the circle? Sometimes, it is not the money value of the possession, but the meaning value.
- How many of you put yourself in the circle? Many times, caregivers and responders do not put themselves in the circle.
- How many of you put people or pets who have died in your circle?
- Were there any surprises about who or what landed in your circle?

This offers a widening perception of who and what can be a part of our circle of meaning.

Essence and Expression Activity

Life is a constant balancing of who one is and what one does. Actions in the world may not always express inner gifts and talents. In the process of finding one's heart's dream, it is vital to identify inner gifts, talents, and capabilities to see if they match outer actions and ways one expends energy in the world. Whenever there is a disparity between essence and expression, there loss of vital life energy.

In this exercise to explore essence and expression, we invite group members to create three concentric circles of increasing size on the paper (Figure 17.1). We give the following instructions.

In the first circle, place the qualities of your essence—all of your gifts, skills, and talents.Right now. Include the inner qualities and gifts that you bring to the world and that you embody, such as compassion, humor, the ability to organize, as well as your developed skills and aptitudes, such as facility with logic or leadership. We invite you to gather this information by internal reflection as well as how others perceive your qualities. What attributes would your best friend, sibling, or the person you have lost identify? Group members can reflect on qualities they see and experience in others. This forms the core of your matrix.

In the second circle, put down your activities and ways you express yourself in the world. How do you expend your energy? Where does your time go and what does your time go to? This includes how you spend all of your day, not just work activity. Do you help others? Do volunteer work? Are you obsessed about cleanliness or order in your home or workspace? Do you procrastinate or worry about the future? Do

Figure 17.1. Essence/expression.

© Copyright material from Darrow and Childs (2020), *Experiential Action Methods and Tools for Healing Grief and Loss-Related Trauma*, Routledge.

you spend time in front of the TV or reading? Are you a fixer or a shopper? Do you garden or take hikes in nature? Do you meditate?

In the final circle, list your dreams and hopes. If you could do or have anything, what would you create for yourself? What are your deepest goals and aspirations? What do you hold most precious? What do you most want to do in your lifetime?

Now, examine the three circles and role reverse with components of the three circles. Questions to ask components in the second circle (what you currently do) include:

- Tell me about yourself—the role you play.
- What do you most like about it?
- What do you least like about it?
- How do you walk in this role and do you feel as you walk?
- What does this role do for (name of the group member)?
- Does your role make (name of the group member) happy?
- Are you using your 'essence' qualities in this role?
- How do you want to be in (name of group member)'s life in six months—bigger, smaller?

Questions to ask third circle roles (the future) include:

- So, this is a future role for (name of group member). How much in the future from (today's date)?
- What are you doing now?
- What is this role doing for (name of group member)?
- What do you feel in your body when doing what you are doing? Do you notice any feelings anywhere—chest, legs, arms, head?
- Does this role make (name of group member) happy?
- What 'essence' qualities are you using in this role?
- Were there challenges you needed to overcome?
- Pretend you are being acknowledged and you want to express thanks. Who or what helped you get here? Who were the most important supports in getting to what you are doing now (such as friends, family, internal strengths)?
- Would you like to hear supportive words from other group members?

© Copyright material from Darrow and Childs (2020), *Experiential Action Methods and Tools for Healing Grief and Loss-Related Trauma*, Routledge.

Heart Hotel

Within each of us lies a 'heart hotel', where we can honor an important person who resides in a room in our heart (Figure 17.2). In the heart hotel, a room can never be taken away because we lose what or who occupied the room, unless we wish it. This exercise provides the opportunity to celebrate what is exceptional and beautiful within our hearts which we can claim and keep. These gifts that we hold in our heart nurture us through the journey of building the 'new normal' of our life. The true work of healing loss or change is to release the pain and trauma of the loss, while keeping the goodness and the meaning in the rooms of our heart hotel.

Label each box as a specific room dedicated to a special individual or life experience. Put the qualities of love and memory you wish to keep in your heart hotel in each room. Make the heart hotel as big as you want. You can use words, symbols, pictures, collages, or colors that represent the essence of what is important for you to claim. This can be done with individuals or in a larger group.

Figure 17.2. Heart hotel.

© Copyright material from Darrow and Childs (2020), *Experiential Action Methods and Tools for Healing Grief and Loss-Related Trauma*, Routledge.

The Village Within: Aspects of Inner Landscape

Within each of us
> There nestles a village.
Full of history,
Personality and
> Varied landscapes.
As we journey down the road of
> Our life,
It is good to take a side dirt path
> For a visit to
> > Your inner village …

We provide this list to large groups. Write, draw, meditate, and create poetry, music, collage, or sculpture about the people and places that live in or are a part of your inner landscape. Above all, enjoy meeting some of the characters and essences of your inner village.

- What is the name of your village?
  - Think of the landscape of your life. What would your village/life be called?
- The village Goddess:
  - Who is the source of your village's energy, story, and purpose?
- The village priestess:
  - How do you interface between the Goddess's energy and the human condition and circumstances?
- The village lover:
  - How are you connected to your passion and beauty and its expression with others?
- The village priest/shaman/holy person:
  - Where do you meet the spiritual? How do you work with the energies of transformation?
- The village mother:
  - How do you nurture/protect/sustain yourself and others in your village?
- What does the village look like?
  - Describe the physical, social and spiritual dimensions of your village landscape.
- The village gossip:
  - How do you spread news? Is there any need to be in the know or to be liked?
- What is the village secret?
  - What do only you know about? What lies in the details of the shadows?
- The village queen:
  - How do you demonstrate and disperse your energy to the world with your feminine power?
- The village king:
  - How do you meet the world with your masculine power?
- The village leader:
  - How do you serve your village in a leadership role?
- The village idiot:
  - How do you allow the sacred fool, the innocent truth to be expressed?
- The village weaver:
  - How do you build bridges and connect to the beauty of the entwining threads of actions and energies?

- The village warrior:
  - How do you ground and protect your village with strength and compassion?
- The village counselor:
  - How do you support the disenfranchised and hurting people in your village?
- The village newborn:
  - What new energy do you bring to the earth? What streams from past lives are present?
- The village seer/mystic:
  - How do you listen to and express the wisdom from the unseen realms into the earth reality of your village?
- The village madam:
  - How do you create pleasure and delight for the people of your village? Is there any manipulation of people or resources you use?
- The village prostitute:
  - How do you give yourself away in the sacred dance of the Goddess's energy? Do you give away too much, or to undeserving sources?
- The village cook:
  - How do you honor and prepare the gifts of the earth to create flavorful and nourishing delights for your body, soul, and spirit, as well as for others?
- The village elder:
  - How are you the wise counsel for problems and people in the village?
- The village crazy person:
  - How do you allow the energies of change and new dimensions to flow through you?
- The village thief:
  - What do you steal from others/yourself? What is your motive?
- The village traveler:
  - Where do you go? What do you bring back when you return?
- The village foreigner:
  - What wisdom or experience do you bring from another land? How do you speak a different language? How are you separate from the prevailing culture of the village?
- The village healer:
  - What do you bring to the transformation process of pain into meaning? What skills do you possess in the healing arts?
- The village nurse:
  - How do you tend to emergent problems and issues of unhealthy/disease in the village?
- The village dreamer:
  - What do you dream? How do you bring the wisdom of your dreams to the village?
- The village visionary:
  - How do you reach for the future possibilities of your village? How do you share these?
- The village artist:
  - How do you express your creativity?
- What is the village legend?
  - What story sustains the spirit of your village?
- The village merrymaker:
  - How do you play? How do you lighten the mood?
- The village clown:
  - How do you use humor and jokes to transform a situation?
- The village social butterfly/extrovert/host:
  - How do you reach out and bring delight to people through activities and events?

- The village nurturer:
  - How do you comfort, support, and bring abundant love to yourself and others?
- The village alchemist:
  - How do you transform the mundane into precious gifts?
- The village hunter:
  - How do you gather energy and resources for survival and living? How do you reach for what you want and/or need?
- The village maiden:
  - How are you the seed bearer of the gifts of potential and the future?
- The village sorcerer:
  - How do you meet the power of all forces—light and dark? How do you integrate these?
- The village witch:
  - How do you walk in the world as a conduit and transformer for the Mystery?
- The village supporter:
  - How do you support yourself and others in your village to be the best they can be?
- The village organizer:
  - How do you do logistics and planning? What are your gifts in creating/synthesizing chaos into order?
- The village virgin:
  - Who is the innocent and untouched, clear beauty that shines from your soul?
- The village teenager:
  - Who is the frightened, brave, daring, and vulnerable you in transition from one state to another?
- The village mischievous child:
  - Who is the playful and bratty part of you that fearlessly challenges the old ways of being?
- The village writer:
  - How do you chronicle the dynamics of your village? How are you a poet for social change?
- What is the village famous for?
  - What is your sweetest accomplishment, your most proud moment?
- The village schoolteacher:
  - How do you teach others and share your wisdom, both in individual contact and group interaction?
- The village philosopher:
  - How do you explore the deep questions of human existence? How do you express that awareness?
- The village truth teller:
  - What is the clear, knowing part of you that can determine the essence of a situation and express it?
- What are the village visions?
  - What are your deepest hopes and dreams for the future? How do you hold these visions?
- The village recluse/hermit:
  - How does the introverted and inward person take care of self and commune with the spiritual realm?
- The village carpenter:
  - How do you build the structures of your life and living? What energy of excitement and artistry do you bring?
- The village ancestors:
  - Who are the ancient ones, the old ones on whose energy you call upon in your deepest moments of struggle or joy?
- The village ritual keeper:
  - How do you create and hold sacred ceremony? What elements do you use? What are your favorite rituals to facilitate?

- Other people who live in your village ...
- What is the history of your village?
- What are the dreams and hopes of your village?
- What is the culture of your village?

The inspiration for this concept came from my work with thousands of people going through life-changing events on their journey. They have taught me the necessity of gathering the resources and personalities of the inner village, and how to identify who is hurting, isolated, or in need within this landscape of our being.

We invite you to use this as a roadmap, as a community gathering, as a mobilizer for healing, and as a conduit for transformation.

How to Use This Tool

- In the present, identify who in your village needs support, and who in your village can give support. Set up a dialogue/village meeting and create an action plan for support.
- Pick a particular villager, whether one who is listed or one who speaks to you, or comes to you, and create a poem, artwork, song, or biography on that villager.
- Gather a family of villagers together and conduct a drama play about a certain event or interaction. This can be done with other people or just with yourself, where you take the different roles of your villagers.
- Invite your villagers to heal a past event together by creating a different ending to the story. What and who needs to rewrite history and bring forward the wisdom and learning from the past?
- Is there a sacred marriage between villagers? Who will be married? What are the vows? Where is the ceremony to be held? Who is invited?
- Pick a villager whom you will be for a day, or for a few hours. Awaken, dress, and do activities this villager would do. Embody his or her life in every way possible. At the end of the exercise, reflect upon what it was like to be that villager. Write a poem, or a journal entry, or a letter to this villager. What are the gifts you received? What have you learned? Also note how your environment or the people around you respond to this villager.

In order to do any processing with your inner village, we first must establish safety to ground and protect the valuable work. What works for you to create the optimum emotional safe place? Look at physical space; do a meditation to envision a safe place, imagining a protective sphere of light, color, sound, or dome around you. Create a ceremony of invocation to call upon protectors, warrior guides, angels, and ancestors to circle around you. When we make an intention to create a sacred space, it actively manifests a powerful and safe container for us.

Light a candle. Ask a trusted friend or associate to be your partner to provide safety and be an anchor as you explore. And remember, do one exercise at a time. Give yourself plenty of time and space to examine and synthesize what you have done. Below is an example of using the village within (or inner counsel) and the essence and expression activity to support rebuilding a life with new meaning after a major change.

A Firefighter's Experience

A firefighter/paramedic, who had gone through an extremely difficult marital separation, was struggling to build a new normal. She had dedicated a great deal of her time and energy to the relationship, but then realized it was both physically and emotionally abusive and draining. This was coupled with the fact that she had been unable to save two small children from a house fire—a critical incident that reminded her of her inability to always save her patients. This was the 'straw that broke the camel's back'.

She began by writing an 'unfinished business' letter, which she then read to her estranged partner. We asked if she could access her village within, to give her the internal resources she needed to survive and heal. She returned with a diorama of a village in which three people were surrounding her (being the wounded lover): the healing and nurturing grandmother, the fierce and protective warrior, and the mischievous child. Their jobs: the grandmother would provide her comfort and unconditional love; the warrior would protect her from returning to the dysfunctional relationship, and the child would distract her and remind her to have fun and not take herself too seriously.

This rebuilt awareness of the internal supports and resources within her inner village—supporting a primary need after trauma for safety. Next, we invited her to do the essence and expression exercise, described above. In three concentric circles, she drew and wrote about her essence qualities (who am I?) at the center, her activities now (how she spent her time and energy in the world), and her hopes and dreams (her potential expression). We invited her to explore what was giving her energy and what was draining her energy. For example, if there was a quality in her essence that was not getting expressed, its energy was lost. If there was something in her expression that did not match her essence, that was another energy drain. In the potential expression of her hopes and dreams, she could call upon her essence qualities that would help her to manifest and activate those dreams, creating a clear stream of energy and power.

Step by step, she was able to build a paradigm for creating a life beyond the pain of loss. First, she needed to acknowledge the depth of her pain and express the details of her hurt. Then she took a meaningful action step, which was creating her village support team. Finally, using these supports, she envisioned a future with meaning and energy that was congruent with her essence.

This is often a theme for first responders, unfortunately. They often are, or become, the caregivers in their own personal lives and families. Many times, they overextend their own life force to save or protect people in their personal lives. When they need support, there is often no one to go to who feels safe or is able to support them in their grief journey. This is why it is so important to establish critical incident stress/peer support programs in every fire, police, dispatch, and Emergency Medical Services (EMS) department. This is also true for healthcare, mental health, and spiritual/social care providers, who all work on the front lines of trauma, death, injustice, and stress every day.

Bibliography

Atkins, S., & Eberhart, H. (2014). *Presence and process in expressive arts work: at the edge of wonder*. London: Jessica Kingsley.

Cameron, J. (1997). *Vein of gold*. Los Angeles, CA: TarcherPerigree.

Cameron, J. (2003). *Walking in this world*. Los Angeles, CA: TarcherPerigree.

Cameron, J. (2016). *The artist's way*. Los Angeles, CA: TarcherPerigree.

Fox, J. (1995). *Finding what you didn't lose*. Los Angeles, CA: TarcherPerigree.

Fox, J. (2002). *Poetic medicine: the healing art of poem-making*. Los Angeles, CA: TarcherPerigree.

Neimeyer, R.A. (ed.) (2012). *Techniques of grief therapy: creative practices for counseling the bereaved*. New York: Routledge.

Thomas, B.E., & Neimeyer, R.A. (eds.) (2014). *Grief and the expressive arts: practices for creating meaning*. New York: Routledge.

CHAPTER 18

GRIEF WORK WITH FRAGILE POPULATIONS

Beyond broken on the bathroom floor

By Rebecca B

I've been broken before
The broken that's so talked about
A heap on the bathroom floor broken
Get me out of my marriage that's killing me broken
My dad's dying... dead...gone broken
The "I've had a rough childhood broken."

There's a broken beyond all that.
An ugly broken.
Messy and unkempt and gut wrenchingly hollowed down to your core
of vast empty
un-know-ing broken.
The kind of broken that scares some.
It's too real, raw, and ugly for them to set their eyes upon.
It turns you upside down and sideways and shakes you like an undertow that
never loosens its grasp.
This broken brings you to your knees to question all you know.
But you do follow.
Haltingly at first.
The geography terrifying.
A new terrain where each step is measured.
The weight of your body falling slowly upon your foot, tentative,
testing...will this new earth hold me?

This beyond broken takes everything to navigate.
Your soul is being shattered.
Glass thrown upon the ground to gather the sharpest shards,
The pieces that scream of your authenticity...your voice...
Your truth...your calling to service.
To share. To shine. To learn. To connect.
To love. To grow.

I'm grateful to my beyond broken. It's led me to the other gorgeous souls who bravely
share their beyond broken too.
So we can heal together and love each other.
So we can grow in the midst of the ugly and raw and messy.
We show up. We divulge. We expunge.
We plunder and soar and some days we hide.
And then we come back and cheer.
For ourselves, for each other.
For vibrancy. For life.

I (Lusijah) was hired to work with the Intensive Outpatient Program (IOP) and Partial Hospitalization Program (PHP) because of my experience using psychodrama tools with grief. The most common issues of members in the IOP and PHP groups are debilitating depression, bipolar disorder, severe anxiety, and substance abuse. Grief in these groups has a broader scope—a consequence of loss of relationships, loss of hopes and dreams, loss of self, loss of faith and beliefs, and loss of life meaning. This is often in addition to unprocessed grief after the death of a loved one. Group members experience a turbulent sea roiling around them, as they grope to rediscover ways to make their lives work again.

IOP and PHP group members have experienced impact to jobs, education, and/or relationships. Often individuals start attending the group after a suicide attempt. Coming to the group is courageous as they openly explore their lives during a time of complete disruption. The structures of their lives which have provided meaning have collapsed and people often enter the groups with hopelessness and fear. They are disconnected from their internal strengths and resources, and they often feel a great deal of shame and guilt about having let others down.

Grief work with a fragile population needs to be different from other grief groups. The group members need to be stable and safe when they leave the group. Although standard grief issues are explored, the focus needs to be more strength-based. In this chapter, we explore key issues in this group followed by use of expressive arts and psychodrama methods.

Sociometry Warm-Ups

As described earlier, in Chapter 3, sociometry tools help people identify connections and commonalities with others. Briefly, sociometry gets people up and moving, interacting, and providing an opportunity for being playful with each other as they explore themes in action. Sociometry activities are very flexible; different warm-ups can be used to suit various types of groups, and prompt questions can explore relevant issues. Clients indicate their most pressing issues and the intensity of those issues (depression, anxiety, don't see a future, etc.). Offering prompt questions on motivation, attitudes, and observation of change and/or progress is also useful. Sociometry is also a great assessment tool for group facilitators to see where individuals are at and whether there are common themes on any given day for the group.

Identifying and Amplifying Resources

Fragile clients in these groups often feel disconnected from their strengths and resources. We have previously described an activity that is especially helpful to this population in Chapter 3 and elsewhere. We invite clients to think about interpersonal (people), intrapsychic (personal qualities), and transpersonal strengths (something greater than themselves, guardian angel, God, someone who is no longer in embodied physical form). We invite clients to let these strengths and resources have a voice with role play and role reversal.

124 Fragile Populations

Making a Lifeline

We are who we are today as an accumulation of all of our life experiences. Group members in IOP and PHP groups benefit from looking at important periods of their lives—their decisions and experiences. In the early days of being in IOP or PHP groups, hopelessness, feelings of failure, and shame are common. This activity adjusts the narrative group members have about the events on their timeline, offering a change in the perspective or the internalized stories they've created about their lives.

Group members are provided art materials to draw a lifeline of important events in their lives. They are also asked to include future hopes and dreams on their timeline. One at a time, group members are invited to make a scarf sculpture of their lifeline. They choose one scarf to represent each life event on their timeline, and they lay them on the floor using their own sense of design. Each person then walks their timeline stopping at each place, being interviewed in the role of themselves at that particular time. Below is a vignette of one such timeline and interview.

> David, a 34-year-old man, was suffering from severe anxiety and depression. He was on leave from a job in the tech sector. He laid out his scarves on the floor.
>
> *Lusijah:* Let's walk your timeline and talk to David at the different ages and life stages on the timeline you've made. (David nods agreement and walks to a scarf.)
>
> *David:* OK. This scarf represents when I was a student at college. I studied computer science.
>
> *Lusijah:* So, speaking to David as student. How is it to be a student, studying computer science?
>
> *David:* It's hard! I struggle. I'm not sure I can do this.
>
> *Lusijah:* Do you like computer science?
>
> *David:* I don't know. I feel confused. I'll be able to get a well-paid job. But I can't say I like computer science. I feel very stressed so much of the time.
>
> *Lusijah:* David, step out of that role now into present-day David. With your greater perspective and maturity, what are your thoughts about this time in your life?
>
> *David:* I wish I had not been as influenced by wanting a good job and I'd been more interested in what was going to make me happy.
>
> *Lusijah:* Do you see this as a waste of your time? Were there any positives from your student experience?
>
> *David:* Well, yes. I completed my degree in something that was difficult. I felt good about myself for having done this. Like, I know I can be persistent, follow my goals, even though it's hard.
>
> *Lusijah:* This knowing about yourself—that you can work to complete hard stuff—seems relevant for you right now.
>
> *David:* Yes. I know I will continue to work towards being healthy again.
>
> *Lusijah* (nods acknowledgment): Let's keep walking.
>
> *David:* This next scarf represents the time that I was drinking too much and taking drugs. It was a bad period.
>
> *Lusijah:* How old are you here?
>
> *David:* Late twenties. It was originally a way to relax from the stress of work. But I over-did. I was high or stoned just about every day. I was not alive. I do not feel good about myself in this time. But I was able to stop. I do feel good about that.
>
> *Lusijah:* Step again into today's David with perspective and maturity and consider what this time or experience was for you on your path of growing as a human being. What were the lessons from this time?
>
> *David:* I don't want to live this way! This time made me realize that numbing myself out is not the way I want to live. This experience gave me understanding about myself, how I wanted to escape

from anxiety. I was able to see what I was doing and I was able to choose the life I wanted—not being drunk or stoned. I am actually grateful for this experience; I am a person with greater wisdom because of this time. I understand that this time, which I am not proud of, still gave me something that made me who I am today.

Lusijah (nodding acknowledgment): I am of the belief that we learn from hard times, not easy times. Some people need a whack from a two by four, others need a wrecking ball from a crane. (Smiling) I also know we keep revisiting personal growth issues which are opportunities to do things differently, and hopefully get it right at some point. Let's go on to the next scarf.

David: This next scarf represents my family, getting married and becoming a father. This has been the happiest period of my life. I love my boys and my wife, and I know I have really let my wife down. She has a lot on her right now, working and taking care of our children, while I am here. I am so grateful to her (begins to cry).

Lusijah (softly): Yes, and you want to do better.

David: Yes, I must find better ways to deal with anxiety. I am very committed to learning and using tools that I am learning here (referring to learning dialectical behavior therapy skills). I am looking at my life, what has brought me to this point. I am not planning to return to the work I was doing. I need to do something else.

Lusijah: I know you are still in the middle of this time of your life, possibly not yet with a great deal of hindsight perspective. Do you have thoughts about the important learning of this period?

David: Yes, I need to find work that makes me happy rather than makes me money! I don't think I thought about this when I was going to university. Computer science was something I was capable of doing it, but I can see now that it never made me happy. I was stressed when I was a student and the stress has continued. Here I am.

Lusijah: Let's move now to exploring a role you see in the future. Imagine yourself in that role now.

David: OK.

Lusijah: Tell me, what are you doing now?

David: I am now in school again, studying to be a therapist.

Lusijah: Wow! Are you happy?

David: Yes, I am happy. This feels like work that resonates with me. I am loving the people-to-people aspect of psychology. I want to do this, I want to support others.

Lusijah: How long ago did you leave the IOP group?

David: It is two years since then. I completed the IOP and started to think and plan about what kind of work I really wanted to do—what would be satisfying, make me happy. I thought about not money but happiness. I love being in school.

Lusijah: How is your family?

David: Everyone is good. My wife and I are doing better than before. I am so grateful for her support. I feel like we are closer, having gone through the time I was in the IOP. She can see I have been able to use what I learned in the IOP group to manage anxiety. There is so much that has changed. I am no longer working in a job that was so stressful.

Lusijah (smiling): Wonderful. Now, for a last thing to do, I would like to invite you to walk the path from today, being in the IOP group, to the day in your future. Here is a pile of scarves. Consider what personal strengths you need to keep close to yourself and what beliefs or attitudes you need to release as you walk from today to the future you envision.

David (spends time choosing scarves): OK, I'm ready.

Lusijah: So just start on one side of the room that represents today, and slowly walk toward the other side of the room that represents your envisioned future. Walk slowly as you name the qualities you want to embrace and drape the scarves around your shoulders. Also, state what you want to release and drop the scarf representing what you want to release.

David walked slowly, putting scarves on, representing love of his family, deeply listening to his inner voice, wanting to grow as a person, and discarding the voice of fear.

Lusijah: From where you are today, having completed the IOP, and now being in school, having identified a life that is more satisfying, what helpful advice do you have for yourself two years ago, when you were at the IOP?

David: Ah David, keep going, believe in yourself. You can make changes and take whatever steps you need to take to turn your life around. I am happy, you will be happy.

Changing Roles

IOP group members examine their life circumstances intensively—their decisions, beliefs, relationships, and what they want to do with their lives. This is a time to take stock of where they've been and envision the future.

In action, we explore this with a variation of the Social Atom (described in Chapter 6), a pen-and-paper sociometry tool that maps out different roles. We can call this the role atom (Figure 18.1). Group members are given a piece of paper and art materials. They place themselves in the center, using a circle for

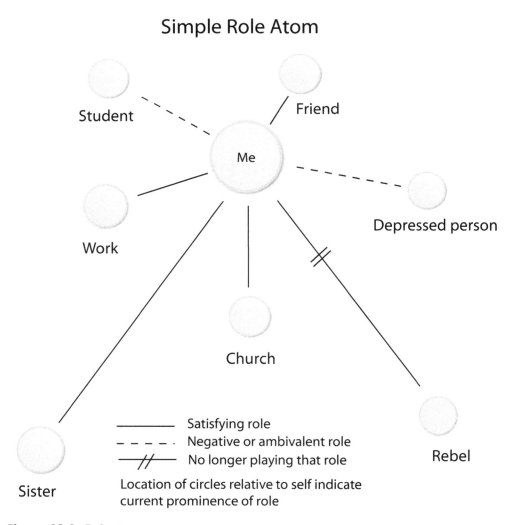

Figure 18.1. Role atom.

women, a triangle for men. They indicate roles they have played, which can include being a child, sibling, parent, student, worker, spouse, and parent. The roles are placed closer or further away from the symbol representing themselves according to prominence of this role right now.

Solid lines represent a positive connection, dashed lines represent current distaste for a particular role, and two short perpendicular lines crossing the line between oneself and a role indicate they no longer have this role. Group members are also invited to include roles they are moving into—encouraging group members to envision a future. The role atom can be further explored in action with interviewing important roles, especially roles that are future roles. Below is a vignette using the role atom.

> Michael, who was debilitated by severe depression, was invited to share his role atom, which contained only three roles—student, member of a spiritual organization, and friend.
>
> *Lusijah:* Let's explore the roles you have here. I will invite you to step into each of these roles and speak from the role's perspective. OK?
>
> *Michael:* OK.
>
> *Lusijah:* Let's start from the role of student. So, Michael as student, tell me about yourself. How old are you?
>
> *Michael:* I'm twenty-one years old. I'm a college student.
>
> *Lusijah:* Do you like being a student?
>
> *Michael* (makes a grimace): It's a lot of work. I am a physics major.
>
> *Lusijah:* Wow! You must be pretty intelligent. What does this role give you?
>
> *Michael:* Well, physics doesn't feel that hard; it all comes pretty easily to me. I feel good about myself, studying physics.
>
> *Lusijah:* Tell current-day Michael what you did for him or gave him.
>
> *Michael:* I showed you that you are smart and can take on and complete difficult things.
>
> *Lusijah:* What a great gift.
>
> *Michael:* Yeah.
>
> *Lusijah:* Let's move now to the role of being a member of a spiritual organization.
>
> *Michael:* I get angry thinking about this. I followed a spiritual teacher from the U.K. I had started to have periods of depression. The teacher told me that following him as a student would cure my depression. It did for a while. I was very happy and was taking on greater responsibility and leadership in the organization. But then the depression came back.
>
> *Lusijah:* I can feel the pain from your experience. You believed that following the teacher would cure your struggle with depression. How are you feeling now about the experience you had as a member of the spiritual group?
>
> *Michael:* Disillusioned. I feel like this teacher lead me on—it was all BS. Maybe all spiritual practices are.
>
> *Lusijah:* This is a very serious loss for you Michael. It's as though a core aspect of your life and beliefs imploded. It has left a vacuum in your life.
>
> *Michael:* Yes, it has.
>
> *Lusijah:* Although this experience was very painful, let's consider whether there are some things of benefit to you out of this experience.
>
> *Michael:* I don't see anything. It was a waste of years.
>
> *Lusijah:* When you were in the group, what were some of the values you lived by? Many spiritual practices value kindness, service to others. Where these values that you incorporated into how you lived?
>
> *Michael:* Yes, definitely.
>
> *Lusijah:* Tell me more.
>
> *Michael:* The lifestyle was pretty simple. I lived for periods at the center of the U.K. Eventually I became a sort of mentor for others. Of course, I tried to be kind and loving toward newer students. I tried to support them in their growth.

128 Fragile Populations

Lusijah: How was that for you? How did you feel inside when you were being helpful and kind to others?

Michael: It felt good.

Lusijah: Do you still have this value, even after you are no longer in the spiritual group? Does this still feel to you like the way you want to live?

Michael: Yes, this still feels good to me.

Lusijah: Does it make sense to you that you get to keep this, to keep the values you learned to live by, even though you are no longer part of the spiritual group?

Michael: Yeah, I guess so.

Lusijah: I wonder if there are ways right now that you can tap into the values of kindness and support of others—whether there are volunteer possibilities that could provide a way to be in service to others?

Michael: Maybe so.

Lusijah: Let's explore the last role, that of friend.

Michael: OK.

Lusijah: Tell me about yourself, your role of being a friend.

Michael: Well, I am not really a friend right now. I just don't want to meet with people. I don't talk to anyone.

Lusijah: Have you been a friend in the past? Do you want to be a friend again?

Michael: Yes.

Lusijah: I think you need to give current-day Michael some helpful advice. What can you tell him that would be helpful so that he can reclaim being a friend?

Michael: You need to reach out to people.

Lusijah: Are there people who know you and care about you? What are their names?

Michael: Yes (names three people).

Lusijah: So, what does current-day Michael need to do? Tell me what he can do for each of the three people.

Michael: You need to call these people and set up a time to meet.

Lusijah: When could Michael do this?

Michael (smiling): This week.

Exploration of Michael's deep wounding and disillusionment with a spiritual practice provided space to talk about several things. The vacuum created by loss of life meaning, and the necessary patience required as a new normal slowly re-establishes itself, require being open to finding new ways to engage with activity that will provide satisfying meaning. Shortly thereafter, Michael started volunteering at the local garden project for the homeless. He also reported following through on reaching out to friends he had lost touch with.

Looking at Self-Defeating Beliefs

Self-defeating beliefs and cognitive distortions are part of the human condition. We all have them in some form and in some intensity. They are prominent symptoms of severe depression and anxiety. So-called negative thought loops are often based on cognitive distortions and self-defeating beliefs. They may be a repeating story, a narrative of failure, wrongness about self, not being good enough, not being respectable, not being likeable, and so on. Cognitive behavioral therapy, developed by Aaron Beck and David Burns, focuses on working with and disabling negative thought loops. The relationship between negative self-talk and depression and anxiety has been well established (Burns, 1999, 2006).

People are especially vulnerable to cognitive distortions and self-defeating beliefs after experiencing multiple losses. The impact of loss of a relationship, employment, serious mental health issues, being forced to put life on hold, and often death of a loved one is cumulative.

Action methods can be used to explore cognitive distortions and self-defeating beliefs. *When Panic Attacks* (Burns, 2006) has an extensive list of cognitive distortions and self-defeating beliefs. A chair is placed at the front of the room to represent a particular self-defeating belief. The person choosing the belief is invited to stand to the left of the chair and take the role of the self-defeating belief, voicing and expanding on the unhelpful belief. Then the person is invited to change roles, moving to the other side of the chair to be the voice that challenges that self-defeating belief. Other group members are invited to jump up to also play both roles, fleshing out the negative self-messages and compassionate wise voice challenging the self-defeating belief.

Intention to Lighten Weight in the Psychic Backpack

This activity is described earlier (in Chapter 10) and is a good activity for fragile populations to look at unresolved issues, including regret or guilt about past actions, anger, and/or negative self-judgment.

Receiving Positive Reflection from Others

Receiving accurate reflection from others is the way we feel seen and understood. Mental health issues rob people of positive self-identity, as they struggle with feelings of guilt, shame, and inadequacy. The honest self-reflection that takes place in IOP and PHP groups creates deep knowing about others in the group. Group members get to see the honesty, pain, humor, wisdom, willingness to keep trying, kindness, and care of others in the group. These traits are often invisible to and unacknowledged by the person who is exhibiting these qualities. This is a valuable and uplifting exercise in which group members give and receive positive reflection as they express appreciation for qualities that they admire and respect in other group members.

Place a big pile of scarves (or sand tray objects) in the middle of the room and tell group members that we are going to let group members honor aspects of others—that the other may not see in themselves. Group members, one at a time, pick a scarf or object that represents the quality they wanted to honor in the other. Each person talks about the quality and then places the scarf respectfully around the shoulders of the other group member. The process is 'popcorn style' as group members are spontaneously moved to pick a scarf and acknowledge someone in the group. We have witnessed that group members themselves keep track—making sure everyone is given positive reflections. This is quite a positive experience.

Forgiveness Activity

Forgiveness of others and of self is relevant work in the IOP and PHP groups. Anger toward someone who has hurt them can be empowering for people who have experienced trauma. Clearly naming a hurtful or harmful action strengthens self-worth and respect and helps people form better boundaries. Although this is a necessary step in the forgiveness process, it doesn't end there. The following activity offers a way to explore forgiveness.

Begin by inviting a group discussion of how people understand forgiveness. (As facilitators, we state that forgiveness is not acceptance that harmful actions by another are OK.) Group members are given publicly available quotes online on forgiveness and invited to choose and discuss any quotes that resonate for them.

After the discussion, provide art materials, and invite group members to draw a picture that represents their current feeling about forgiveness. Group members know which person or event in their own lives sits most heavily on them. We ask members to choose a color that represents how they feel and to begin the drawing with their eyes closed, making an initial gesture or sweep of motion on the paper. This keeps group members in their feelings, rather than going to an analytical part of themselves. After the completion of this drawing, group members are given another piece of paper and asked to do another drawing in the same way, this time asking them to draw a picture that represents how they would like to be with forgiveness of the person or event. The final step invites group members to do body sculptures or poses that represent the first and then the second drawings. Discussion and sharing follow, focusing on the differences in how the two drawings and poses felt.

Hero's Journey

The recovery from grief and loss is a heroic journey—a crisis that requires change and growth. Tolkien's *Lord of the Rings* is a familiar story which chronicles an important mission that will determine survival or destruction of life itself. Each character in the fellowship of the rings plays a necessary role or has special personal qualities which are necessary to complete the mission, while other characters create obstacles. These characters serve as a metaphor for the qualities and traits needed in a heroic journey, as well as qualities that hinder or get in the way of successfully completing the mission. These qualities might be people in our lives or internal personal traits.

Invite group members to consider some of the main characters of the fellowship of the rings and to describe the qualities each character brought to the mission or hindered it. Below is a list of the characters in the fellowship with descriptions. Group members can enlarge on these qualities or attributes.

Frodo: simple, humble, willing, afraid, not knowing the future, persistent
Samwise: loyal, giving, supportive, patient
Merry and Pippin: humorous and playful
Gandalf: wise, patient, having the larger view, the protector, having self-awareness of his own weaknesses
The dwarves: earthy, hard-working, willing to fight
Saruman: power-hungry, deceitful
The elves: ethereal, not of this world, intuitive
Aragorn: humble, noble, aware of duty
Boromir: afraid, secretive, vengeful
Orcs: stupid, violent, mindless
Gollum: broken, greedy, self-absorbed.

After exploring the qualities of the characters in *Lord of the Rings*, invite group members to make a drawing of their own heroic journey. The drawings can include personal qualities or people who have made up their fellowship—both helpful and hindering. After group members are finished with the drawings, ask follow-up questions:

- What came up for you as you were doing the drawing?
- Are there characters in *Lord of the Rings* with whom you identify?
- Can you identify people in your life that fill similar roles to those in the *Lord of the Rings*?
- How does the role of Gandalf show up in your life?

Invite group members one at a time to make a representation of their journey using scarves to represent characters/internal strengths of their heroic journey, making a statement, asking for help, or saying a word of thanks to each member of their fellowship. After everyone has had an opportunity to make a representation of their journey and group members have heard about the make-up of each other's fellowship, invite group members to ask to borrow characters/internal strengths from each other, in order to make their fellowship stronger.

Bibliography

Burns, D. (1999). *Feeling good*. New York: Harper.
Burns, D.D. (2006). *When panic attacks*. New York: Broadway Books.
Tolkien, J.R.R. (2012). *The lord of the rings*. Boston, MA: Houghton Mifflin Harcourt.

CHAPTER 19

FAMILY DYNAMICS IN LOSS AND CHANGE

To understand how a family responds in crisis, first visualize the family system. A family is more than the sum of its members. The family becomes another entity, very much like another person with a unique personality and a set of individual coping mechanisms. Work with individual clients is also family counseling, because clients bring in their entire family with them as they walk through the door.

In grief work, the family can be any group that is bound together by ancestry, occupation, common beliefs, mutual support, or by caring and love. There are work families, biological families, heart families, and spiritual families. The family dynamic is composed of relationships between each other individually and each person has a relationship to the whole family (considered another individual), as described by two of the pioneers of family dynamics, Virginia Satir (1984), and John Bradshaw (1990). The basic message is that, when a family loses a member, the others will attempt to bridge the gap. Each family member is dealing with their individual loss in their own way, and no two people in the family are experiencing the same loss in the same way. Kissane and Hooghe (2011) note the importance of facilitating awareness of family strengths and connection between family members while working with the reality of individual differences among surviving family members.

In a family, when stress, loss, illness, or death affects one member, every other member is also affected in a significant way, due to the complex interactions between family members. Add the element of time, years of relating to each other, and certain patterns of behavior have become established, particularly in crisis. *Life's Last Gift* (Garfield, 2017) and *Last Acts of Kindness: Lessons for the Living from the Bedside of the Dying* (Keyssar, 2011) are superb books on support in the dying process.

As explained by MaryAnne Schreder (referred to elsewhere as MaryAnne Kelly) in *Bereaved Children and Teens* (1995), the family is also influenced by external forces, environment, home, neighborhood, culture, religion, economic status, extended family relationships, and mobility.

Stress and grief are the normal human responses to loss of a loved one and critical incidents. Each individual experiences stress and responds with different behaviors. In families, people often react to each other based on the other's behavior, rather than taking the time to acknowledge the emotion or back story behind the behavior. We provide examples in Table 19.1.

Table 19.1 Types of behavior, and the feelings behind them

Behavior	Feelings behind behavior
Aggressive, belligerent	Angry, helpless, scared, guilty
Withdrawn, quiet	Scared, depressed, guilty, sad
Complaining	Feeling abandoned, invalidated, scared
Cheerful, optimistic	Denial, scared, guilty
Work performance down, controlling	Helpless, scared, angry, guilty
Hysterical, frantic	Scared, sad, overwhelmed, guilty

Family members may share similar feelings, but their behaviors can alienate them from one other. A way to support a family facing a death or critical incident is to point out the difference between feelings and behaviors. Then, create a safe atmosphere to acknowledge and express the different reactions and behaviors—and to validate that all are normal.

When working with families, it is important to set a structure for how to acknowledge the loss. This is very similar to group ground rules. We suggest these guidelines for the process:

- Establish confidentiality to create safety.
- Invite each member to take a defined length of time to discuss what has been the most difficult (usually it will be five to eight minutes, depending upon the size of the group. You can use a small hourglass, or an alarm on your phone),
- Encourage 'I' statements, insist that family members not talk over each other, not confront other family members, and not characterize others' experience.
- When the family member's time is up, no one is allowed to critique the family member who was speaking. Then move on to the next person, who shares how it has been for him or her.
- As family members listen to each other, they gain an understanding of each person's perspective on their grief, and it lessens judgment and unites the family.

Next, we suggest these follow-up questions, using the same guidelines:

- How has your life changed since this has happened?
- What has been the most difficult aspect of dealing with this crisis/death/illness?
- What is most difficult for you right now?
- What do you miss about the way things were?

What do you need to get through this right now, and who in your family can support you? At this point, we ask each family member to ask the person directly if he or she is willing to help. Even if family members can only get some of what they need, they build support nets of safety within the family.

- What are you most concerned about in the future?

For each family member, the magnitude of the loss varies—how the crisis has changed the member's life and what he or she misses from that particular individual who is ill or has died is overwhelmingly personal. Each person is covered in their own overcoat of pain. It is sometimes useful to have family members list what they received from that person and what they have lost. Each person is losing and missing an essential relationship, and each family member has to compensate for their own lack—as well as the gap left in the whole family unit. These adjustments generate a great deal of strain in the daily life of a family.

Validating the magnitude of these changes in detail enables family members to become more aware of their situation. They can then mobilize their internal and family resources to build a positive, cohesive support system with each other. Family intervention/grief counseling breaks the judgment cycle and creates understanding and empathy with each other's situation and feelings.

A father, a well-known minister in their community, had died from a long-term illness. No one in the family had been expecting Dad to actually die. They were in shock and extremely angry, with themselves and with other family members. The mother was overwhelmed with grief and felt unable to take care of their many friends, loved ones, and children who were missing this beloved man. Just getting the family together in the same room proved to be a nearly insurmountable challenge. At the beginning, they immediately began to argue, dramatically with shouts and threats. Fellow counselors shared that they could hear their voices two houses away!

We needed to get them under control, so we invited them to please sit, and take a deep breath, releasing all of the pent-up tension and frustration. We then validated their grief and established ground rules: confidentiality, no cross-talk, everyone gets a voice, and no judgment from anyone else. We let them know we couldn't fix it, or make it better, and that they were actually the best support for each other. We also made it clear that acceptance does not necessarily mean agreement. To accept each other, all that is needed is for them to honor each other's grief journey as true for them.

Then we were able to move forward with the story of Dad. We invited them to share the quality of Dad they most admired and asked them to identify what support Dad might give to them individually. We asked them to also say how specific family members could help them. As each person identified what they needed from each other, the atmosphere melted, and at the end of the session there were, amazingly, some hugs and outreaches to each other.

Family Dynamics Exercise

Each person takes the role and behaviors of a family member he/she has the most difficulty experiencing or interacting with. Each person interacts coming from that role. As the role play progresses, people often find that they are more alike than different, even though behaviors are quite diverse. This is an excellent role play to do with a family after you have spent several sessions with them.

Typical family behaviors

Angry, belligerent, aggressive, irritable
Sick humor, jokester, gallows humor
Suzie sunshine—perky—"Let's look on the bright side"
Withdrawn, quiet, isolated
Emotional, crying, whiney
Incident commander, bossy, overbearing
Overbearing nurturer, nagging, interfering
Hovercraft

Children and Youth with Grief

When young people are forced to cope with the harsh realities of illness or death, they grieve and often feel as deeply and powerfully as adults. Often they are 'protected' or pushed aside by well-meaning adults. This can lead to a sense of isolation and a belief that there is no safe haven—no place where their feelings can be shared.

Adults struggle to deal with serious illness and death. Amidst unfamiliar physical and psychological feelings, adults and children face sadness. Though less sophisticated in expressing or masking complex, conflicting feelings, children still struggle. They benefit from sensitive, informed support along their own grief journey. They express feelings when encouraged. There's no magic to help a grieving child, but there are some invaluable tools—gifts to a grieving child—for dealing with common expressions of grief.

An intervention with a firefighter's family resulted in a powerful action step. The firefighter had been diagnosed with stage four cancer. His wife and children were struggling with the news, and everyone was reacting differently. When asked, what do you need from each other to get through this difficult time? the five-year old son (youngest in his family) responded, "I need an afternoon alone with my Daddy!" We asked the father if that would be possible. He responded warmly, "I think that's exactly what I need as well." So, Josh created a tea party for his father, complete with cups, milk, a tea pot, and cookies. After they finished tea, he took his dad out to the small back yard and demonstrated how he was practicing his 'hoops' with the portable basketball set-up. After a while, Josh commented to his dad, "You're a little tired. I'm going to put you to bed." So he guided his dad to bed, with his favorite stuffed toy to keep him safe and comfy, while reading him a 'bedtime' story. After the success of this magical afternoon, the rest of the family were able to schedule 'Daddy dates', before he became too ill to interact with them. They each had the opportunity to bear witness to the dad's love and legacy before he died. This came from the wisdom of a five-year-old who was asked what he needed in the midst of his dad's illness.

The Gift of Listening

To listen as someone processes grief requires total presence, and a willingness to engage all the senses—see, hear, feel what is said, and not said. In listening, we need to leave behind preconception and prejudice, expectation and exasperation.

Listening to a child express facts and feelings about his or her loss is not about waiting to interject with pearls of wisdom. It is about opening our hearts, opening our minds, and opening our ears as the words flow and falter. The gift of validation: a child's grief is as individual as a fingerprint. Expressions of grief—shock, anxiety, anger, guilt, sadness, regression—weave a common cloth, but experience is as unique as each child.

- Children may show no outward sign of sadness, playing much the same as always. This does not mean they are not sad.
- Children may react with disproportionate intensity to issues seemingly unrelated to their loss.
- Children can ask questions that make adults squirm, wanting details about how their loved one died, or what happens to buried bodies.
- A child is inevitably the center of his or her own universe. Children may ask,

"Is it my fault? Am I going to die too?" "Why did Mommy leave me?" "Didn't Dad love me?"

Almost any response to grief is valid. Acknowledging a child's feelings is a powerful gift. Keep your answers open-ended, inviting the child to express feelings and fears.

"That must feel terrible…"
"What special memories do you have?"

Avoid trap words—could've, should've, would've. They can imply disappointment.

The Gift of Acceptance

Grieving takes time—time and energy. Although the experience of loss is universal, it is inevitably life changing. Some changes are temporary and immediate; others take time and appear gradually. Acceptance is key.

Consider how most people react to tears—offering tissues with a kindly, "There, there now, don't cry." Without meaning to, these words signal that tears make others uncomfortable, that crying should stop. To listen without judgment conveys acceptance and respect of the child's experience, a critical component for healing grief.

The Gift of Honesty

The language of grief is universal. Yet, in this country we offer euphemisms. Concerned about creating additional anxiety, instead of saying, "Mommy (or Daddy or your friend P.J.) died," we substitute polite terms—passed away, went to God, isn't coming back. But children are literal creatures. Imagine how easily such statements may be intensifying a sense of abandonment or creating false hope. Keep it simple, honest, and direct.

How Can I Help?

Grief is often misunderstood, especially when it comes to children. It is common to feel that a child is not grieving the right way or needs to be expressing him- or herself differently. Grief is a spiral of feelings and experiences. It is not a straight line with a beginning and an end. There is often a wall of silence around the painful issues of death, dying, and grief. It can create a sense of disconnect, of treading water without a lifeline. This is especially true for children and adolescents.

The Centre for Living with Dying Healing Heart Program is a grief support program for children, adolescents, and families, and for the caregivers who support them. We offer three age-appropriate support groups for youth (littles, middles, and teens), as well as a concurrent group for the adult caregivers (usually the surviving spouse/parent). The caretaker group assists adults to support children through the grief process, while giving them a safe place to receive support and process their own grief. Meeting concurrently with the different age groups helps break down the walls of isolation that are common for children and adolescents. The meetings also provide a bridge over which children can talk and traverse their solitary sadness.

Helping Children Cope with Loss and Trauma

Children will experience a variety of emotions in response to loss or trauma. Some retell personal experiences over and over again while others refuse to discuss the loss at all. Both are normal. In the wake of a disaster or major loss, the following is a list of common reactions along with suggested responses for caring adults.

Withdrawal

After a disaster, a child may refuse to interact with others or to join in activities.

Suggestions

- Gently set up a time to talk with the child, acknowledging that you understand how difficult it can be to share feelings.
- Engage in some physical expression together such as drawing or playing with stuffed animals or puppets.
- Talk about your own feelings or how you might feel in their situation.
- Explain that their feelings of anger, sadness, guilt, embarrassment, relief, and love are normal.

Belligerent Behavior

Some children act out by displaying uncharacteristic or intensified aggression and toughness. They may become uncooperative at home or at school. They may pick fights.

Suggestions

- Often, children act angry or belligerent because they feel helpless, hurt, or hopeless. Their tough behavior is an attempt to feel strong and safe.
- Set up a time and place to talk one-on-one.
- Do not embarrass or humiliate the child.
- In simple, direct language, reassure the child that you realize he or she is going through a horrific time.
- Share how you are affected by the child's behavior. Explain that they may be alienating others who could support them.
- Do not be afraid to ask direct questions.
- Many children, including teens, may not even know why they are angry.
- Talk about your own personal loss and anger.
- Above all, help them understand that they have a right to their own feelings.

© Copyright material from Darrow and Childs (2020), *Experiential Action Methods and Tools for Healing Grief and Loss-Related Trauma*, Routledge.

Depression

Some children may actually become depressed by exposure to talk and images of war. Eating or sleeping habits may change. They may appear drained, despondent, or moody.

Suggestions

- It is important to discuss signs of depression directly. Depression is a natural part of trauma, but if unresolved, strong feelings can evolve that drastically lower a child's ability to function.
- Shift the focus to living one day at a time.
- Ask what the child needs right now to get through the day—addressing specific needs, feelings, and issues to lessen the overwhelming 'dark cloud'.
- Limit exposure to media coverage and talk of war.

Regressive Behavior

A child's behavior will often regress in unsettling times. They may need to be held or kept close constantly, and they may be especially fearful and afraid to be left alone. Even teens may be frightened to sleep alone or become afraid of the dark.

Suggestions

- Again, reassure children, letting them express their fears, and allow them to ask questions.
- Be clear and honest.
- Make no promises you cannot keep.
- Keep as much consistency in routine and schedule as possible.
- Physical touch can be very reassuring.
- Let children know there are resources to support them and keep them safe.
- It's OK to allow children to regress a little, then gently move them back into a normal routine, step by step, as they feel comfortable.

Protective Behavior

Children may try to protect themselves and you by acting strong and grown up. They may try to appear unaffected by the situation.

Suggestions

- Protective behavior is one way a child tries to regain a sense of self-control, but such behavior may cover true feelings.

© Copyright material from Darrow and Childs (2020), *Experiential Action Methods and Tools for Healing Grief and Loss-Related Trauma*, Routledge.

- Validate their gestures of loving protection and explain that it is OK to be a child who needs loving care. It is OK to allow loving adults to provide that care.
- Be a reliable role model.
- Children pay more attention to what we do than what we say. It is OK for children to see adult expressions of sadness, anger, and helplessness. It provides permission for them to also express these difficult feelings.

Children, like adults, may have a delayed response to loss, so it may be months before any of these feelings are expressed or even manifested. This is normal. A child may appear to be coping well immediately, then suddenly regress. It may take a while for them to begin to feel safe in their world again.

Information to Share with Children

- Even with all the terrible things that have happened, this is still one of the safest places to live.
- If you are at school when a disaster happens, remember that teachers are experts in what to do in case of an emergency, and want to hear how you feel.
- Hugs, games, silly movies, music, and even a stuffed animal (a 'trauma buddy') can help us feel safe again. It's OK to be happy and to laugh even in sad and scary times.
- Everyone needs to talk and listen to others. Parents, teachers, and friends want you to share your feelings. Don't be afraid to ask questions—your friends are probably feeling the same things you are.
- Get plenty of sleep and eat nutritious food.
- Remember that no matter how big your questions and fears are, your family or community will take care of you.

When a beloved teacher died, our team member asked the fourth-grade class this question: "What makes you feel better when you have had a rough time or a difficult day?" One student responded, "I love a nice bowl of cereal." Another stated, "I want a big bowl of ice cream." Another commented, "A bowl of my grandma's rice and beans." The final student mused, "What I need is a big bowl of friendship." This was an eloquent statement in line with the findings of Kelly McGonigal and co-authors (2019) that tending and befriending in stressful circumstances raise oxytocin levels and reduce stress and isolation. Children and youth in grief can offer deep wisdom and honesty to caregivers. When given the safe place to express and process their feelings, children serve as an inspiration to all of us.

Bibliography

Bradshaw, J. (1990). *Homecoming: reclaiming and championing your inner child*. New York: Bantam Books.

Garfield, C. (2017). *Life's last gift*. Las Vegas, NV: Central Recovery Press.

Grollman, E.A. (1993). *Straight talk about death for teenagers: how to cope with losing someone you love*. Boston, MA: Beacon Press.

Keyssar, J.R. (2011). *Last acts of kindness: lessons for the living from the bedside of the dying*. San Francisco, CA: Transformations in Care.

Kissane, D.W., & Hooghe, A. (2011). In R.A. Neimeyer, D.L. Harris, H.R. Winokuer, & G.F. Thornton (eds.), *Grief and bereavement in contemporary society: bridging research and practice* (pp. 287–302). New York: Routledge.

McGonigal, K., Puddicombe, A., & Harris, D. (2016). *The upside of stress: why stress is good for you and how to get good at it*. New York: Avery.

Satir, V. (1984). *Satir step by step: a guide to creating change in families*. Mountain View, CA: Science and Behavior Books.

Schreder, M. (1995). In E. Grollman (ed.), *Bereaved parents and teens: a support guide for parents and professionals*. Boston, MA: Beacon Press.

CHAPTER 20

STRESS, TRAUMA, AND CRITICAL INCIDENT STRESS MANAGEMENT

The Birth of the Bay Area CISM Team

As a young woman of twenty-one, MaryAnne Kelly survived the suicide death of her husband, who took his life with a high-powered rifle in the living room of their home on the morning of Mother's Day. In the cold dawn of that day, her life and destiny were irrevocably changed. The first responders who helped her that day were the 911 dispatcher, who stayed with her on the phone, the young police officer who helped her through the investigation, and the kind paramedic who offered his care and support. After that, the healthcare community did not know what to do. MaryAnne went to her medical doctor, who gave her pills to help her calm down and sleep, to a priest who told her to pray, and finally to a psychiatrist who recommended she get a hobby to help her forget her husband's death and her own subsequent trauma. When none of these suggestions worked, MaryAnne sat in the bathroom with the pills in her hand, realizing she had three choices: to die, to go crazy, or to find a way to help people in grief. She took the third choice, which became the Centre for Living with Dying.

About five years after the Centre for Living with Dying began, MaryAnne Kelly and Janet Childs realized that responders needed more help on the front lines in the aftermath of stressful events/critical incidents. MaryAnne never forgot the initial support she received after her husband's suicide—how the responders became her anchors of safety and support in those first few moments. She often talked about the dispatcher, the police officer, and the paramedic and how each of them had brought her comfort that day. Subsequently, reading her local paper one day, she noticed the name and photo of the young police officer who had assisted her that day. She had hoped he was getting a commendation for his good service. Instead, MaryAnne read in the paper that this officer had died by suicide in a very similar way.

So began the Critical Incident Stress Management (CISM) Team. In the first days, we called ourselves the Bay Area Responders Crisis Intervention Team. When we asked first responders what was needed, we discovered that the best support often comes from peers. Empowering resilience within their personal lives and strengthening team support among themselves are critically important.

At the same time, the International Critical Incident Stress Foundation (ICISF) was started on the east coast of Maryland by Dr. Jeffrey Mitchell, a retired paramedic who became a psychologist, and wanted to support his co-workers in stress management. Everly and Mitchell (1999) wrote the seminal book on CISM as a concept for emergency responders. When the term 'critical incident stress management' became well known, our team changed our name to Bay Area CISM Team. We then became a regional team, training department and agency teams around the San Francisco Bay Area and California. We have worked with healthcare providers, police, dispatch, fire, medics/EMS, social services, probation, corrections, therapists, and community workers. As of 2020, we are thirty-nine years old.

Our CISM team provides help to both responders/caregivers and communities. In this chapter, which focuses on the responder experience, we provide education on the dynamics of stress, trauma, grief, loss, and change, as well as effective CISM practices. Many of these concepts have been validated by Laura van Dernoot Lipsky and Connie Burk in *Trauma Stewardship* (2009).

First, we offer definitions of critical stress, which is the natural byproduct of working with victims and survivors. There are four types of stress:

1. Critical incident stress: this type is incident-specific—focused on the aftermath of any event which causes unusually strong emotions in the responder/professional, either during the incident or later. This stress has the potential to interfere with their ability to function, either on the scene or later.
2. Delayed stress response syndrome: this is commonly diagnosed as post-traumatic stress disorder. We think a more accurate term is post-traumatic stress injury. Delayed stress response can occur (weeks, months, years) after stressful event(s).
3. Cumulative stress: working in a high-stress occupation and experiencing multiple critical incidents can amplify impact to responders, creating a domino effect to personal and professional functioning, particularly when stress is not addressed effectively.
4. Occupational stress: the administrative systems and command structures in the occupation are not responsive or validating to employees, which increases the already existing stress levels. We term this 'organizational betrayal'.

Critical incident stress is initially imprinted on several sensory paths and can create a trauma response in the body (Levine, 2005; van der Kolk, 2014). Auditory, visual, and kinesthetic senses process information about the incident and drive appropriate responses. Responders monitor and manage the incident from start to finish, but often have the least amount of opportunity for closure. Figure 20.1a shows typical immediate and delayed reactions in the aftermath of a tragedy. Figure 20.1b can be used as a handout for responders to name their own immediate and delayed reactions.

Critical Incident Stress Management/Critical Incident Stress Response (CISR)

CISM/CISR provides immediate and ongoing response, through prevention (pre-incident education on stress and stress management), intervention when a critical incident occurs, and support through the recovery process, which includes ongoing training. This encourages and provides a structure for effective recovery from critical incident stress, post-trauma stress, and cumulative stress for emergency responders, public safety personnel, healthcare providers, social workers, therapists, caregivers, and victims/witnesses.

Goals include:

- Normalize feelings in the face of abnormal stress.
- Lessen stress responses—mental, emotional, physical, social, and spiritual.
- Accelerate recovery of personnel to former level of functioning.
- Allow personnel to talk about the stressful experience.
- Obtain an overall view of the incident.
- Build camaraderie and support among team members who worked the incident together.
- Provide stress survival skills and resources for the future.
- Begin to cognitively make sense out of the horror and trauma.
- Give meaning to the difficulties faced during and after the incident (primary and secondary trauma).
- Provide a safe and neutral environment to wind down before making the transition to personal life.
- Affirm the value of involved personnel and acknowledge any meaningful aspects of the incident.

Typical Reactions in the Aftermath of Tragedy

A critical incident is any event that causes unusually strong reactions in the responding personnel or survivors. These reactions/responses can occur immediately or in a delayed fashion.

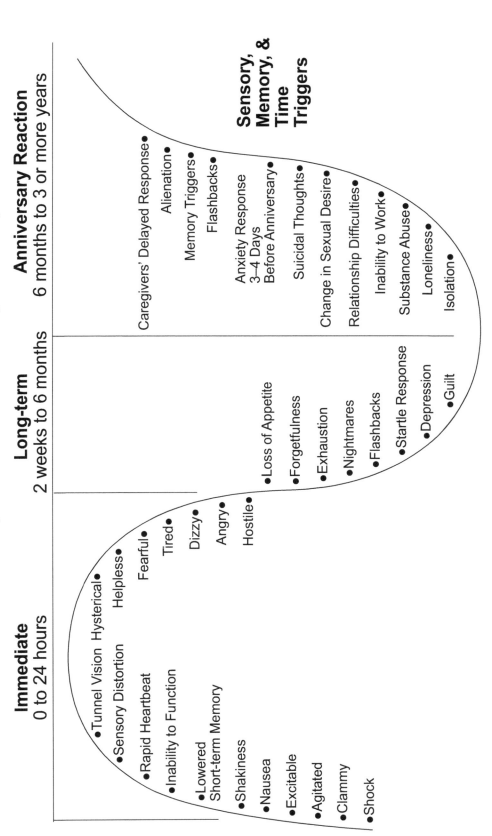

Figure 20.1a. Typical reactions in the aftermath of a tragedy.

© Copyright material from Darrow and Childs (2020), *Experiential Action Methods and Tools for Healing Grief and Loss-Related Trauma*, Routledge.

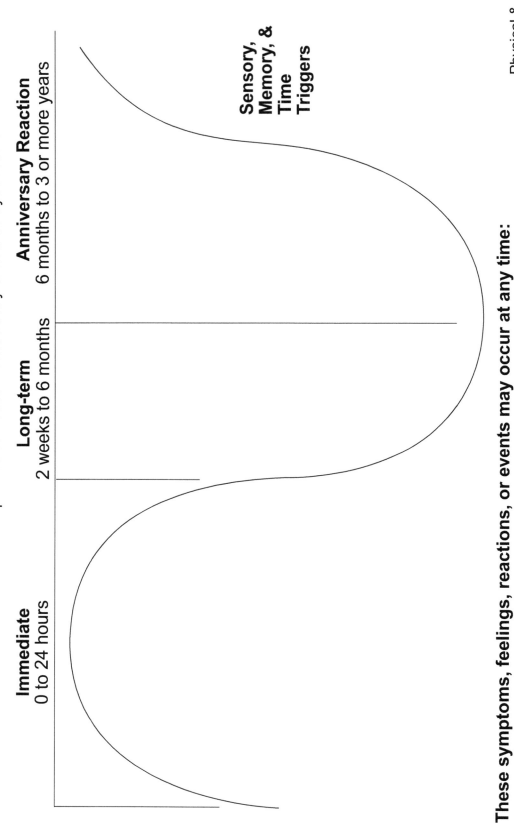

Figure 20.1b. Personalized reactions in the aftermath of a tragedy.

Pre-Incident Education and Training

When we are able to provide information to responders and caregivers before a critical incident, it can build resilience and comfort for them in a critical incident response. These include the following components:

1. Generate educational updates on stress and stress management.
2. Provide support and training for command staff and supervisors.
3. Create a CISM team.
4. Provide support services and pre-incident training for family and significant others.
5. Create a peer counseling program.
6. Have information on resources for professional counseling/therapy/emergency action plan program.
7. Develop a process to provide crisis interventions and debriefings for citizens and community (network with other agencies).
8. Develop a process for on-scene support services.
9. Develop a process for debriefing the debriefers.
10. Provide resources for setting up memorial services/celebrations of life.

Critical Incident Management/Response

Effective CISM/CISR (which we use interchangeably) practices include immediate and follow-up support of affected personnel. Steps may include crisis interventions, defusings, debriefings, check-in debriefings, and training on the effects of the critical incident.

- Crisis intervention: immediate emotional support at times when a person's own resources appear to have failed to adequately cope with a problem or life situation.
- CISR (formerly known as debriefing): an organized approach to supporting emergency service personnel and survivors who are involved in emergency operations under conditions of extreme stress in order to assist in mitigating long-term emotional trauma. The debriefing process provides a format in which personnel can discuss their feelings and reactions, thus reducing the stress that results from exposure to critical incidents. All CISRs are strictly confidential.

CISM/CISR changes the dynamics of how a caregiver or responder processes trauma, stress, and grief. The structure of CISM/CISR gives the opportunity for a group or individual survivor of trauma to acknowledge, express, act, and reconnect. This structured format creates safety and freedom for individuals and the group to identify triggers, to be able to hear others' experience of the trauma, to put the puzzle pieces of the incident together, to hold space for each other, and to identify a proactive action step. We make it clear from the beginning that we are not meeting with first responders to eliminate pain. We are together to make meaning of the pain and process the stress as a team, rather than having to work at this in isolation. We are here to mobilize support for each other in a concrete and visible way.

In group interventions, prepare your participants for safety by doing these steps:

- Know your audience.
- Prepare to validate the specific issues of stress.
- Assure the group that we know we can't make it 'better'.

- Meet and greet before the official meeting.
- Use language that your participants will relate to.
- Mobilize your group to mutual support by reminding them that they are the best support for one another.
- Explain what is going to happen in the process of CISR.
- State ground rules (see below), and that the group is going to talk about what happened, including what was the most powerful aspect of the incident, and ways that individuals can take care of themselves and each other.
- Encourage participants to take care of themselves in whatever way works for them.
- In individual support, there is more room for self-disclosure. In group work, be very conservative about what you share from your personal experience, or your experience as a facilitator. People might take this as minimizing.
- When there is a participant who is agitated or interruptive, validate his or her experience, and then open it up to the rest of the group by asking, "Can anyone else relate to this experience, thought, or feeling?" This activates and empowers the entire group, as well as connecting the individual to the group. Also, safety is maintained. We call this 'groupify'. If an individual is escalating and is unable to continue to participate, ask them what they need right now, and if needed, assign a support person to be with them, as they leave the group intervention. Do not just send them away or banish them from the group without supportive presence from another person. Hopefully, the support person would be a co-facilitator, but if needed, deputize a capable group member, so that work can continue with the group.
- Brainstorm with responders about action steps they may need to do—ways they can effectively take care of themselves and teammates/co-workers.
- Thank them for the honor of being with them during this difficult time and remind them that they made a difference by their presence on the front line.

Group Ground Rules: The Guidelines That Create Safety

- Group members agree to confidentiality.
- Group is not therapy.
- There should be no critique or tactical/procedural analysis of the incident and any individual's actions.
- Automatic attendance—all involved personnel are encouraged to attend.
- Participation is not required.
- There is no rank or hierarchy of command—everyone is equal.
- Meetings usually occur twenty-four to seventy-two hours after the incident but may occur later.
- Meetings are two to three hours in length.
- There should be no notes or paperwork.
- A safe, comfortable environment is provided.
- Food and drink are made available.
- Theres is no media, no tape recorders.
- Personnel not involved with incident are not allowed at CISR.
- Only trained CISR peers and mental health professionals will conduct debriefings.
- Establish a paradigm that the group is the best support for each other—based on the fundamental belief of CISM that people who do the same work understand the nuances of the stress response for that particular profession.

Introduction

After establishing the ground rules, stating the purpose of the meeting, and validating the potential impact of the incident, the team facilitators ask these questions.

Fact Phase

- What happened? Discuss the specific details of the incident or situation.
- What was your role, how did it come down, how did you respond?
- How did you find out about the trauma or death?
- Can anyone take us through what he/she did at the incident?

This helps people to put the puzzle pieces together. All are encouraged to share what their role was, because it helps the rest of their team complete their picture of the incident. This is most effective if it can be done chronologically, but it is not necessary. We wait for people to volunteer, so they do not feel pressured.

Thought Phase

What were first thoughts about what happened? Ask questions and explore issues that surfaced in the aftermath: "What thoughts ran through your head as you were responding to the incident?"

This encourages people to consider what they imagined had happened. Even imagination creates a neural pathway in our brain. Many times, imagination can be worse than the actual incident scene. Hearing everyone's thoughts can help to foster understanding for where fellow team member's perceptions and perspectives originated. Many times, after a CISR, we have taken responders who were not present at the scene to responders who were present, to explain what happened and help facilitate correction of what was imagined.

Reaction Phase

- What were the immediate and delayed feelings and physical reactions to the incident?
- What was the roughest?
- When was the "Oh, no" moment when you knew that it was going to be a bad one?
- What was the most powerful aspect of this incident? What hit you the hardest?

These questions allow people to express the details of what impacted them the most, which fosters support and camaraderie amongst the participants, and creates bonds between team members.

Normalizing Phase

Share physical, emotional, thinking, and relationship reactions you have experienced. Talk about what is normal. Remind people that they are normal, and their reactions are normal in the face of abnormally traumatic events. Ask people, "How has it been for you since the incident?" This invites expression of the signs and responses to stress both at home and at work. It normalizes the stress response and gives the CISM Team facilitators a chance to validate the reactions.

Memory Phase/Landmine Phase

Discuss previous incidents that this incident may have brought up. Trauma and grief know no time—so it doesn't matter how long ago the previous incidents happened. If it was never resolved, it is as if it happened yesterday. Debriefing for these older incidents is important to address at this time.

- What is in your trauma/grief backpack (Figure 20.2)?
- Has this incident reminded you of past incidents, either personal or work-related?

This is the deepest part of the CISR, as people are able to acknowledge what past experiences have been triggered.

Education Phase

Have the group discuss what has worked to help them survive in the aftermath and get back on their feet. Talk about tools for dealing with stress—before, during, and after. Share resources for ongoing assistance. Brainstorm about what people can do for each other and themselves to bring some healing or resolution. Letting people share their stress reduction tools with each other is empowering. Even if these tools are shared with a sense of humor, it gets the ball rolling. One dispatcher shared that she would draw the water to the perfect temperature, then add scented oils to the water, put on soft music and dim the lights, and bring a plate of her favorite chocolates. She expressed this in such detail, it brought the concept of the bubble bath alive.

Explore and plan action steps, both on a group and individual basis. For example, after an eighty-car collision on a freeway, one of the paramedics shared that he was going to visit the family of the person he had not been able to save. It gave him a way to validate his sorrow for the family—to convey the fact that he cared. He later reported that it went far better than he had hoped. He was embraced by the family; they invited him to the funeral of their loved one and honored his efforts to save their son.

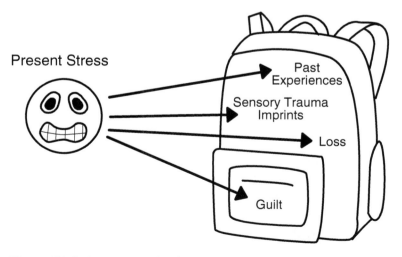

Figure 20.2. Past trauma backpack.

Meaningful Aspects of Incident Phase

Next, we invite the group to identify any meaning that might be derived from surviving the incident. Even in the midst of tragedy, and even death, explore the meaningful aspects in the aftermath, such as good teamwork, appreciation of co-workers, appreciation of the beauty and fragility of life, and the importance of living life to the fullest. It might also be a sense of the preciousness of life, the heroism of actions taken, or that we are together in this moment supporting each other through this crisis. This phase gives team members a chance to convey gratitude to one another.

Closure Phase

Finally, we close the CISR with reminders of the ground rules established at the beginning, the resources available to support personal stress, and the reminder that each person is the best support for each other. We invite team members to do something that is totally self-indulgent and rejuvenating for themselves in the next twenty-four hours. Do a wrap-up exercise if it feels right. We invite people to take turns stating an intention to let go of trauma, pain, guilt, or anger, and so forth, and to claim a positive quality they want to take with them. Stress confidentiality and the importance of maintaining that safety bond with each other after the group debriefing is over.

Re-entry Phase

Because the group has worked on stress in a very powerful way, a break is needed. Invite participants to stay and share in food and conversation with each other. This is a powerful bonding time of debriefing, where individuals who may not have talked in the group may feel more comfortable. Group members are also able to reinforce what they learned and encourage each other in a non-threatening atmosphere. We also offer handouts on stress and stress reactions to normalize their experience.

Building Sensitivity among Co-Workers

When someone is coming back to work after a loss, describe the person and situation, and then ask these questions:

- What do you think _____ might be feeling/thinking/experiencing?
- What do you imagine they might need right now?
- What do you need when you are going through a crisis or rough time?
- What might we do to support _____?

This is effective to use with supervisors/managers in the workplace. It bonds co-workers together and enables people to support each other. It equalizes power dynamics and creates a sense of unity and communal strength.

Demobilization after a Major Critical Incident or Mass Casualty Event: Crisis Management Briefings

Definition of demobilization: response that occurs after a major critical incident.

First establish a venue that is near the staging area of the event, so that personnel can go to a safe environment, shielded from media, public, and other distractions.

- Have food and snacks available, preferably away from the exit door.
- Create a safe and comfortable place for people to rest or lay down.
- Provide handouts with simple coping tools (see Chapter 5).
- Allow people to mingle informally, creating small support groups.
- As the support person, interact in a non-invasive way. Gently introduce yourself and offer to serve food or drink.
- Inform people there will be a CISR in seventy-two hours, or however long the incident response has lasted. (For example, if the incident was two weeks long, including recovery, the CISR will occur two weeks after the incident ended.)
- The same ground rules apply to demobilizations as to all responses—confidentiality and no critique of actions or reactions.
- Give accurate, specific information about the incident as needed or as requested.

Normalize and validate experiences and reactions. Avoid asking lots of questions. Offer simple ways to care for self. Encourage people to tell their family and loved ones what they need, or what they don't need, when they go home. Prepare them for the possibility of the long-term responses they may experience. Discuss ways they can pace themselves.

Affirm that the people in the room are the best support for each other, because they have survived the incident. If it feels right, acknowledge the power of simple stress survival skills: breathing, movement, and hydration.

If possible, get people working in similar disciplines to be available for supporting the responders.

When a demobilization center is functioning for a long time, have letters written by children for responders, or have stuffed animals, and/or comfort items available for them to take home. This is also valuable for Urban Search and Rescue (USAR) teams, who may be responding from out of the area.

Key Points

- Remember, people will be in shock, exhausted, and possibly uncommunicative. Don't push yourself upon them, particularly with verbal dialogue, debate, or questions.
- Validate their skill and courage and acknowledge the horror of this incident.

The power of supportive people in a demobilization makes a huge difference.

Defusing

Definition of defusing: response given to involved personnel in the aftermath of a critical incident within zero to twenty-four hours.

Defusing is a shortened form of the CISR, in which the same ground rules apply. The usual length of time is twenty to forty-five minutes. It is usually done within eight hours of a critical incident using the following steps. Multiple defusings for different groups of emergency/public safety personnel may be offered for the same incident.

Introduction

State the ground rules and the purpose of defusing. Acknowledge participants' courage in participating in defusing.

Exploration

Ask involved personnel what happened. Discuss details of their experiences and reactions. Reassure them as needed. Do not disagree with the perceptions of participants.

Information

Normalize experiences and reactions. Discuss stress survival skills (breathing exercises, diet, recreation, sensory trauma release, etc.). Address the issues of family and job, and potential delayed reactions that may occur in the future. Reassure them that they are capable. Triage how they will take care of themselves when they get home or leave the workplace. Ask the question: "What are you going home to?" This allows colleagues to know what is happening with their co-workers and to offer meaningful, immediate support. Give resources for ongoing CISM.

Key Points

- Be honest in your role. Discuss the value in coming together as a team who worked the incident, to talk about it, without critique, judgment, or discussion of job performance.
- Acknowledge issues of unfinished business with the incident. Are there any action steps that need to be done, as a team or individually?
- Express your concern and empathy for what they have survived.
- Acknowledge and validate the positive support and intervention they performed, just by their presence, their response, and their willingness to do this type of work.
- Validate that they are each other's best support system now and in the future, when others around them may not fully understand the magnitude of the incident or the impact of the aftermath.

Critical Incident Stress Response (Formerly Called Debriefing)

Definition: critical incident stress response (CISR) is a psycho-educational structured discussion with involved personnel about the critical incident in the aftermath.

Key Points

- Acknowledge that stress and critical incidents are an occupational hazard. While people cannot control the incident, they can control how they respond to it. Participants can be urged to be easy

152 Stress, Trauma, and CISM

with themselves and allow others to support them in whatever ways feel right. What people do in the aftermath for themselves and each other can help the recovery process.

- The body knows no difference between physical injury and emotional trauma. So, by treating stress with the same importance as a physical injury, people survive and recover faster and with fewer long-term reactions.
- There is no simple procedure for dealing with stress because each person reacts differently and needs different things at different times. Because people are impacted on physical, emotional, mental, social (relationships), and spiritual levels, their entire life is affected. Urge participants to be patient with the process of healing, reminding them that they have been injured. The key is to listen to the body and stay in the present moment as much as possible. Beware of 'futurizing'—paying undue attention to the future.
- Provide examples of action steps to heal unfinished business. This might include lighting a candle, writing a letter, or visiting the family of the victim who died. Share brief stories to illustrate strategies to address stress reactions. Do not do this too soon as it can be perceived as minimizing the present incident.

Follow-Up CISR

Check in with responders after a CISR has been conducted, to follow up and determine if any secondary trauma has occurred, or if further support is needed. This lessens the possibility of isolation in the aftermath. This is done on anniversary dates or a few weeks/months after the incident. Determine if any action steps need to be taken, such as a ceremony of life, tree planting, revisiting the incident scene, creating a trust fund for family members, contacting victims, or the reporting party, and so on.

Key Points

- Explore how responders' lives have been impacted since the incident.
- Discuss the power of landmines (something or someone who unexpectedly triggers painful memories or trauma reactions) and anniversary dates. To quote Army General Schwartzkopf, "A man who doesn't cry, scares me." An interviewer had inquired if he was ashamed or embarrassed to shed tears on national TV after the death of his mother.
- Plan action steps that may still need to be taken.
- Explore the spiritual or life-changing impact this incident has created. Discuss examples.

Landmine CISR

A modified CISM/CISR is used when past incidents remain unresolved for responding and affected personnel. It can be done for a cluster of unresolved incidents or can focus on a specific incident from the past.

Key Points

- State clearly that it does not matter how long ago the incident occurred. If it was never dealt with in a humane or positive way, it is as though it happened yesterday. Trauma knows no time.

Stress, Trauma, and CISM **153**

- Acknowledge again that this is not therapy. Proceed carefully, and let participants know that it is not easy to dredge up feelings and issues from the past and, at all times, they have control over what they discuss and how.
- Discussing past incidents gives participants some distance and perspective and also unites co-workers who survived the incidents and the aftermath.
- This is also a time to do a review of unfinished business or of any personal or family aftershocks since the incident(s).

When the critical incident involves grief counseling with survivors, grieving non-responders, or people in the community, we ask different questions in the phases of the unfolding CISR.

Grief Counseling CISM Steps

- Introduction: validate the impact of the loss/death.
- Fact: explore death notification. How did you find out?
- Thought: examine pre-death events. When was the last time you had contact with the person who died?
- Reaction: what hit you the hardest? What is currently the most challenging aspect of what you went through? Encourage sharing memories of the person who died—the good, the challenging, the redemptive. Bring up the image of the heart hotel (Figure 17.2).
- Signs: how has it been since you found out about the death? What indications of grief have you noticed in yourself and in your family or co-workers?
- Landmine/memory trigger: what are reminders of past incidents/situations of grief or loss? What is in your backpack (Figure 20.2)?
- Education: identify action steps to honor the person who died. Explore how to take care of self and each other.
- Meaningful aspects: what would you want to give/receive from person who died?
- Re-entry: discuss how we as a community can continue and strengthen support.

Serving a community in the aftermath of a major incident, the CISR questions are as below:

- Introduction: validate the impact and magnitude of the loss/death/disaster. Address survivor guilt.
- Fact: what were the actual facts, as opposed to the media portrayal of the incident?
- Thought: how has it been to re-enter your home/work life after surviving the incident? Discuss the culture shock of re-entering life.
- Reaction: what was the most difficult? What memory stayed with you?
- Signs: what reaction or sign seems persistent since the incident?
- Landmine/memory trigger: reminders of past incidents/situations. Acknowledge that it may be difficult to know what past events might be triggered by the present event.
- Education: action steps to honor the incident and your part in it. Explore how to take care of self, each other, and loved ones. Others can suffer vicarious trauma from your involvement.
- Meaningful aspects: lessons learned in the aftermath. What is important in your life?
- Closure: you are the best support team for each other. You made a difference. Protect yourself; create safety for yourself, for family, friends, and co-workers, and for your community.

When a teacher or student has died, or is living with a life-threatening illness, we often recommend putting a large piece of butcher paper on a library wall or in the quad. (In special circumstances, such as suicide, care needs to be taken to not over-memorialize or glamorize, potentially creating a situation of suicide contagion.) The shared messages and memories are precious reminders of the gifts the person gave in his or her life span. When my (Janet) son died suddenly many years ago, our family received many cards of condolence, which were comforting and healing. Years later, we kept only a few cards, but the long strip of art paper on which students had recorded their memories, wishes, and thoughts about Leroy was a treasure.

Tips for Self-Care for Responders and Healthcare Providers

1. Breathe. Breathing is an immediate way to center you in the midst of crisis situations and intense feelings. Consciously breathing gives you a moment to pause and gather your own thoughts and feelings. Breathing grounds you in the here and now.
2. Stay in the present moment as much as possible. Deal with feelings and needs that require attention now. Focus others on the present moment as this will enable them to take control over their immediate situation. Help them to prioritize what is the most important or most difficult issue right now.
3. Do what you need to do to complete the intervention or action. As feelings and reactions come up, acknowledge them and make a bargain with yourself that you will attend to them at a later time. When a break time does come, honor your commitment to deal with the feelings and issues inside. Exercise; scream as loud as you can into a pillow; hug a stuffed animal or a real pet; allow yourself to be held or cradled; or let yourself cry in a safe place for a few minutes.

These simple actions will relieve the immediate physical pressure of the reactions inside your body.

4. If you need to say goodbye to a patient/victim who has died, allow yourself to touch the body, bring flowers to the body, cleanse or prepare the body for removal. By honoring the body of our patient, we instinctively are physically expressing our care. Say out loud any last messages you wish to share.
5. Light a candle in honor of that person's life or send your good wishes to the person you are remembering or who is on your mind. The action step of lighting a candle, writing a letter or card, framing a photograph is a positive response to the experience of worry, pain, or loss.
6. If you have a shift of co-workers that is fairly consistent, you can establish a special place in your staff room or lounge where you can memorialize those patients who have touched you in a deep way. Have flowers, a candle, any significant objects, and a bulletin board where favorite photographs, drawings, poems, or thank you letters can be posted. This is another way to share the sorrow and the love with fellow workers without talking.
7. Establish a 'secret code' with co-workers whereby you can wear a visible symbol, only recognizable to them, that indicates you are grieving or having a rough day. This sign might be a small ribbon you can wear in a specific color, or even a special color of ribbon. It might be a special pin or piece of jewelry. Talk to co-workers and see what would be appropriate and life affirming for all of you.
8. Remember when you are journeying with people in pain, as the professional, you enter into the landscape of their life. When you are complete, it is important to step back on your life's road with all its frustrations, joys, and love. When you find yourself over-identifying with a patient, begin to notice all of the physical ways in which you are different from them: eyes, hair, body type, color, personality, face, and so forth. This is a quick way to gain some perspective. Remember, we have no right to 'rob' anybody of their pain. For whatever reason, that we may never understand, their circumstances are what they are. We can offer our unconditional, non-judgmental presence.
9. A quick way to release pain that has collected in your body is to imagine the pain draining out of the soles of your feet into the earth. Then imagine a healing light coming in from the top of your head, filling up your body with healing, comforting energy, completely immersing every cell of your body

© Copyright material from Darrow and Childs (2020), *Experiential Action Methods and Tools for Healing Grief and Loss-Related Trauma*, Routledge.

with love. It sometimes helps to take your shoes off and actually feel the earth beneath you, providing solid strength and gentle support.
10. Nature is a powerful healer and, even on a stormy day, it can be very refreshing to walk, even for a few minutes, in the fresh air. Animals are also amazingly healing in their free expression of unconditional love and regard, and their physical presence can anchor us.
11. Music is incredibly useful, because it bypasses the intellectual barriers of reason and goes straight to the heart. Use music to bring up feelings of grief deliberately, while you are in a safe place to cry, rage, write, or draw. Play songs or watch movies that remind you of specific people or situations you are missing. Find the music that expresses your deepest emotions. Play your own music. It can be a great avenue of expression. Everyone can sing, play rhythm instruments, or dance. It is a way to let your body act physically in a creative way. On the other side, if holiday, religious, or sentimental music is painful, give yourself permission to take a break from listening.
12. When the stress or emotions are held inside, you have a log jam. Sometimes it is more effective to watch a movie or read a book or news article about someone else's suffering. It can give permission to release the tension and overflow, without having to deal directly with your issue or incident. It makes it easier sometimes, when it is too difficult to face your problems directly. It can be a safety valve and a pressure release.
13. Talk with co-workers or friends who understand your profession. Attend a CISR or grief support session. Take a break and spend at least a few moments discussing your reactions, any memories of past incidents, and your sense of the outcome of your efforts.

Managing stress involves honoring the grief process—the natural response to any change or loss in our life—whether it is positive or negative.

Trauma Release Meditation

This meditation is an opportunity to acknowledge and release some of the trauma you may have experienced. This is a useful meditation immediately after surviving a critical incident. It is a time to re-center, re-group, and re-ground your mind, body, and spirit in the present moment.

First, find a safe and quiet place. Do not do this meditation while you are driving or operating any machinery. Either sit or lay down in a comfortable position. Become aware of your breathing. There is no need to change it; simply pay attention to the in and out of air, the flow of oxygen moving through your body.

Now, draw your attention to your favorite place. Close your eyes if this feels right and comfortable. This is very useful if it helps you to visualize and sink into this meditation. As you notice your breathing becoming more regular, you are aware of your body relaxing. You are completely supported by the chair or couch or floor. There is no need to support yourself by yourself. You are lovingly supported completely right now.

Now allow yourself to drink in the beauty of your favorite place through your five senses. Notice the sounds, sights, textures, aromas, colors, and feeling of your favorite place. Allow yourself to sink into the safety and comfort of your favorite place.

At this time acknowledge that you are safe, and you are OK. Become aware of your body sensations. Notice what is the most powerful right now. Ask yourself this question, even though it may change a few moments from now: "What is the most difficult right now?" What is affecting you the most? What has the most impact for you, right now? What is the most powerful sense? Is it what you have seen, what smells have stayed with you? What sounds? Textures? Or feelings? What has stuck with you in your awareness? Simply pay attention to what is true for you right now. No judgments, just acceptance and space for whatever is so for you right now.

Just allow yourself to create a safe container for whatever is going on for you. Even though you may have conflicting feelings and reactions, just allow the entire truth of what is. There is no need to critique, judge, or minimize the impact upon you. Acceptance of our reactions does not necessarily mean agreement. Feelings just are—they are not right or wrong.

As you are acknowledging this place, this state of being for you, remember that you are safe. You have survived. You have experienced a trauma that has brought awareness of the power of your presence on the earth right now in this moment. With every breath, realize that you, in this moment, are alive. You are a survivor. Experience the power and truth of that right now.

Allow yourself to take another deep cleansing breath, and listen to what you need right now to support you in surviving this incident. Do you need to talk with someone? Do you need to go home and hug your loved ones? Do you need to spend some time in nature? Do you need to write down your thoughts, reactions, or feelings? Do you need to connect with someone who may have survived the incident with you? Do you need to connect with a spiritual comfort anchor? Do you need to just allow for the reactions and thoughts that are coming up to be there? Even though we may be feeling angry, sad, withdrawn, or numb, it does not mean we have to act upon these reactions. They are what they are: simply feelings. And the more we allow them to be expressed and acknowledged, the more we defuse them, and lessen the impact they have on our lives, both now and in the future.

For our next step, become aware of anything, any thought, any feeling or reaction that might be a burden for you right now. Although you may not be able to release the entire burden, ask yourself, what am I willing to let go of right now? Maybe a piece of the pain, the guilt, the helplessness, the frustration,

158 Stress, Trauma, and CISM

the sadness, the numbness, the regret over anything unsaid or undone that may be weighing you down at this time. With the next breath, allow yourself to release the burden as you breathe out. Feel the weight being lifted out from your body and released back into the universe, where it is transformed into positive energy for the world to use.

And now, prepare yourself to be engulfed and enveloped by love and protection. From your highest spiritual source, call down the healing energy you need to be filled up and renewed. Imagine a wonderful light in the color that feels right for you this moment cascading down on you, from the tip of your head to the bottom of your feet and toes. You are completely surrounded by this soothing and powerfully healing light. Imagine you are in a cocoon of this energy three feet out in every direction from your body. You are totally surrounded in this radiant light. And everyone around you is affected positively by this beautiful aura around you. Your life flows effortlessly. Your interaction with others is smooth, loving, and fulfilling. You are claiming the beauty that is in your life now, even as you have survived this trauma.

You return your awareness to your breathing and find that you have come back from your favorite place and you are present here and now, feeling light and refreshed, rejuvenated and renewed. Your body feels completely integrated and grounded, while also feeling light and flexible. You take another deep and renewing breath, and move forward on the moment-by-moment journey of your life today, this hour, this moment, now… Remember what you need to do to take care of yourself. Be gentle with yourself and keep the loving presence of healing light around you and in your consciousness. Welcome back. And as you move forward in your activities in the world, do something healing and life affirming for yourself, something fun and lighthearted that connects you back to the good in your life. Welcome back. Welcome back.

Heart Meditation

We are taking a journey today, to the landscape of our heart. We rarely take time to be within this sacred land, where love is grown, as a seed into a flower, as a flower into a fruit, as a fruit into mulch to feed the earth, as the earth builds the seed from a dream of love in the heart.

Allow yourself to let go of the cares and worries of the day. Let your mind and body rest in these moments we are taking this journey. Become aware of your breathing—the slow ebb and flow of your breath as it inhales rich oxygen, as it exhales what is no longer needed. Each moment is rejuvenating your body and your life. There is no need to change the rhythm; simply pay attention to the natural way your body takes care of you in each moment. What does your breath tell you about where you are energetically right now? Allow yourself to close your eyes and settle your body into a comfortable position. Feel yourself being supported by the environment around you. Notice you are relaxing into the present moment. There are no worries or responsibilities. You are here, in total peace and complete relaxation.

Now, lift your hands to your heart and feel your heartbeat, as your heart pumps the blood to every cell in your body, bringing nourishment and removing waste. As you experience the drumbeat of your heart, know that every second, your heart works with your breath to bring you life. Rest in that automatic and wonderful way your heart takes care of you. Honor your heart, this moment, and your life.

Now we are going to envisage a road in front of you. This is the road to the landscape of your heart. As you begin walking on this road, notice what is around you. What are the colors, aromas, sounds, and textures of your landscape? What animals, plants, or scenery fill your image? Are you in the city, on the beach, at the desert, in the mountains, by a river or lake, near trees or a forest? Whatever is present for you, acknowledge it. This is the beginning awareness of the wisdom and depth of your heart.

As you walk down the path, you come across a dwelling. It can be a palace, a monastery, or a cave. What type of dwelling is it? This is the home of your heart. Go to the entrance way and gently open the door of your heart's dwelling. What do you see, hear, smell, or feel as you enter?

Now, as you are in the home of your heart, what appears in front of you? What does your heart look like? Who and what are in your heart's dwelling?

Now it is time to speak to your heart. Ask any question that has been in your consciousness. What does your heart say? How does your heart respond? There may be words, or simply intuitions, sensations, or thoughts that enter your awareness. Listen … listen … listen. Feel … feel … feel. Allow the truth of your heart to speak to you.

When you feel complete, thank your heart, for revealing itself to you and for entering into a dialogue. Before you leave this dwelling of your heart, notice that your heart has a gift to offer to you. Receive this gift as a reminder of your connection and relationship with your heart. In gratitude, take this gift as a remembrance of this sacred time with your heart.

As you leave to walk back down the path, take one last look at the home of your heart. And breathe … breathe … breathe …

Now your footsteps fall gently on the path, back through this inner landscape of your sacred life. Allow the joy, relief, or river of emotions to flow. This is your time to be in communion with all that is true for you right now.

As you feel ready, notice that the path leads back to the place you are right now. Allow yourself to stretch and move your body, becoming aware of your surroundings. Breathe and listen to your body's song; the rhythm of your heartbeat and breath as you enter into this reality of your life. Take the wisdom, the gifts, and the loving connection of your heart with you as you journey forward into the world.

And know you can always return to the landscape of your heart to share a moment of loving wisdom and deep sharing. In gratitude, we thank these moments of communion and reunion with our heart.

Stories from the Front Lines

Throughout the years, our Bay Area CISM Team has gathered many stories in the wake of providing CISR. Names and situations have been changed to protect confidentiality, but all participants have given permission for their stories to be shared. In fact, they have wanted to get the word out to other responders and caregivers that they are not alone.

Administrative Betrayal

Some years ago, a police officer shared his experience with an officer-involved shooting (OIS). What happened to him after the shooting was even more stressful than the shooting. His weapon was confiscated in front of the public and the media, with no replacement provided. He was transported in the back of a patrol unit and sequestered in an interrogation room at the police department for four hours, with no contact with his family. He was then placed on administrative leave for several months during his internal affairs investigation. He was subsequently cleared of wrongdoing. When he came back to work, no one would talk with him. This was a secondary trauma. He stated a powerful message: "I can handle it when the public doesn't like me, I can handle it when the media doesn't like me, but what I can't handle is when the very department that I put my life on the line for does not support me. That is the biggest betrayal."

So now, fast forward to more recent times. Procedures have changed. One recent incident of an OIS occurred with an officer who was freshly off field training. He was confronted and shot a suspect who was threatening the lives of several citizens. He was immediately removed from the scene and taken to a neutral location. His weapon was immediately replaced. His peer support officer was with him, and his

160 Stress, Trauma, and CISM

Lieutenant asked him if he would like anything to drink. The officer stated that he would love some hot chocolate. The Lieutenant went to several places to find hot chocolate, unsuccessfully. He finally went home to his spouse, who made a special pot of Oaxacan hot chocolate, which he brought to his officer. This officer now refers to the incident as 'my hot chocolate call'. He remembers the kind treatment that he received from his co-workers, which soothed the initial trauma he experienced. This kindness created meaning out of a difficult call.

Building resilience and hope in response to stress experienced by law enforcement personnel can be improved upon. There is much more we can do individually and in the workplace in partnership with healthcare professionals, including group interventions with CISM. When the trauma of critical incidents is handled correctly, our officers and their significant loved ones are better able to build meaning and purpose from the stress they survive together.

Our team has worked with officers across the state and the country. We were able to support officers and dispatchers after 9-11 and after other major disasters. There is one theme: when officers are cared for as human beings and structure is brought forth to take care of their needs, they can sustain life to a fulfilling retirement.

The following vignettes demonstrate themes in this chapter.

Dispatcher and the Eight-Year-Old Reporting a Home Invasion

Acknowledge/Express/Act/Reconnect

We worked with a 911 dispatcher who took a call from an eight-year-old, who reported that her mom had been beaten up. The dispatcher walked her through the process of medical support for her mom. The dispatcher told us that this was the best caller she had ever had in her career, and that she was touched by this call. Subsequently, it was discovered that the mom had died from her injuries. We were able to do a CISR for our dispatcher, and she felt heard and validated. Then a very powerful connection occurred. At our Healing Heart Group, one of our grief groups for families and their children in grief, Andrea, from the youngest group, approached me and said, "Janet, you work with the 911 people. Say thank you to my 911 lady. She helped me with my mom who died."

I realized that this might be the same incident as the one we responded to at the Communications Center, so I asked her how her mom died. She confirmed that it was a home invasion. I called our dispatcher and shared the message from Andrea. I then asked Cindy, our dispatcher, if she would like to contact Andrea directly. She affirmed that it would be healing to connect, and they met. After that, Cindy put Andrea up for a county Citizen's Hero award. On the Board of Supervisors floor, with the Sheriff describing the heroism of Andrea, Andrea suddenly left her seat, and walked up to the Sheriff and asked, "Don't you think my dispatcher should be giving me my award?" The sheriff was accommodating and allowed Cindy to present the award to Andrea. This is the magic of follow-through and completing action steps as inspiration arises. It also teaches us as a community how to acknowledge, express, act, and reconnect with each other in the midst and in the aftermath of critical incidents.

After Disaster: Finding Family/Spouse Support

Our CISM team did a critical stress response for family members and children of first responders after they returned from deployment after Hurricane Katrina.

We worked with the eight-year-old son of a first responder, after his father had been deployed with the USAR team. We asked him, "How do you know when your parent has had a bad day?" He immediately responded, "I can tell by how hard his feet hit the driveway when he comes home from work." When we inquired what he normally did when his dad came home, he stated, "I wait for him by the window near the front door. When he is in a bad mood, I run and hide." When we asked what he wanted to do, he made it very clear that he wanted to give his dad a hug.

Later in the day, we were debriefing the responders in the USAR team, and I approached the father of the little boy. I mentioned to him that I could not break confidentiality, but that his son seemed amazingly dialed into when he was having a bad day. He looked at me with annoyance and said. "He doesn't know at all when I am having a bad day. When it is a normal day, he is waiting by the window for me. When I have had a bad day, he is nowhere to be found." I offered to him an opportunity to have a discussion with his son about that very issue.

He called me up about a week later and reported that he and his son had worked out a plan for when he was having a bad day. When his day was rough, he would intentionally walk hard on the sidewalk up to his front door. His son would wait for his dad, and when he entered the doorway, his son would ask, "Hi, Daddy, thirty seconds or sixty?" Then whatever his dad replied, they would count up together, one to thirty or one to sixty. Then he would ask his dad, "One hug or two?" They had worked out a functional action step of providing support to each other.

This is the power of breaking the conspiracy of silence and stopping the default reaction of hiding in one's own overcoat of pain. Solutions can be found to create mutual support systems when we ask the questions: What is the most difficult right now? What do we need from each other right now? In families and in grief/crisis situations, it simply takes a moment, where safety is created to build healing.

Car Fire: Healing Action Steps

In the Los Angeles area, an officer was driving to a police funeral when he noticed a car fire on the freeway. Normally in these situations, people have already gotten out of the vehicle. However, when he pulled up to the scene, bystanders were yelling that people were still in the car. He radioed for assistance and immediately tried to get the people out of the car. He was unsuccessful with the passenger, as the car was fully engulfed in flames. However, he managed to extricate the driver and performed emergency medical procedures. She was airlifted to the hospital and died four hours later. He was left with the knowledge that both young women died as a result of the car fire.

He began to have symptoms of post-traumatic stress injury. He couldn't sleep, suffered repeated visual images of the car fire, and began drinking heavily. His dispatcher noticed the officer showing up for his shift disheveled and bleary-eyed. She told him to take a day off and encouraged him to come to the Bay Area CISM Team to get help.

In the CISR, he had the opportunity to acknowledge the various dimensions of his stress. He found out after the incident that the two young women had been sniffing nitrous oxide to get high. One of them decided to have a cigarette, and kaboom! The car exploded. With this added information, he was not only sad that he could not save them, he was extremely angry. The car could have exploded and injured or killed first responders trying to help.

We invited him to write an unfinished business letter to the young women. After five pages of intense expression of conflicting feelings, thoughts, and reactions, he put down his pen and stated, "I feel fifty pounds lighter. I had no idea I was carrying all of that in my backpack." We then asked him about doing an action step to bring meaning and a sense of resolution to the incident. We often call this the period at the end of the sentence.

162 Stress, Trauma, and CISM

When he returned to Southern California where the incident took place, he called us and shared his action step. He had gone back to the scene of the car fire and brought two red roses, one for each of the young victims of the fire. He placed them on the ground and declared, "I forgive you and I forgive me. I release you and I release me." When he had completed this action, he reported that he felt a great deal of peace and relief. It was not that the incident was forgotten. It was a way of making meaning out of the pain.

He thanked us, saying he felt he could move forward in his life and career. Three days later, he called us back again, telling us he had received a letter from the mother of the driver. She thanked him for rescuing her daughter so she could say goodbye to her in the hospital. The mother stated in her letter that she had been trying to write this message for months. The letter was dated on the same day that our officer did his action step with the roses. When we are able to do our action steps, it may free up the energy for others to be able to do what they need to do to bring a sense of completion to the trauma.

Dispatcher and the Elderly Caller

The Backpack Effect

A 911 dispatcher called our Bay Area CISM Team after experiencing a routine call from an elderly woman whose husband had probably died in his sleep. The dispatcher mobilized a response as soon as she could but realized that the husband had probably been dead for a number of hours before help arrived. She could not get the call out of her mind. She realized she needed to have a CISR around this call, although in most cases, this type of call would be considered routine. However, our Bay Area CISM Team teaches that any incident that affects us, either immediately or in the aftermath, is potentially a critical incident for us.

She asked if the responding officers could also come and they agreed, although both reported that it was a routine call. When in the CISR, our facilitator asked the dispatcher, "What hit you the hardest about this call?" She responded that it was the sound of the reporting party's voice.

"What about her voice?"

"She sounded just like my grandmother."

"In what way? How did this remind you of your grandmother?"

"When I was eleven years old, I was home alone with my grandmother and she dropped dead of a massive stroke in my arms. It took two hours for responders to get there and four hours for my family to get back home. I think I became a dispatcher to get responders there faster after a critical incident. Also, I was not allowed to go to the funeral because my family thought it would be too upsetting for me. So I never got to say goodbye to my grandma."

When the officers heard this story, the older officer spoke. "The old woman did not get to me, but the old man who died did. He reminded me of my uncle. My uncle was supposed to pin my badge on me at the graduation of my academy, but he dropped dead of a massive heart attack three days before the ceremony. I want to thank this wonderful dispatcher for calling us to attend this CISR, because I didn't say a word to anyone because it was just a routine call."

We asked the dispatcher and officer what action step they could take. The dispatcher decided to honor her grandmother with a celebration of her life and her love—twenty-six years after her death. She also checked in with her elderly caller to ask how she was doing and gave her resources for grief counseling at the Centre for Living with Dying. The elderly woman was so touched, she sent the dispatcher a bouquet of flowers and a box of designer chocolates.

The officer took his first badge to the military cemetery where his uncle was buried. As he buried his badge at his uncle's grave, he stated, "You couldn't pin the badge on me, but I can give you my first badge in honor of you, and all of the support you gave me to become a police officer."

Both responders were energized and renewed by performing these concrete action steps in the aftermath of their critical incident.

Warrior Ceremony after an Officer-Involved Shooting

Healing Support from Chosen Family

Ceremonies have been utilized over the span of human existence to bring meaning and resolution to major incidents, especially in the aftermath of trauma, death, crisis, illness, and grief. This work with a police officer is a powerful example of the healing and transforming nature of ceremony. Below is an example of ceremonial healing. The concept was gifted to us by one of our Native American responders, who is a member of our CISM Team.

Our CISM Team provided a critical incident response defusing support in the aftermath of an OIS, in which two officers were injured. The officer who fired the shots had the driver's license of the person he had been forced to shoot. He had kept it in his wallet for several months. It created a 'frozen moment', in which he kept reliving the seconds before the shooting, wishing he had been able to do something different.

We gathered together his trusted comrades; we performed a cleansing and releasing ceremony. The officer held the license and said everything he needed to say to the deceased. We then lit a fire in the fire pit. As he threw the license in the fire, the officer named what he wished to release. His comrades backed him up with affirmations. Each of his fellow officers named and affirmed a quality in him to sustain him as he moved forward in building his new normal. It was not only an affirmation, but a blessing and a strengthening of his net of support for the future. He was taken back into the 'tribe' and given meaningful support that only his fellow officers could provide.

Subsequently, we have been made aware of a wonderful program called Soul Injury Veteran and First Responders (www.soulinjury.org or www.OpusPeace.org). The Fallen Comrades Ceremony includes veterans' families and other important civilians to help veterans. While Memorial Day honors those who died in military service, the Fallen Comrades Ceremony honors those who survived and carry the burden of their dead comrades' memory. Based on Native American warrior welcoming-home rituals, the ceremony restores hope for healing the soul injury that veterans and first responders often carry. Safe sanctuary is provided for them to mourn the losses they have sustained, such as comrades who died in battle, loss of physical/mental health, loss of the self they had prior to the trauma, assault that occurred within their own ranks, or an unfair administrative action taken against them.

Hanging of an African American Man

The Backpack Effect

A police sergeant Charles, having responded to a hanging of an African American man, was left with a lingering unease, and the inability to get the image of the man out of his head. It was only by acknowledging that something was stuck in his consciousness that he could begin to process it. In a CISR, he was able to express the details that stayed in his awareness. The way the body of the man was hanging

164 Stress, Trauma, and CISM

reminded him of a memory. His great uncle, who had lived in Mississippi, had been lynched in a tree and found dead by his family. The sergeant was reminded of a Billie Holiday song, *Strange Fruit*. He realized he had never honored or said goodbye to his uncle. As an action step, Charles traveled back to his family's home in Mississippi and paid homage at the grave of his great uncle, erecting a marker, which stated "You are not forgotten. We honor your sacrifice, which gave us our freedom." Not only was this healing for him, but his entire family felt empowered and strengthened, which turned the memory of unspeakable pain into courage, strength, and hope.

The final step, the reconnect process, is as important as the first three. The reconnect grounds us into what is still good and meaningful in our lives, even in the aftermath of trauma, disaster, and grief. It also lifts us into the spiritual meaning of our struggles and losses. It can be as simple as eating something that we really enjoy or going out into nature and allowing the elements to soothe, comfort, inspire, and excite us into engagement with our lives. It can be reconnecting with people and pets who love us and to whom we can express our gratitude. It can just be a moment in which we are quiet, honoring our self for the work we have done with our pain to bring meaning.

Approaching the Healing Journey

A dispatcher, Bianca, demonstrated our four components to healing. She was monitoring an officer in pursuit on an unmarked fire road. She heard his car crash and tumble down into a ravine. The last words she heard her officer say was that he was bleeding from his head—and then the radio went dead. She did not know what happened to her officer, but her immediate visualizations were alarming. Her three thoughts: he had bled out from his injuries, his car had rolled over and crushed him, or the suspect had doubled back to the officer and shot him. She thought he had died. Meanwhile, she had to mobilize support to find him. This all happened within seconds. An intuitive sergeant happened to look down the ravine. He discovered the officer's car and called for life flight to rescue the officer, who was taken to the hospital in a serious condition.

If we use our triage questions, what is the first thing Bianca needed to do to take care of her stress? She needed to see the officer, to see that he was OK. Unfortunately, she had to work until the end of her shift. When she told her Lieutenant about her wish to visit the officer, he stated, "Good job responding and finding the officer. We don't need you any more." To which she responded, "You may not need to see me, but I need to see the officer." When she went to visit the officer, he thanked her for coming, exclaiming, "You are the only face I want to see. I was in serious trouble. Thank you for saving my life."

Bianca was able to acknowledge her stress, to express the details of her trauma, and to complete an action step, by visiting the officer.

This is sometimes not the end of the stress cycle. As time went on, Bianca felt the need to discuss the details of her visualizations about the officer that night. She came to our Bay Area CISM Team for a CISR and learned, as she told the story again, that she was stuck in the imagined picture she had. As she described the details, she experienced the frozen moment/trauma of her visualizations. Then she asked the officer to take her to the scene and tell her exactly what happened. This fieldtrip enabled her to release her picture of what could have happened with the real scenario of what had actually happened.

By doing the four-component process—acknowledge, express, act, reconnect—we uncover and peel layers of stress and unresolved trauma, until we reach the core issue. By expressing the details of the imprinting that has occurred, we can identify an action step. This action step can be done solo, or it might be accomplished with both internal and external support systems.

The Conspiracy of Silence

We live in a death- and grief-denying society. Many cultures demand that we deal with our issues of grief, loss, and illness on our own. We typically get three days' bereavement leave for the death of an immediate family member in the workplace and one day if you are a child in our school system in the state of California. This gives a clear message that we are to be 'over it' by the time we return; thus, we will most likely be isolated as we navigate the grief journey. If the deceased was diagnosed with a stigmatized disease, such as HIV, or the death had controversy, such as suicide, homicide, or an unusual accident, we are further marginalized and alienated from natural support systems.

The Centre for Living with Dying is dedicated to breaking the conspiracy of silence and dispelling the condition of isolation in the aftermath. So, how do we deal with the conspiracy of silence? Here are some steps to manage the aftermath of difficult or controversial loss. These circumstances arise, for example, when we are asked to provide support at a school, and the cause of death is controversial (suicide, homicide, or accidental, e.g., autoerotic asphyxiation) and we are not given permission to tell the truth about the death. Likewise, sometimes we are asked to support the family of a seriously ill person, and we are not allowed to address the full nature of the illness, or the fact that it is life threatening.

Tools to Respond after Controversial Deaths

- Establish guidelines of confidentiality.
- Establish a practice of no critique of actions or reactions.
- Validate fear.
- Build trust.
- Be honest:
  - If there are no details of the death, illness, etc.
  - If the specifics of the cause of death are unknown.
  - If the cause of death is still being determined.
  - If there is no permission to discuss the details of the death.
- Open up discussion:
  - How did you find out about the death?
  - When was the last time you had contact with the person?
  - What are the different reactions you have upon hearing of the death/illness?
  - What goes through your mind as you focus on the news of the death?
  - What's been the hardest about this death/crisis?
  - What action steps do you need to do to bring some healing to this tragedy?
  - How can you support each other through this critical incident?
- Validate, validate, validate: how hard it is to not know the details of the death, and how difficult it is for the imagination to run wild. Bring it back to the present moment. This is what we do have control over—how we can support each other with as much caring and loving regard as possible.

Remember: Reaching out to others for support and being easy on ourselves can enable us to survive the pain.

CISM: Grief Support in the Technological Age

Many times, in creating a safe place for grieving and traumatized individuals, media and social media can create secondary trauma in the aftermath—or it can be a tool for connection. Although there are valid

166 Stress, Trauma, and CISM

concerns about using social media, email, and text as a means of death or trauma notification, this avenue of communication can also provide support.

Texting is a good example of a tool that can be utilized for initial, intermediate, and ongoing support of people facing trauma. Many years ago, I (Janet) was personally opposed to using text as a communication tool. I have now learned from experience that, for some people, particularly introverted, technologically savvy, thinking types, texting can be a safe and comforting avenue to give and receive support. Texting is a mainstay of communication amongst our youth and many emotional support and therapy services that now utilize text. The platform gives the gift of time to meditate upon what has been written, and also the option to respond when and if you are ready. When in person or by phone, there is an expectation to immediately respond, with text and email, we have the ability to sit with the shared information which might allow more empathy and freedom of expression to occur. In the context of this book, we wish to acknowledge that we are not experts on this topic. Yet it is one that needs to be studied and explored as we move forward in the caregiving community.

I had the privilege of supporting a young man, who was studying in the area to become a social worker. Shaun's mother had been murdered in addition to him having suffered other past losses and trauma. I had seen him a couple of times in person and we had developed a good therapeutic connection; however, he was uncomfortable talking about his experience face to face. After determining that it was a more comfortable communication method for him, we began to text. The texts I received from him were poetically descriptive of his inner process and he was able to articulate the range of emotions and experiences. Shaun wrote a poem/rap in honor of his mom and shared that with me in the body of a text. He reported in real time about his action steps when he returned to his home state to honor his mom and support his devastated family. We were even able to utilize action methods with the empty-chair technique for him to have a dialogue with his mom, through text. We have learned that it can be a tool for healing, connection, and transformation.

In working with a family, in the aftermath of the suicide of their son, we discovered that one of the best ways friends and loved ones could support them over the long term was to give a quick and short text message of comfort and camaraderie, every day or couple of days. It became an anchor of grounding support when difficult moments arose during the day.

Text is also a way we can honor anniversary dates by sending a quick message of hope and healing, demonstrating that we have remembered this could be a potentially rough time.

As we write this, we are responding to shootings at our iconic Garlic Festival in the Silicon Valley area, followed by more shootings throughout the country. We are reminded of the power of compassionate presence and deep commitment to reach out in these times of suffering and trauma. The random acts of kindness and outreach, the acts of bravery and courage, and the deep tenacity to hold to our commitment to each other, our community, and our world touch my soul in a deep way and reminds me why we do the sometimes challenging, deeply fulfilling, powerfully healing work we do. CISM truly makes a different in so many ways.

Bibliography

Everly, S. Jr., & Mitchell, J.T. (1999). *Critical incident stress management: a new era and standard of care in crisis intervention* (2nd ed.). Howard County, MD: Chevron.

Gilmartin, K. (2002). *Emotional survival for law enforcement: a guide for officers and their families*. Tuscon, AZ: E-S Press.

Kirschman, E. (2018). *I love a cop: what police families need to know* (3rd ed.). New York: Guilford Press.

Lansing, K.M. (2012). *Rite of return: coming back from duty induced PTSD*. Chattanooga, TN: High Ground Press.

Levine, P. (2005). *Healing trauma: a pioneering program for restoring wisdom to the body*. Boulder, CO: Sounds True.

van der Kolk, B. (2014). *The body keeps the score: brain, mind, and body in the healing of trauma*. New York: Penguin Books.

van Dernoot Lipsky, L., & Burk, C. (2009). *Trauma stewardship: an everyday guide to caring for self while caring for others*. San Francisco, CA: Berrett-Koehler.

CHAPTER 21

GRIEF TRAINING FOR CLINICIANS AND CAREGIVERS

Listening, just listening, and holding another's story with loving presence and compassion may be the most important gift that can be given to a person overwhelmed by grief. We give this article to our grief volunteers.

Listening as Healing
Margaret Wheatley, December 2001
Reprinted with permission from Lion's Roar

You are reading this in December, but I have written this just a few days after September 11th, 2001. I have tried to imagine what the world feels like now, two months later, what else might have happened, what has changed, how each of us feels, if we are more divided or more connected. In the absence of a crystal ball, I look to the things I believe to be true in all times and for most situations. And so I choose to write about one of these enduring truths: great healing is available when we listen to each other.

Listening is such a simple act. It requires us to be present, and that takes practice, but we don't have to do anything else. We don't have to advise, or coach, or sound wise. We just have to be willing to sit there and listen. If we can do that, we create moments in which real healing is available. Whatever life we have experienced, if we can tell our story to someone who listens, we find it easier to deal with our circumstances.

I have seen the healing power of good listening so often that I wonder if you've noticed it also. There may have been a time when a friend was telling you such a painful story that you became speechless. You couldn't think of anything to say, so you just sat there, listening closely, but not saying a word. And what was the result of your heartfelt silence, of your listening?

A young black South African woman taught some of my friends a profound lesson about listening. She was sitting in a circle of women from many nations, and each woman had the chance to tell a story from her life. When her turn came, she began quietly to tell a story of true horror—of how she had found her grandparents slaughtered in their village. Many of the women were Westerners, and in the presence of such pain, they instinctively wanted to do something. They wanted to fix, to make it better, anything to remove the pain of this tragedy from such a young life. The young woman felt their compassion, but also felt them closing in. She put her hands up, as if to push back their desire to help. She said: "I don't need you to fix me. I just need you to listen to me."

She taught many women that day that being listened to is enough. If we can speak our story, and know that others hear it, we are somehow healed by that. During the Truth and Reconciliation Commission hearings in South Africa, many of those who testified to the atrocities they had endured under apartheid would speak of being healed by their own testimony. They knew that many people were listening to their story. One young man who had been blinded when a policeman shot him in the face at close range said: "I feel what has brought my eyesight back is to come here and tell the story.

I feel what has been making me sick all the time is the fact that I couldn't tell my story. But now it feels like I've got my sight back by coming here and telling you the story."

Why is being heard so healing? I don't know the full answer to that question, but I do know it has something to do with the fact that listening creates relationship. We know from science that nothing in the universe exists as an isolated or independent entity. Everything takes form from relationships, be it subatomic particles sharing energy or ecosystems sharing food. In the web of life, nothing living lives alone.

Our natural state is to be together. Though we keep moving away from each other, we haven't lost the need to be in relationship. Everybody has a story, and everybody wants to tell their story in order to connect. If no one listens, we tell it to ourselves and then we go mad. In the English language, the word for 'health' comes from the same root as the word for 'whole'. We can't be healthy if we're not in relationship. And 'whole' is from the same root word as 'holy'.

Listening moves us closer, it helps us become more whole, more healthy, more holy. Not listening creates fragmentation, and fragmentation is the root of all suffering. Archbishop Desmond Tutu describes this era as a time of 'radical brokenness' in all our relationships. Anywhere we look in the global family we see disconnection and fear of one another. As one example, how many teenagers today, in many lands, state that no one listens to them? They feel ignored and discounted, and in pain they turn to each other to create their own subcultures. I've heard two great teachers, Malidoma Somž from Burkino Faso in West Africa, and Parker Palmer from the United States, both make this comment: "You can tell a culture is in trouble when its elders walk across the street to avoid meeting its youth." It is impossible to create a healthy culture if we refuse to meet, and if we refuse to listen. But if we meet, and when we listen, we reweave the world into wholeness. And holiness.

This is an increasingly noisy era—people shout at each other in print, at work, on TV. I believe the volume is directly related to our need to be listened to. In public places, in the media, we reward the loudest and most outrageous. People are literally clamoring for attention, and they'll do whatever it takes to be noticed. Things will only get louder until we figure out how to sit down and listen. Most of us would welcome things quieting down. We can do our part to begin lowering the volume by our own willingness to listen.

A school teacher told me how one day a sixteen-year-old became disruptive—shouting angrily, threatening her verbally. She could have called the authorities—there were laws to protect her from such abuse. Instead, she sat down, and asked the student to talk to her. It took some time for him to quiet down, as he was very agitated and kept pacing the room. But finally, he walked over to her and began talking about his life. She just listened. No one had listened to him in a long time. Her attentive silence gave him space to see himself, to hear himself. She didn't offer advice. She couldn't figure out his life, and she didn't have to. He could do it himself once she had listened.

I love the biblical passage: "Whenever two or more are gathered, I am there." It describes for me the holiness of moments of real listening. The health, wholeness, holiness of a new relationship forming. I have a T-shirt from one conference that reads: "You can't hate someone whose story you know." You don't have to like the story, or even the person telling you their story. But listening creates a relationship. We move closer to one another.

I would like to encourage us all to play our part in the great healing that needs to occur everywhere. Think about whom you might approach—someone you don't know, don't like, or whose manner of living is a mystery to you. What would it take to begin a conversation with that person? Would you be able to ask them for their opinion or explanation, and then sit quietly to listen to their answer? Could you keep yourself from arguing, or defending, or saying anything for a while? Could you encourage them to just keep telling you their version of things, their side of the story?

It takes courage to begin this type of conversation. But listening, rather than arguing, also is much easier. Once I'd practiced this new role a few times, I found it quite enjoyable. And I got to learn things I never would have known had I interrupted or advised.

I know now that neither I nor the world changes from my well-reasoned, passionately presented arguments. Things change when I've created just the slightest movement toward wholeness, moving closer to another through my patient, willing listening.

Your Caring Presence
(Ways of effectively providing support to others)

1. Be honest about your own thoughts, concerns, and feelings—particularly your helplessness—and your honest desire to support in whatever manner best meets their needs.
2. When in doubt, ask questions:
   - How is that for you?
   - How do you feel right now?
   - Can you tell me more about that?
   - Am I intruding?
   - What do you need?
   - What's been the most difficult for you?
   - When is the hardest time of day?
3. When you are responding to a person facing a crisis situation, be sure to use statements such as:
   I feel…I believe…I would want/need…I acknowledge…
   Say something rather than nothing. Let them know it's good to see them. Gently acknowledge the loss, rather than ignoring it.
   What not to say:
   - You should/shouldn't…
   - I know just how you feel…
   - Everything will be OK. Don't worry, be sad, cry, be angry, scared, etc.—these are statements that may not give the person the opportunity to express his/her own unique needs and feelings.
4. Stay in the present as much as possible. Examples:
   - What do you need right now?
   - What would best support you right now?
   - How is that for you right now?
5. Listening is profoundly healing. You don't have to make it better. You don't have to have the answers. You don't have to take away the pain. It's their pain. One has to experience it in one's own time and in one's own way.
6. People in crisis need to know they have decision-making power. It may be appropriate to support them in exploring options and/or alternatives.
7. Offer any practical assistance you feel comfortable giving. Offering to take care of the small details of daily living is particularly comforting to people in crisis. It relieves them of one more burden. Again, ask permission, and offer specific suggestions of help, such as doing laundry, bringing dinner on a certain night, vacuuming, doing dishes, and so on.
8. If the situation warrants it, feel free to refer the individual to an additional appropriate agency. Help them to build a network of support services.
9. Reach out beyond the initial stages with cards, letters, or phone calls to check in. This validates the long-term grief process and lets them know you care.

© Copyright material from Darrow and Childs (2020), *Experiential Action Methods and Tools for Healing Grief and Loss-Related Trauma*, Routledge.

Different Cultural Responses to Loss and Grief

Definition of culture: The integrated patterns of human behavior that include thoughts, communications, actions, customs, beliefs, values, and institutions of racial, ethnic, religious, or social groups.

People who provide support are influenced by their primary culture as well as the one in which they currently live. Many of our automatic perceptions will be based on these two frames.

Points to Remember

- Try to release cultural assumptions and ethno-centric perceptions of how death and grief occur. Be open to gain wisdom from clients and respond to what is needed in the present moment. Enter into a partnership with grieving people by collaborating with them to determine what is the best and most helpful action.
- Get a feel for those participating in the preparatory grief, death, and aftermath. How are they responding? Empathize.
- What are the philosophies about death, dying, and grief in their culture? For example, what happens to the soul and personality? What are the beliefs around a deity or higher power?
- How do people learn about death, dying, and grief as children, including behavior, traditions, taboos, values, and attitudes?
- What are the rituals, ceremonies, and actions that reflect the culture and its values in the death and dying process?
- What happens immediately after death? What is done with the body? The funeral or grief ceremony? Burial?
- What ceremonies or acknowledgments happen at intervals in the grief process after the death? What are these time frames and what is done?
- How has acculturation affected the grief rituals, responses, behaviors, and social support? For example, what if certain ceremonies cannot be completed in the primary culture? Or perhaps are overly expensive? What is the aftermath? What can be done as a substitute action step?
- We can learn about grief from several sources from different cultures, but the most powerful wisdom comes from the people we are serving. We can educate ourselves about different cultural traditions but remember there are also family traditions and community traditions. All need to be validated and supported. When in doubt, focus on the family traditions.
- Be careful about judging grief expressions: muted, excessive grief, somatization, or violent grief.
- Explore the meanings of grief and death and also be aware of the multiple losses (job, home, friends, traditions, etc.) that can occur in the aftermath of death, particularly for families from a different country or culture.
- Death and grief outside of the mainstream: homicide, suicide, AIDS death, for example is minimized, and can cause specific secondary trauma.
- Grief is a normal reaction to the death of a loved one, but individuals from culturally diverse groups in our countries may be grieving for significant losses on a chronic basis. Such populations may be dealing simultaneously with the loss of their homeland, personal belongings, family members, economic status, professional identity, cultural traditions, language, and sense of self. The chronic and deep-seated nature of such unresolved grief may complicate the bereavement process in terms of intensity and duration. Not only will culturally diverse populations grieve differently over the death of a loved one, but they may be grieving for other significant losses at the same time.

172 Training for Clinicians and Caregivers

- There are a variety of ways that people and cultures perceive death, and this affects how they assign meaning and cope with loss. Typically, the time and depth of relationship will determine the depth of the grief response. As deeply as we love, so do we grieve.
- Lack of cultural understanding and sensitivity to cultural diversity in death and grief causes more problems than language barriers.

Tips for Response

- Many cultures do not feel comfortable sharing the intimate emotions and thoughts in their grief with people who are not familiar with their culture.
- The workplace is usually not a safe place to talk about personal issues or feelings. If you are from a different culture than the mainstream, there is a tendency to feel isolated, as well as fearful of judgment about how you are handling the loss.
- Around the world, there are many rich cultural traditions for healing loss and coming together as family and community in the grief journey. Many times, individuals will give up the root traditions in order to more fully assimilate into the American mainstream culture. This can cause conflict in a family, or even within an individual, when choosing which traditional customs to use, integrate, or let go.
- When interacting with persons whose culture is unfamiliar to you, be as gentle and non-intrusive as possible, while letting them know you care and wish to support them. Ask questions about issues or customs you are unfamiliar with, as well as appropriate ways you can support the person and their family during the grief process.
- Another way to communicate concern and caring is through a handwritten note. It can be very brief and simple. A note acknowledges the person's loss and gives permission for them to grieve. If possible, avoid expressing your own cultural/religious viewpoints in the letter, especially if they are different from the grieving person's. By being non-judgmental and supportive, you give the gift of human kindness.
- Even in the same culture or religion, there are individual differences. Be willing to listen to the specifics of what each person and/or each family needs to do. Sharing the details empowers and supports them in whatever they need to do to heal.
- Most of all, be sensitive to the changing needs of the grieving person and try not to take their moods personally. Be yourself and be honest.

Worksheet for Bridging the Gap between Self and Other

Explore the dynamics of cultural humility and how we can raise our awareness of separation and judgment when we are sitting with a client.

Cultural Humility

- Value diversity.
- Cultivate the capacity for cultural self-assessment.
- Be conscious of the dynamics inherent when cultures interact.
- Integrate cultural knowledge.
- Adapt your caring response to reflect an understanding of diversity between and within cultures.

How You Identify Self

- Economic status
- Political point of view
- Ethnic origin
- Sexual orientation
- Partnership status
- Gender
- Work/professional role
- Relationship roles
- Spiritual orientation
- Life goals
- Health/wellness attitudes
- Background: grief, trauma, and stress events
- How do others respond to you?
- Within your culture? From another cultural perspective?
- How do you identify 'other'?
- Who do you consider to be different from you? What is their background?
- Who, or what situation would be the most difficult or frightening to respond to?
- What experiences have you had in working with people from ethnic groups, socio-economic classes, religions, age groups, or communities different from your own?
- What were these experiences like? Give an example of a particularly difficult experience and a particularly rewarding experience from working with a person from a very different background/life view.

How can we be a bridge for healing, while taking care of self? Determine 'buttons', or 'hot spots', that might create distance. For example, if someone has grown up in an environment where smoking was an accepted behavior, and has asthma as a result of second-hand smoke, he/she might have an issue with smokers. Knowing that, how can the person create the safe environment for both in counseling? He or she might express the need for a smoke-free setting for meetings. The person is building a bridge for a deeper connection, by setting appropriate boundaries. We invite trainees to consider their own buttons and steps to establish safeguards:

- List of potential issues
- List of possible safeguards and action steps.

Immediate Responses in the Crisis Response to Potential Suicide

- Sounds like things are kind of rough right now.
- Can you tell me more about what's happening?
- What's hitting the hardest right now?
- You must have cared about _____ a lot.
- It's not easy dealing with all the losses and changes that are happening.
- What do you miss right now?
- I can relate to what you are going through. But I don't know what it's like for you. Can you tell me?
- I know that I can't control or stop you from hurting yourself. You have the power. That is always an option. I'm hoping we can take a look at other options as well, given that you always have the choice.
- If you were in my shoes, what would you ask right now?
- What is the question I most need to ask you right now?
- If you were giving advice to someone in your shoes, what would you say?
- I know I can't fix it for you, but together we can talk about options.
- You have the most wisdom about what you need.
- Let's focus on what is happening right now.
- I'm very worried/scared that you are very serious. Let's work together now to make it safe. What can we do?
- I'm really thirsty/hungry. How about you? Let's take a short break and get some food.
- Let's take a deep breath together. You've been through a lot.
- Tell me about your hobbies. What do you like to do for fun?
- Listen to me. We are working together on this. Work with me.
- You know, I don't know much about what is happening. Can you tell me what's the roughest right now?
- You know, you are having a natural reaction to a lot of stress and grief in your life.
- Sometimes, we get hit by stuff in our past ... We call it the backpack. So, when something hits us in the present time, we are reminded of what happened before.
- We only have to deal with one issue, one feeling at a time.
- Emotional trauma is just like a physical injury to the body. You wouldn't walk around with a broken arm and leave it uncared for. The same goes for a broken heart.
- I am here for you to help work this out.
- Sometimes, things can become overwhelming. I know it's not easy to do, but let's focus on what is in front of you right now.
- Are you thinking of hurting yourself? Have you thought about suicide? Is life so hard right now that you've thought about ending it? Are you thinking about killing yourself?
- What family members do you have? Do you have any kids/children? Who are the people that are close to you?
- Sometimes, when I am in a bad place, it's hard to reach out to people who might care about me. I kind of want to protect them, so I don't let them see my pain. I'm wondering, has that happened for you?
- When was the last time you had something to drink (not alcohol) or something to eat?

© Copyright material from Darrow and Childs (2020), *Experiential Action Methods and Tools for Healing Grief and Loss-Related Trauma*, Routledge.

An Activity for Working with Trauma after Violence

Violence is an energy that is likely to touch all of us at some point in our lifetime. It is a physical reality that can stay with us for a long time and it can totally change our beliefs, self-esteem, and security in the world. It is imperative that we talk about the physical presence of violence and fear as we gradually work to regain our power and our purpose in life. When working with violence or traumatic incidents, it is useful to explore feelings, thoughts, and perceptions of violence: What does violence mean to you? Here are a series of questions to explore in writing, drawing, and dialogue:

1. How do you define violence?
2. What would you consider to be a violent act?
3. Have you experienced violence in your past? What are your memories of that time? How did you respond? How did you feel? How did others respond to you?
4. How do you feel/respond when you hear of a violent death?
5. Have you ever felt violent or had violent thoughts or fantasies? If so, how did you respond to those feelings?
6. How do you feel about and respond to an individual whose loved one has died suddenly or violently? Describe what would be most difficult or fearful for you in being with such a person.
7. How do you take care of yourself in the aftermath of violence?

© Copyright material from Darrow and Childs (2020), *Experiential Action Methods and Tools for Healing Grief and Loss-Related Trauma*, Routledge.

Death Notification/Trauma Notification

- Accurate information:
  - Disposition of incident
  - Victim's name—correct pronunciation
  - Accurate identification of relatives—next of kin
- Attire—understated professional—muted colors
- Breathing and preparation before notification
- Roles of notifiers
- Identify self:
  - Identify person: Are you the family of_____?
- May we come in?
  - Get the person to sit down if possible
  - Find out who is in the house, i.e., children
- We have some hard/difficult news/information to share
- Discuss progression of event/incident:
  - For example: Your loved one was in an accident; they were transported to the hospital. Everything was done for them to help them survive. Unfortunately, they died.
- Explain in three different ways/at three different times that their loved one has died.
- Give information to the survivor: what happens to the body, and so on, to the best of your ability. Make your responses short and clear.
- If asked about suffering, one of the truths about traumatic injury or death is that the body naturally goes numb as a survival instinct, so the pain we may imagine our loved one going through might be more profound than what actually occurred for them.
- Share any last words from the victim that were positive for the family/loved ones. They will hang on to those words in the long grief process afterwards and derive comfort from them.
- Mobilize resources to be with the loved ones.
- Assure them that their grief reactions are normal and natural, no matter how crazy they may seem.
- Remember to debrief yourself and each other after the notification.

Refer loved ones to ongoing support agencies, such as grief counseling programs or advocacy groups, victim assistance, Mothers Against Drunk Driving, or local United Way.

Finally, when you leave, assure them that their grief response is normal—and that you care about the death of their loved one. Even though you deal with trauma every day, their loss is important. Most of all, demonstrate that you care by being there as a non-judgmental support.

Bibliography

Neimeyer R.A. (ed.) (2012). *Techniques of grief therapy: creative practices for counseling the bereaved.* New York: Routledge.
Wheatley, M. (2001). Listening as healing. Shambhala Sun (now Lion's Roar Foundation). Halifax, Nova Scotia, Canada: Lion's Roar Foundation.
Worden, J.W. (2009). *Grief counseling and grief therapy* (4th ed.). New York: Springer.

CONCLUSION

Final Thoughts

The essence of this guide is to support people who work in the field of grief and loss-related trauma. We hope this work will ultimately help bereaved people and those affected by loss-related trauma to claim ownership and control of their own healing. In a word, the key to this work is love. Connection to the love that existed before loss and the love of family and friends is a powerful resource for healing, guidance, and support to find a new normal.

The grief groups at the Centre for Living with Dying offer soothing compassion and interpersonal connection. Groups catalyze transformation; they break the conspiracy of silence about loss, trauma, and grief in our society. The way we attend to grief, both personally and with each other, informs the spirit of compassionate response we bring to life's changes and challenges.

In this guide, we offer a variety of tools to manage stress and grief. We have included the handouts we provide to clients. These provide helpful information and normalization of the process and components of grief and we give readers permission to use them in work with individuals and groups. In addition, we include effective strategies in dealing with these life issues—culled from the forty-plus years of experience in helping children and adults face grief, loss, serious illness, and stress at the Centre for Living with Dying.

We found that talking is sometimes not enough to transform grief. Telling the stories of loss touches on the pain but does not create insights to transform how that pain is held. Action methods which emerge out of psychodrama principles and techniques are a multi-dimensional response to grief. They engage mind, heart, and soul and often result in new insights. They are effective in group and individual process.

We also include tools for coping and stress management for first responders and caregiving professionals that we use in our Bay Area Critical Incident Stress Management (CISM) Team. Caregivers and responders on the front lines are the first contact with trauma. They play a critical role in our community. Our CISM program provides support and training for first responders. An essential aspect of this support is working with and clearing first responders' 'backpack' of past losses, so that they can be compassionately and fully present.

For readers who wish to use action methods in their work with grief and loss-related trauma, we encourage further study in psychodrama theory and methods. There are numerous psychodrama training programs throughout the U.S. and many other countries. In addition, we invite you to attend trauma and CISM workshops.

Let us not forget the deep questions of the soul and spirit that emerge in the wake of traumatic and painful incidents:

- What is the purpose of my life? Of this event?
- How do I survive? Now? Later?
- What do I believe? About myself? About the universe?
- How can I be fully immersed in every moment of precious life I have?

178 Conclusion: Final Thoughts

We leave you to explore these questions, to discuss, to meditate upon, and to experience what arises. May your life be richer, and may you gain the capacity to reach every being you interact with, bringing the aromatic fragrance of hope, of survival, and ultimately of love. This is the deep work we are called to bring to ourselves and to the world.

In deep gratitude for all you are and all you bring.

Lusijah and Janet

APPENDIX I

RESEARCH OVERVIEW OF PSYCHODRAMA

Historically, psychodrama as an effective therapeutic modality has needed more validation. According to Kipper and Ritchie (2003):

Questions concerning the scientific basis of the clinical application of psychodramatic techniques have been raised primarily because of the infrequency of research publications that validate the clinical observations.

Four investigators have published studies (D'Amato & Dean, 1988; Kellermann, 1982; Kipper, 1978; Rawlinson, 2000) that pointed out that, although there are positive indications about the efficacy of psychodrama, including changing maladaptive behaviors, building empathy for others, decreasing problematic symptoms of various disorders, and increasing well-being, many studies lack methodological rigor. In the Kipper and Ritchie (2003) meta-analysis of twenty-five experimentally designed studies, they concluded that clinical improvement with use of psychodrama was similar to or better than what has been commonly reported for group psychotherapy. They also concluded that the specific psychodrama techniques of doubling and role reversal are effective therapeutic interventions. Elliott et al. (1998) found that psychodrama was as effective as psychodynamic and cognitive behavioral therapy (CBT) modalities and could be considered a best treatment for survivors of trauma.

More recent literature has focused on defining consensus techniques used in classical psychodrama. Cruz et al. (2016,2018) performed a review of books and articles, identifying eleven core techniques: soliloquy, doubling, mirror position, role reversal, resistance interpolation, sculpture, social atom, intermediate objects, games, sociometry, and role training. These have achieved consensus among practitioners and will hopefully form a basis for future research evaluation of psychodrama techniques. Fortunately, since the beginning of the twenty-first century, more articles and books have examined the use of psychodrama with specific populations and issues, including adjustment disorders, attachment disorders, substance abuse, mood disorders, psychosis, and trauma.

Among the difficulties of research on the efficacy of psychodrama, and for that matter most other therapeutic modalities, are questions posed by Gonzalez et al. (2018).

Are specific therapeutic models and schools more efficient than others? Does the person of the therapist make a difference? What is the importance of the client's characteristics? How should we measure the impacts of treatment? Is psychotherapy, as a practice, becoming more effective in general over the years? What is the role of deliberate practice in the improvement of the therapists?

Meta-analysis studies indicate that there is a preponderance of articles and books by clinicians based on 'in the trenches' observations, including this book. While controlled study with acceptable questions and criteria is needed to gain widespread academic acceptance, in the field, the results of using action methods drive continuation of its use. In our own work, we clearly witness relief of symptoms among individuals suffering from grief. There are two issues (at least) with performing rigorous studies of the efficacy of psychodrama. The first is that clinicians themselves create a variable that cannot be controlled. Each clinician is different. Given this reality, how does one set a control comparing different types of group psychotherapy? Secondly, the Heisenberg uncertainty principle serves as a metaphor here. The need for defined measurement with specific questions and criteria results in a change in the system. Specifically, the required facilitator/director spontaneity to follow the client is a fundamental aspect of psychodrama, choosing—in the moment—which tool or technique to use. Changes or restriction in the room for spontaneity and clinical judgment of the facilitator/director of psychodrama may well serve to diminish the validity of the study. The relationship between spontaneity and good outcome is apparent in looking at many of the vignettes in this book. This observation does not diminish the desirability of studies that validate psychodrama that meet the bar of methodological rigor, however; it just points out the difficulties and challenges of doing so. Relevant controls, assessment criteria, and questions that allow flexibility for clinical judgment of psychodrama are needed.

Elliott (2002) suggested three critical questions in his psychodrama work with single case studies:

1. Are individuals in psychotherapy changing?
2. Is therapy responsible for change?
3. What in therapy is causing change?

These important questions focus on the specific tools or techniques; however, because of the nature of psychotherapy, they do not contain a true negative control. One cannot match up subjects who share identical issues with identical emotional/psychological temperaments to accurately compare and demonstrate a causal relationship of growth and change with psychodrama (and for that matter any therapeutic modality). At best controls are statistical, akin to an epidemiological approach.

Encounter Groups: First Facts (Lieberman et al., 1973) was the seminal study that looked at the effectiveness of group process. This exhaustive study compared groups with facilitators of diverse orientations, including classic T-group, gestalt, psychodrama, psychoanalytic, transactional analysis, eclectic, Rogerian, synanon (aggressive, confrontational), personal growth, and tape-led groups. There were two groups of each type with different facilitators for each orientation. The results demonstrated that it was not possible to definitively rank the best approach. Rather, the study defined important qualities in the facilitator that made for successful groups with high engagement and participant learning. The four facilitator qualities were:

1. Emotional stimulation—the emphasis is on revealing feelings, challenging, confronting.
2. Caring —offering friendship, affection; leaders express warmth, support, and praise, and demonstrate real concern for members of the group.
3. Meaning attribution—leaders provide explanations about how to understand and interpret, and frameworks for change.
4. Executive function—limit seeking, rule setting, goal setting, management of time and pacing or stopping, suggesting procedures for the group or person.

The study concluded that facilitators with high degrees of caring and meaning attribution with moderate emotional stimulation and executive function had the best outcomes for learning and change with the fewest negative outcomes.

Interestingly, among the two psychodrama groups, the group leader who had received training from J.L. Moreno was the most highly rated for competence as a group leader and for participant learning, while the other psychodrama group leader received low ratings across many criteria, including competence as a group leader. This may reflect uneven psychodrama training at that point in time.

More recent studies have considered the neurobiology of experiential action methods. The advent of the MRI has demonstrated neuroplasticity, that is, the capacity for change in the brain, linked to creating new neural pathways. Cozolino (2016) proposed changing what is going on in the brain is linked to successful therapeutic outcomes. Greenberg (2013) reports on meta-studies that demonstrate therapeutic experience that stimulates reflection in the context of heightened emotion has greater success in the treatment of depression, anxiety, trauma, and emotional regulation issues. As a holistic therapy, psychodrama engages heart, mind, body, and soul—which creates new understandings and insights which form changes in the brain.

Thoughts for Further Study

A questionnaire could be administered at the beginning of meetings to be answered by individuals and the therapist/facilitator. The questions could ask about progress in the identified tasks of mourning based on contemporary grief theory, explored in Chapter 2.

1. Client use of self-care strategies
2. Processing the specific issues of grief
3. Movement toward finding a new normal
4. Finding an enduring connection with the deceased in the midst of embarking on a new life.

Bibliography

Cozolino, L.J. (2016). *Why therapy works: using our minds to change our brains*. New York: W.W. Norton.

Cruz, A., Sales, C., Moita, G., & Alves, P. (2016). Towards the development of helpful aspects of Morenian psychodrama content analysis system (HAMPCAS). In C. Stadler, M. Wieser, and K. Kirk (eds.). *Psychodrama. Empirical research and science*, vol. 2 (pp. 57–67), Wiesbaden: Springer. doi: 10.1007/978-3-658-13015-2_6

Cruz, A., Sales, C.M.D., Alves, P., & Moita, G. (2018). The core techniques of Morenian psychodrama: a systematic review of literature. *Frontiers in Psychology*, 9:article 1263.

D'Amato, R.C., & Dean, R.S. (1988). Psychodrama research: therapy and theory: a critical analysis of an arrested modality. *Psychology in the Schools*, 25: 305–314.

Elliott, R. (2002). Hermeneutic single-case efficacy design. *Psychotherapy Research*, 12:1–21. doi: 10.1080/713869614.

Elliott, R., Davis, K.L., & Slatick, E. (1998). Process experiential therapy for post traumatic stress difficulties. In L.S. Greenberg, J.C. Watson, & G. Lietaer (eds.), Handbook of experiential psychotherapy (pp. 249–271). New York: Guilford Press.

Gonzalez, A.-J., Martin, P., & Pedroso de Lima, M. (2018). Studying the efficacy of psychodrama with the hermeneutic single case efficacy design: results from a longitudinal study. *Frontiers in Psychology*, 9:article 1662.

Greenberg, L.S. (2013). Anchoring the Therapeutic Spiral Model into research on experiential psychotherapies. In K. Hudgins & F. Toscani (eds.), *Healing world trauma with the Therapeutic Spiral Model: stories from the front lines* (pp. 132–148). London: Jessica Kingsley.

Kellermann, P.F. (1982). Outcome research in classical psychodrama. *Small Group Behavior*, 18:459–469.

Kipper, D.A. (1978). Trends in the research on the effectiveness of psychodrama: retrospect and prospect. *Journal of Group Psychotherapy, Psychodrama and Sociometry*, 31:5–18.

Kipper, D.A., & Ritchie, T.D. (2003). The effectiveness of psychodramatic techniques: a meta-analysis. *Group Dynamics: Theory, Research, and Practice*, 7(1)13–25.

Lieberman, M.A., Yalom, I.D., & Miles, M.B. (1973). *Encounter groups: first facts*. New York: Basic Books.

Rawlinson, J.W. (2000). Does psychodrama work? A review of the literature. *British Journal of Psychodrama and Sociometry*, 15:67–101.

APPENDIX II

RELATIONSHIP OF EXPERIENTIAL ACTION METHODS AND THEORY WITH OTHER MODELS OF PSYCHOTHERAPY

Psychodrama inherently contains and overlaps with elements of other modalities, which we will briefly present here. For a more extensive review of the relationship of psychodrama and other modalities, we refer readers to *Empowering Therapeutic Practice: Integrating Psychodrama into Other Therapies* (Holmes et al., 2014), which includes chapters by clinicians using psychodrama with different therapeutic orientations.

Cognitive Behavioral Therapy

The affinity between cognitive behavioral therapy (CBT) and psychodrama is clear in the distilling statements of its founders, Aaron Beck, the originator of CBT, and Zerka Moreno, co-creator of the methods and theoretical foundations of psychodrama.

> The goals of cognitive therapy are to correct faulty information processing and to modify dysfunctional beliefs and assumptions that maintain maladaptive behaviors and emotions.
>
> (Beck & Weishaar, 1989, p. 28)

> Psychodrama is not just for recreating a disturbing experience. It is meant to do, undo, redo, and integrate, producing closure. Subjective perceptions may be distorted in ways only others can reveal to us, therefore in that corrective interaction, we can accept and integrate the correction.
>
> (Moreno, 2013, p. 28)

In our hands, with a focus on grief, psychodrama shifts perspectives and entrenched beliefs that drive distress. Role reversal, auxiliary roles, and doubling offer the individual an opportunity to view their perspectives from outside themselves and to experience a broader perspective that is often corrective. Individuals receive these new perspectives in what is known as the 'trance' or altered state of reality (Sheiffele, 2014) of psychodrama, a state that has body, mind, heart, and soul activated. Thoughts and feelings are explored *here and now* with the protagonist taking roles, witnessing their own role, and hearing other messages or points of view. Use of psychodrama with individuals and in groups has time and again demonstrated the powerful difference between inviting clients to consider 'what he/she would say' vs. saying what he/she is saying. Both come from the internal knowing the client has of another person. The method of delivery to a client in the psychodrama trance is transformative. They have holistically (heart, mind, body, soul) experienced a new perspective rather than intellectually considered a new perspective. All of the vignettes and activities in this book demonstrate how use of action methods with specific grief topics creates a change in thoughts and beliefs that cause distress, much like CBT.

Narrative Therapy

Persistent grief is influenced by the stories, meaning, or narratives that survivors have about the death of a loved one. *Restorative Retelling* (Rynearson & Salloum, 2011) explores the importance of restructuring the narrative after violent death. We have noticed that narratives are often related to guilt, anger, and loss-related trauma. They have stories about what survivors did or didn't do or say and things they may have done or said in irritation. Unexpected deaths often leave the survivor regretful that they couldn't say "I love you" one last time or convey how important the loved one was. There are images either actually seen or imagined that are seared into memory of the survivor surrounding the actual death of the loved one, that we refer to as 'frozen memories'. We have seen that these memories are often traumatic and very painful and difficult to address. Working with psychodrama on narratives is transformative. The process of enactment creates a felt sense of the wise presence of the loved one. Through role play, speaking and hearing the caring and compassionate words of the deceased, the story shifts, thinking about an event is altered, and a new narrative is created. The individual experiences new insights about the frozen moments, usually including compassionate acceptance of self and others. This ultimately reduces anguish.

It has been speculated that the effectiveness of psychodrama to transform entrenched or distressing thoughts and narratives is related to how the human brain works.

Fear and anger are imprinted more readily than pleasant experiences, which is adaptive to human survival. Intense experiences are stored as memories and a felt sense of these experiences can be evoked even many years later. Psychodrama enactment goes to those stored memories and creates a new narrative directly related to this stored memory. Kate Bradshaw-Tauvon (2014) noted that the process of working with trauma with psychodrama may be similar to the adaptive information processing with eye movement desensitization and reprocessing (EMDR). The same is true for individuals who have experienced the death of a loved one and loss-related trauma.

We aren't aware of a neurobiological study that delineates what happens in the brain due to the action aspect of psychodrama, and such a study might well be impossible. It seems magical to see a psychodrama process in which those memories and the stored emotional responses are activated and through use of action/experiential methods changed—like a light switch. The protagonist has a new experience connected with his or her grief—a new way of thinking about the same event. With insight, the stored narratives are rewritten—permanently.

The principles of narrative therapy are best illustrated in the chapters on guilt, anger, frozen memories, and unfinished business with vignettes about death of spouse/partner and parent. In one account of a full psychodrama, the stored memory of panic and guilt was transformed for the protagonist using the mirror position, that is, stepping back and seeing the scene enacted being played by others. She was able to witness the love for her partner that went alongside the intensity of seeing her partner die.

Transpersonal

Our strength-based approach identifies and amplifies interpersonal, intrapsychic, and transpersonal roles. Transpersonal strengths, that is, something outside of this material plane, are chosen by the individual and can be guardian angel, spirit guide, God, Jesus, or someone in the realm of spirit. Although we don't state this when inviting individuals to identify a transpersonal strength, we have found that these roles universally offer more insightful and compassionate perspectives.

Continuing bond, one of the tasks of mourning discussed in Chapter 2, is not only a transpersonal concept, it is a biological reality. This is the foundation of what has been effective for grief work. Deceased loved ones are and will always be a part of the survivor on a cellular level. We contain in memory our felt sense of the person who has died. We can access, even in ambivalent relationships, a loving, supportive,

184 Other Models of Psychotherapy

and wise aspect of the one who has died. Bringing the voice of this aspect of the loved one is universally soothing and healing. The vignettes in frozen memories are particularly good examples of using a transpersonal strength.

Another transpersonal aspect of psychodrama is found in reparative work. Reparative psychodramas work with creating a new experience in which the survivor has been hurt by the one who died. This works with the individual's own religious or spiritual beliefs. Reparative work suggests that some amount of essential goodness, perspective, and wisdom might exist within the one who has died and that these qualities remain or are more available after he or she has been freed of their life burdens, medical illness, mental illness, or addiction. The vignette in Chapter 15 on reparative work with surplus reality is a good demonstration of this.

Motivational Interviewing

Stages of change in motivational interviewing are particularly relevant in the readiness for survivors to make changes (Miller & Rollnick, 2013). Forward projection and doubling are tools of psychodrama which help build clarity about the value of change. Doubling statements that accentuate the entrenched attitude are often enough for the individual to see that their attitude is not something they want to stay frozen in. (See vignettes in Chapter 9 on anger.) Also, forward projection—imagining a time in the future—offers a vision for a happier future.

Existential Therapy: Finding Acceptance and Meaning

Finding acceptance about the death of a loved one is a key component to resolving the persistent thoughts and feelings that cause ongoing distress and suffering. Acceptance of the inability to change the past, along with compassionate recognition of the inevitable mistakes and insensitivity by our species, helps take the edge off anger and guilt. Forgiveness works. Examples are given in the vignettes in the chapters on guilt and anger.

Bibliography

Beck, A.T., & Weishaar, M. (1989). Cognitive therapy. In A. Freeman, K.M. Simon, L.E. Bentler, & H. Arkowitz (eds.), *Comprehensive handbook of cognitive therapy* (p. 28). New York: Plenum Press.

Bradshaw-Tauvon, K. (2014). Psychodrama informed by adaptive information reprocessing (AIP). In P. Holmes, M. Farrall, & K. Kirk (eds.), *Empowering therapeutic practice: integrating psychodrama into other therapies* (p. 203). London: Jessica Kingsley.

Holmes, P., Farrall, M., & Kirk K. (eds.) (2014). *Empowering therapeutic practice: integrating psychodrama into other therapies*. London: Jessica Kingsley.

Miller, W.R., & Rollnick, S. (2013). *Motivational interviewing: helping people change*. New York: Guilford Press.

Moreno, Z.T. (2013). *The quintessential Zerka: writings by Zerka Toeman Moreno on psychodrama* (p. 285). New York: Routledge.

Rynearson, E.K., & Salloum, A. (2011) Restorative retelling: revising the narrative after violent death. In R.A. Neimeyer, D.L. Harris, H.R. Winokuer, & G.F. Thornton (eds.), *Grief and bereavement in contemporary society: bridging research and practice* (pp. 177–188). New York: Routledge.

Sheiffele, E. (2014). Hypnotherapy altered states of consciousness, and psychodrama. In P. Holmes, M. Farrall, & K. Kirk (eds.), *Empowering therapeutic practice: integrating psychodrama into other therapies*. London: Jessica Kingsley.

APPENDIX III

SPECIAL ASPECTS OF GRIEF

Death of a Dream: Survival after Divorce, Separation, and Relationship Change

The death of a relationship is very similar to the loss of a loved one through death. The main difference is that you may still have to interact with a former spouse in regard to life issues such as children, finances, and practical issues, which creates a secondary trauma, and can make separation more complicated and difficult.

Life after divorce or separation is a journey. It is a step-by-step process of rediscovering yourself and rebuilding your life without the relationship. It is a spiral of emotions, revelations, painful losses, and new beginnings. If we treat it as a grief process, it may be easier to manage it, and acknowledge that ultimately, at all times, we have the power to determine how we build the new 'normal' of our life.

There are the physical and legal changes you need to expedite, once you have made the serious life decision to separate. There are the emotional, relationship, and life-meaning changes you will navigate, once your separation is final. What we have discovered through the years of providing stress and grief support is that your entire circle of meaning is impacted. How we respond to these changes will form how we recover and gain wisdom from the pain.

Dimensions of Divorce: Once Two, Now One...

- Physical: home, daily routine, financial, sexual, job
- Emotional: relationships, children, in-laws, family, sex life, friendship, confidant, dream sharing, self-esteem
- Social: friends, activities, hobbies, job, family, image in community
- Spiritual: life promise, belief in goodness, relationship to core beliefs, future hopes.

The journey includes:

- Disbelief about the reality of the separation
- Ruminating and destructive mind chatter about all the would haves, could haves, and should haves
- Guilt about what we did or didn't do or sense of failure
- Anger and resentment about what our spouse has done, or is doing
- Paralyzing loneliness, isolation, and fear of the future
- Experiencing the liberating freedom to only be responsible for self
- Stepping back into old behavior patterns of helping, supporting, or arguing with our former spouse.

All of these are normal and natural reactions.

Steps to Healing

Divorce can throw us out of control. Divorce management is moving to claiming back our control over our life, our process, and our feelings. We only have to deal with one issue at a time. Focus on:

- What's the most difficult right now?
- What do I need to do right now to survive it?
- How can I get support to do what I need to do?

This is inner work of transformation and reclaiming our life, our self, and our dreams:

- Acknowledge.
- Express.
- Act.
- Reconnect.

1. Accept what is, rather than what you think it should be.
2. What meanings we attach to events are not always the facts. Take a step back and breathe.
3. Try to separate the facts from your perception of the worst-case scenario.
4. Try not to get stuck in the repetitive mind chatter. Acknowledge it, honor it, and do not try to rationally argue with it. Then, let it go.
5. Begin the process of forgiveness—of yourself and hopefully your former spouse. Acceptance does not mean agreement. However, do not rush this. It may take some time. Always start with yourself.
6. Accept and love yourself, for all that you are. Try to acknowledge yourself as you would a best friend who was struggling with a rough situation. Make a list of your good qualities and ask friends and family to do the same. Use it as ammunition, when your self-esteem is faltering.
7. You are the only one who is responsible for you. Also, remember you are not responsible for the well-being of your former spouse or anyone else.
8. Take care of yourself physically. Eat well, exercise, be around uplifting people, get as much rest and sleep as you need, do fun and interesting activities that give you a chance to experience the joy in living.

When relationships are at risk for break-up or separation:

- Death of past passion, good memories, mutual respect and regard
- Idealization of marriage relationship or committed relationship is shattered
- There is violence or abuse: physical, emotional, mental, sexual, or spiritual
- We look at our significant other and we see a 'monster in the bed'
- We have lost contact with ourselves, our own sense of being and purpose, as well as what brings us happiness
- We are dependent upon our partner's moods, needs, and actions to determine our state of mind, be it peaceful, happy, loving, disappointed, angry, or fearful
- We have other losses or changes we are coping with in our life:
  - Personal illness
  - Issues with children
  - Job change or financial crisis
  - Aging or ill parents or family members

- Internal changes in goals and/or dreams
- Any major loss or critical incident
- There is betrayal, breakdown of trust, or lies being told
- Grief, joy, or life events are not shared with your significant other, but shared with others instead—be it friends, co-workers, or strangers (example: over the internet).

Tools for Managing the Downward Spiral

- Create an affirmation of your goodness, wholeness, or life goals that are positive. Use it when the negative self-talk kicks in.
- Make a list of gratitudes: what is good about your life right now?
- Reach out to friends and loved ones who do care and will support you in stopping the negative spiral of thoughts and emotions. Set these up ahead of time.
- Suffering is in the resistance to the pain. Let the sorrow, anger, or pain flow. Allow yourself to express what is true for you right now. Honor it.
- Exercise—physical movement helps the body deal with the stress.
- Drink water and eat regularly—about four to six times a day to keep blood sugar even.
- Give yourself a treat to honor that you have survived another day.
- Remember that different stages and decades of life present different stressors for you as an individual and in your relationship. Learn about them. Get information and compile knowledge from others who have survived your life stage.

Surviving the Holidays

1. Acknowledge that there is no magical solution for eliminating the pain you are feeling.
2. Accept that you have definite limitations this year and that it is not wrong—it just is.
3. Realize that you must look at your true priorities and determine what is truly meaningful for you, understanding and accepting that these may differ for family and friends.
4. Give yourself permission to let go of the 'shoulds' and 'have tos' this year.
5. Many changes in your life are painful and unwelcome and you are entitled to grieve over them. Give yourself permission to do so and then try to see if some of the changes can be transformed into challenges. The challenge is to survive—and find a new approach to life. This includes the holidays.
6. Know that it is OK to say, "No, I can't this year."
7. Release the guilt over what you cannot control this year.
8. Make your needs around the holidays known to friends, family, or anyone who can provide support—especially emotional support.
9. Try to find constructive things to do at least some of the time.
10. Remember, those around you are also struggling with their own pain. You are responsible for taking care of you, just as they are responsible for taking care of themselves.
11. Talk with family and friends about personal choices. Sometimes exploring together can bring creative ideas about how to survive and co-create a new and meaningful normal.
12. Be aware of your use of alcohol or other substances. Pay attention to changes, especially increase in use. In the end, this can make matters worse.

Remember: If any activity takes more energy than it gives you, let it go for this year. You can always return to it next year.

Symbolic Ways to Remember Our Loved Ones

- Purchase a special remembrance candle. Place it in a prominent place. Burn it all day or at special selected times.
- Place a special flower or bouquet on a table by a photograph.
- Attend a religious ceremony.
- Spend spiritual quiet time alone.
- Visit the cemetery.
- Have family members or friends write a special card or buy a special ornament—or you do it.
- Light candles for loved ones or special people throughout the holidays. It is important to honor the living as well as those we have lost.
- Purchase a new special frame for your loved one's photograph and display the newly mounted picture in a prominent position.
- Make a memorial contribution in his/her name.
- Share photo albums with family members and friends, recalling happy memories.
- Buy a gift to or from your loved one.
- Plant a living memorial shrub or tree.
- Give a toast at a holiday meal or ask someone else to do it.
- Help someone less fortunate than you.

INDEX

action methods to soften guilt 80–81
action methods for work with anger 59
action methods for work with faith issues 107
action methods for work with fear 47
action methods for working with sadness 53–54
action methods for work with unfinished business 66
action steps in the aftermath of loss 82–83
action tools in work with loneliness 38
activity for working with trauma after violence 175
adaption of Maslow needs hierarchy after trauma 85
anger 55: action methods to work with anger 59; guilty
   anger 55; managing anger 56–58; steps for processing
   anger 57
approaching the grief journey 3: acknowledge loss 6;
   act 7; express feelings 6; reconnect 7

backpack effect 3
Beyond broken on the bathroom floor, Rebecca B. 122–123

cascade effect of trauma/support 3
causes of suicide 86
Centre for Living with Dying 8
ceremonies of leave taking 105: examples of leave-taking
   rituals 107
comfort anchors, comfort tasks 34
conspiracy of silence 165
contemporary grief theories 9
creative expression activities for larger groups 110: circle
   of meaning 112–113; essence/expression activity
   114–115; exploring trauma in the body 111; heart
   hotel 116; poetry with grief 111; the village within:
   aspects of the inner landscape 117–120; using music
   with grief 110
cultural humility 104

daily log personal check-in process 25
death of a dream: divorce, separation and relationship
   change 185–187
doubling, amplifying statements 60

faith and the grieving process 103: action methods,
   working with faith issues 107; cultural humility
   with faith issues and traditional practices 104;
   forgiveness 108
family dynamics in loss and change 132: behaviors and
   feelings behind behaviors 132; belligerent behavior in
   children 137; children and youth with grief 134–135;
   depression in children 138; family dynamic exercise
   134; gift of acceptance with children 135–136;
   gift of honesty with children 136; gift of listening
   to children 135; ground rules for working with
   families 133–134; Healing Heart program, working
   with families 136; helping children cope 137–139;
   information to share with children 139; protective
   behavior 138–139; questions for family members
   133; regressive behavior in children 138; withdrawal
   behavior in children 137
fear 45: action methods for work with fear 47;
   dimensions of fear 45
feel wheel 89
four components to healing 6; see also healing
   feelings
frozen moments 70: vignettes: frozen moments: day of
   death 72–76; What are frozen moments? 71

grief support in the technological age 165–166
grief training for clinicians and caregivers 167: activity
   for working with trauma after violence 175; cultural
   humility 104; death notification/trauma notification
   176; different cultural responses to loss and grief
   171–172; how you identify self 173; immediate
   responses by caregivers to potential suicide 174;
   Listening as healing, Margaret Wheatley 167–169;
   tips for responses to those from different cultural
   backgrounds 172; worksheet for bridging the
   gap between self and other 172–173; your caring
   presence 170
grief work beyond the acute stage 94: envisioning the
   future 96; finding new meaning 96; gratitude for the

loved one 101; life meaning atom 99; reparative work with surplus reality 102; working with dreams in action 94

grief work with fragile populations 122: changing roles with fragile populations 126; forgiveness activity with fragile populations 129–130; hero's journey with fragile populations 130–131; identifying and amplifying resources 124; looking at self-defeating beliefs with fragile populations 128–129; making a lifeline with fragile populations 124; receiving positive reflection from others 129; simple role atom 126; sociometry warm-ups with fragile populations 123; vignette, with role atom 128

grounding with the body double 53; *see also* safety and containment structures

grounding and stress reduction tools 33

group warm-ups 14–17; *see also* sociometry

guilt 77–79: action methods to soften guilt 80–81; guilt exercise 79; guilt reality list 79; resolving guilt 78–79

handouts: activity for working with trauma after violence 175; circles of meaning 112–113; comfort anchors, comfort tasks 34; daily log personal check-in 26; dimensions of fear 45; dimensions of sorrow 50–52; essence/expression 114–115; grief and the heart 19–22; grounding and stress reduction tools 33; guilt is… 77–79; healing feelings: tools for survival 30–31; heart hotel 116; helping children cope 137–139; immediate responses by caregivers to potential suicide 174; issues and dynamics around suicide 86–87; managing anger 56–58; normal symptoms, feelings, and reactions to loss 24; self-care toolbox 32; surviving violent death 91–92; tools for coping 28–29; tools for finishing business 63–64; What are frozen moments? 71; What is loneliness? 37; What is unfinished business? 63–64; your caring presence 170

heart hotel 5: handout, heart hotel 116

identifying and amplifying strengths and resources 13

life meaning vs. happiness 10

Listening as healing, Margaret Wheatley 167–169

loneliness 37: action tools in work with loneliness 38; social atom 38; sociodrama to explore isolation 43; supporting better understanding and communication 43; What is loneliness? 37

meditation, asking the loved one for help 103–104

mementos, honoring the loved one 82–83

normal symptoms, feelings, and reactions to loss 24

psychodrama 12: doubling 12; identifying and amplifying client resources 13–14; J.L. Moreno, founder of psychodrama 12; relationship of psychodrama with other models of psychotherapy 182; role reversal 12; surplus reality 13

psychodrama with trauma 14, 47; *see also* safety and containment structures; Therapeutic Spiral model

questions in the midst of trauma 93

research overview of psychodrama 179

sadness 49: action methods for working with sadness 53–54; dimensions of sorrow 50–52; gentle reminders with sadness 51–52

self-care toolbox 32

self-compassion 76

social atom 38

sociometry 12, 14: group warm-up 14; line spectrograms 14–16; locograms 15–16; sociometry as an assessment tool 14; sociometry tools for group building 14; step-in circle 16

special aspects of grief 185

steps to formulate ritual of leave taking 106

stress, trauma, and critical stress management (CISM) 141: administrative betrayal 159–160; building sensitivity among co-workers 149; CISM stories from the front lines 159; crisis intervention group ground rules 146; crisis intervention group process 147–149; critical incident management/response (CISR) 142; critical incident stress 142; cumulative stress 142; debriefing, critical incident stress response 151–152; defusing, shortened CISR group process 150–151; delayed stress response syndrome 142; follow-up CISR 152; grief counseling CISM steps 153–154; heart meditation 158–159; landmine backpack 148; landmine CISR 152–153; occupational stress 142; personalized reactions in the aftermath of a tragedy 144; pre-incident education and training 145; tips for self-care for responders and healthcare providers 155–156; trauma release meditation 157–158; typical reactions in the aftermath of a tragedy 143; working with communities after major incident 153–154

surviving the holidays 187

symbolic ways to remember our loved ones 188

symptoms of grief 5

tools for coping 23, 28–29

tools for managing the downward spiral 187

tools to respond after controversial deaths 165

unfinished business 62: action methods, working with unfinished business 66; metaphorical rocks 66; tools for finishing business 63; unfinished business backpack 66; unfinished business meditation 65; What is unfinished business? 63

unique issues after violent death and suicide 84, 86–87

vignettes: acknowledge, express, act, reconnect 160; approaching the healing journey 164; backpack effect 162–164; better understanding and communication 43–44; children with grief 134–135; cultural differences with grieving 105; daily log personal check-in 27; envisioning the future 96–101; exploring trauma in the body 111; family dynamics 133–134; finding family/spouse support 160–161; frozen moments: day of death 72–76; healing action steps 161–162; lifeline with fragile populations 124–126; loneliness using social atom 39–43; reparative work with surplus reality 102; using feel wheel after violent death 90; using music with grief 110; working with anger 59–61; working with dreams 94–95; working with faith issues 108; working with fear, identifying supports 47–48; working with sadness 53–54; working with the village within 120–121; working with violent death 84

violence 88: creating a safe space for family work 85; surviving violent death 91–92

warrior ceremony 163

What is grief? 3

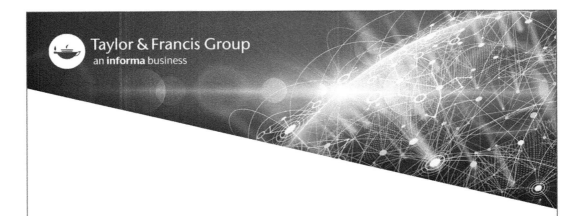

Milton Keynes UK
Ingram Content Group UK Ltd.
UKHW030716210324
439785UK00004B/7